35

Prosperous Paupers & Other Population Problems

Prosperous Paupers & Other Population Problems

Nicholas Eberstadt

TRANSACTION PUBLISHERS
New Brunswick (U.S.A.) and London (U.K.)

Library of Congress Catalog Number: 00-028703
ISBN: 1-56000-423-1
Printed in the United States of America

Library of Congress Cataloging-in-Publication Data

Eberstadt, Nick, 1955-
    Prosperous paupers, and other population problems / by Nicholas Eberstadt.
      p. cm.
    Includes bibliographical references and index.
    ISBN 1-56000-423-1 (alk. paper)
    1. United States—Population.   2. Communist countries—Population.
3. Population. 4. Population forecasting. I. Title.

HB3505 .E25   2000
304.6—dc21   00-028703

To the memory of

Michael Anthony Scully

Contents

Acknowledgments

The essays and studies assembled in this volume were originally published in the mid- and late-1990s. Throughout that decade and most of the previous one, I pursued my research under the joint aegis of the American Enterprise Institute (AEI) in Washington, D.C., and the Harvard Center for Population and Development Studies in Cambridge, Massachusetts. This may sound like a case of dual loyalties, but it has been a most happy and rewarding endeavor for me—and so it remains. Fondest thanks are due—once again—to Christopher C. De Muth, AEI's president, and to Lincoln C. Chen, longtime director of the Harvard Center, for all they have done to encourage and abet my work.

Over the years in which these chapters were written, I was aided in my diverse investigations by a succession of wonderful research assistants. I must first mention Mr. Jonathan B. Tombes—tireless, erudite, and gentlemanly—who often seemed to know what I would need before I knew myself. In this book, my debt to Jonathan is especially deep. I should also like to thank warmly my two other assistants during the course of these chapters: Miss Gwendolyn A. Wilber and Miss Kelly L. O'Neal. In addition to their research skills, both young ladies had the knack of radiating calm and good cheer no matter what manner of chaos they were presented. With Gwen now off to make her mark in law, and Kelly hers in politics, I have no doubts that their talents will serve them both well.

I wish also to acknowledge my great appreciation to the institutions that have so generously supported this book. To the Sarah Scaife Foundation—a faithful sponsor of so many of my research projects—my special gratitude is due yet again. I should also like to thank the Earhart Foundation and the U.S. Institute of Peace for grants that permitted me to produce studies included in this volume. Finally, I would like to note that the Pfizer Corporation and the Philip M. McKenna Foundation kindly provided the funding that permitted me to complete this work.

The following chapters have been reprinted with the permission of the publishers/publications through which they originally appeared. For some of the chapters in this volume, the text has been somewhat revised, and chapter 8 and 11 bear new titles:

Ch. 1: "Prosperous Paupers and Affluent Savages: The New Challenges to Social Policy in America," *Society*, Jan/Feb 1996.

Ch. 2: "Why Babies Die in D.C.," *Public Interest*, Spring and Fall 1994.

Ch. 3: "Daniel Patrick Moynihan, Epidemiologist," *Population and Development Review*, June 1997.

Ch. 4: "Mortality and the Fate of the Communist States," in *Science with a Human Face: In Honor of Roger Revelle*, (Cambridge, MA: Harvard University Press, 1997).

Ch. 5: "The Soviet Way of Death," *World Affairs*, Fall 1995.

Ch. 6: "Health and Mortality in Central and Eastern Europe: Retrospect and Prospect," in *The Social Legacy of Communism*, (Cambridge: Cambridge University Press, 1994).

Ch. 7: "Demographic Shocks after Communism: Eastern Germany, 1989-93," *Europe-Asia Studies,* May/June 1994.

Ch. 8: "Justifying Population Control: The Latest Version," *Population and Development Review,* June 1995.

Ch. 10: "Population Prospects for Eastern Asia to 2015," Johns Hopkins SAIS *Policy Forum Series*, November 1998.

Ch. 11: "What If It's a World Population *Implosion*? Speculations about Global *De-Population*," *Public Interest,* Fall 1997.

Introduction

The entire modern world—from the affluent United States to the poorest of the low-income regions—is beset today by a broad and alarming array of "population problems." That proposition, at least, is taken as self-evident in much of our current public and intellectual discourse. Around the globe, leading scientists, academics, and political figures now attribute all manner of miseries—poverty, hunger, social tension, even political conflict—to contemporary demographic trends. According to these authorities, the size, composition, and rate of growth of population routinely poses direct and major threats to human well-being. That same argument further posits that a society's "population problems" should be addressed by interventions aimed specifically at altering its demographic rhythms.

The essays collected in this volume represent a dissent from this modern-day canon. My objection is a simple one: such thinking about "population problems" all too often forgets about *human beings*.

As we will see, the very conception of "population problems" is inherently ambiguous and arbitrary, lending itself to faulty analysis and inappropriate diagnoses. In the following pages, I also argue that much of the prevailing thinking about "population problems" is plainly careless—rooted in faulty analysis and sometimes even based on the most evident of misconceptions. Such careless thinking about "population problems," I submit, is a result of inattention to, or indifference toward, the fundamental unit in all populations: the individual human being.

These themes run commonly through the separate studies that comprise this book. Their correlative is the volume's recurrent finding: in the diverse settings assayed in the following eleven chapters, phenomena identified as "population problems" reveal themselves again and again to be, at heart, *ethical* problems—or ethical problems transmuted into political problems through the power of the state. In the ensuing pages, we will see this to be the case in the United States, in the territories

1

of the Soviet bloc, in low-income regions of the globe, and for the world as a whole.

The three initial chapters focus upon what some would call the "population problems" of the United States. Chapter 1, "Prosperous Paupers and Affluent Savages," examines the nature of poverty in modern America.

Ours, I argue, is a new and very modern sort of poverty, which progressive American minds from earlier generations did not anticipate. Indeed, they would hardly have imagined our current circumstances, where, in the most affluent society the world has ever known, immiseration blights millions of lives.

This modern variant of immiseration, however, is rooted in individual behavior rather than strict financial need. It is characterized by the spread of criminality, illegitimacy, and dependence, and by the embrace of such practices by persons who would not, in the historic meaning of the word, be regarded as "poor." Call it "poverty," by all means: but the troubling social syndromes that travel under this rubric in our country today have less to do with a lack of financial resources than with a lack of moral resources—or so my argument.

Just as the poverty problem has evolved in unfamiliar new directions in modern America, so, too, has the health problem. Chapter 2, "Why Babies Die in D.C.," analyzes the infant mortality problem in our nation's capital, which is acute. The infant mortality rate is higher in Washington than in any of the fifty states; in the late 1980s and early 1990s, D.C.'s infant mortality rate was actually higher than it had been years earlier.

The prevailing public health paradigms would attribute Washington's infant mortality problem to a lack of material and medical resources, that is, to poverty and inadequate access to health care. That explanation, unfortunately, is wholly inadequate to explain the situation. Washington's infant mortality problem is primarily a black infant mortality problem because Washington is a predominantly black city. As it happens, black Washingtonians constitute one of the nation's most affluent African-American populations. And yet they suffer by far the highest black infant mortality rate of any federal region in the country.

Why should this be so? As I demonstrate, Washington's infant health problem appears to be very closely associated with three distinct, but in practice overlapping, phenomena: fatherlessness; welfare dependence; and violent crime. By contrast, income and educational levels appeared to be rather weak predictors of infant health risk in the nation's capital. The traditional "structural" factors for explaining infant mortality, it seems, were giving way to new factors—factors relating more directly to particular modalities of behavior and life-style. In Washington, I suggest, we may be witnessing the emergence of a new American paradigm for infant health risk: a paradigm defined increasingly by risks accruing from parental behavior. Such a paradigm, of course, could only pose terrible new challenges to our society.

Chapter 3, "Daniel Patrick Moynihan, Epidemiologist," reviews the contributions of America's leading intellectual-in-politics to our understanding of three contemporary public health hazards: traffic injuries, violent crime, and drug abuse.

Perhaps surprisingly, death from violent causes has been assuming a steadily increasing prominence in the mortality structure of postwar America. Understanding the dynamics—or as epidemiologists would say, the etiologies—of these three behaviorally rooted dangers may bring us closer to mitigating them, and Moynihan, as I demonstrate, has brought his polymath insight to each of these areas.

No less important than those specific insights, I would propose, has been his subtle, but more general appreciation of the inherent tension at the very heart of the quest to reduce behavioral harm through social and medical interventions. Moynihan warns that "Epidemiologists have powerful insights that can contribute to lessening the medical trauma, but they must be wary of normalizing the social pathology that leads to such trauma." In the final analysis, as the eminent epidemiologist Dr. H.O. Lancaster has written, a rise in deaths from violent causes reflects a "lessened appreciation of the sanctity of human life"; consequently "the prevention of a proportion" of such deaths is not so much a medical problem as "a moral problem."

The next four chapters concentrate upon the communist and postcommunist societies of the former Soviet bloc—and their death trends.

Overwhelmingly, current commentary about "population problems" focuses on birth rates rather than death rates. To me, that emphasis seems somewhat curious. After all, it happens to be vastly easier to identify genuine and severe "population problems" that devolve from mortality trends than ones caused by fertility trends.

From a normative standpoint, it is worth recalling that the consequences of fertility trends are quite ambiguous. There is no obvious, a priori answer to the question of whether it should be preferable for a birth rate to rise, decline, or hold steady. And there is no widely accepted social consensus about a desirable direction for human birth rates.

The situation is entirely different when it comes to mortality rates. Throughout history and across cultures, better health and longer life have been cherished goals and treasured outcomes for individuals, families, and societies. Premature death, for its part, is almost universally regarded as tragic. Irrespective of a society's given survival patterns, reducing mortality is virtually always a strong preference and a high priority.

It is by no means self-evident that every country with a rising fertility level is automatically beset by a "population problem." It is incontestable, on the other hand, that a rising mortality level would be taken as a problem by any modern society so unfortunate as to suffer it.

By such a criterion, Central Europe and what is now sometimes termed "Eurasia" have been subject to incontestable demographic problems for several decades. For much of the Cold War era, mortality rates throughout the Soviet bloc were on the rise, with the most dramatic increases occurring within the Soviet Union itself.

It should go without saying that long-term increases in mortality are highly anomalous for industrialized societies not at war. For humanitarian reasons—but hardly those alone—the former Soviet bloc region's unsettling demographic trends deserve much more attention than they have received to date.

If we had devoted more attention during the Cold War to Soviet and Eastern European mortality trends, the collapse of the Soviet Empire and the Soviet system itself might have come as rather less of a surprise. This I argue in Chapter 4, "Mortality and the Fate of the Communist States." It is a striking fact that all of the communist countries to experience long-term rises in mortality are no longer communist, whereas for China, Cuba, and Vietnam—the Marxist-Leninist states where communist power has been maintained—secular mortality declines still prevail.[1] Chapter 4 outlines the reasons for suspecting that conjunction to be more than utter coincidence.

Soviet bloc demographic and health trends are examined in greater detail in chapters 5 and 6, "The Soviet Way of Death" and "Health and Mortality in Eastern Europe." The systemic nature of the Soviet bloc's demographic malaise is underscored by a variety of factors—one of the more compelling being the great diversity of peoples that have registered this single, strange, and unnatural affliction. The area from Leipzig to Vladivostok includes a multiplicity of "European" languages, cultures, and histories; levels of economic and material attainment within that region also vary markedly. Nevertheless, every one of the many "European" peoples under the sway of Moscow and its Warsaw Pact came to report a cessation of health progress, and then a sustained retrogression in health conditions, among broad segments of the general population. The proximate causes of these mortality reversals were all the same: an alarming upsurge in deaths attributed to cardiovascular disease (CVD) and to injuries (including suicide). Many of the contributing factors were also collective. One of these—a dangerous increase in heavy drinking of hard spirits—was widely reported and easy enough to measure.

Other possible contributing factors were far more difficult to gauge. An individual's outlook and attitudes—including his or her satisfaction with life and expectations for the future—may have a direct bearing on both susceptibility to illness or injury and prospects for subsequent recovery.[2] Unfortunately, no reliable quantitative indicators of such trends in "mental health" are to be found for the Soviet bloc (or any other area). Even so, given what we know about the behavioral patterns that contributed so directly to elevated mortality risks within the Soviet bloc, it seems only reasonable to infer that the advent of the Soviet bloc's health crisis was associated with a profound shift in popular viewpoint, toward one more redolent of pessimism and despair. Perhaps it should not surprise that a political arrangement so manifestly inhumane as Soviet-style communism should ultimately elicit from ordinary human populations such inhuman demographic trends—trends so seemingly at odds with the deeply held preferences of ordinary human beings.

Although Soviet-style systems might plausibly have qualified as public health hazards by the end of the Cold War, the termination of Soviet-style rule did not result in an immediate turnaround in health trends for all the populaces of the former Soviet bloc. Quite the contrary: the collapse of communism was associated with immediate and sometimes acute increases in death rates for broad segments of the general population. In some places, like troubled Russia, these postcommunist mortality crises continue to this very day.[3] But postcommunist "demographic shocks" also shook populations far better-poised than Russia for achieving a successful socioeconomic "transition" away from communism.

Chapter 7, "Demographic Shocks in Eastern Germany, 1989-1993," examines the reverberations of German unification in the population trends of the former German Democratic Republic. Although living standards for the former East Germans jumped dramatically with their integration into the Federal Republic, fertility levels underwent an immediate collapse. Still more paradoxically, despite general and substantial improvements in consumption levels and in the quality of medical care that unification heralded, death rates for most age groups rose in the immediate wake of unification, and overall life expectancy in Eastern Germany, for a time, *declined*.

Many lessons may be drawn—or proposed—from this East German experience. One of them, quite simply, is that live human beings are not a clean slate. Perverse, distorted, and literally sickening as the rules of life may have been under late Soviet-style rule, adjusting to radically different ones posed grave challenges to nontrivial portions of the general population. Those travails were impressed upon local mortality trends. With the political and economic liberalization of the former Soviet bloc region, it seems reasonable to expect an eventual convergence of mortality levels within greater Europe. But Soviet-style rule was a gruesome, and prolonged, historical detour; the attainment of Western European health levels in what was the East may have to unfold over similarly historical time horizons.

The final four chapters in the book explore more global population questions. Two of those chapters address "population problems" today; the other two speculate about some of the possible "population problems" of tomorrow.

In the estimate of many of today's respected public voices, the premier "population problem" of our time is rapid population growth—and, more particularly, rapid population growth on the part of the world's poorer peoples. The appropriate—indeed urgent—intervention required by rapid population growth, these voices advise, is effective anti-natal policy: measures capable of successfully depressing levels of childbearing.

In many quarters today, this diagnosis and this prescription are taken as utterly unexceptionable. Viewed a bit more clinically, however, it is readily apparent that proponents of these anti-natal policies are championing an intervention that happens to be in continuous search of a justification. Chapter 8, "Justifying Population Control: The Latest Argument," outlines and analyzes the shifting arguments employed in the advocacy of what was once forthrightly called "population control" policy.

A generation ago, the rationale for anti-natal population policies was held to be primarily economic: lower fertility and slower rates of population growth were said directly to accelerate the tempo of material advance and ease the burden of poverty. Years of subsequent economic research, however, have failed to generate the sort of empirical support that would be necessary to substantiate that proposition. Sophisticated proponents of anti-natalism recognized that it was incumbent upon them to make a new case for the policies they preferred. Their new arguments have included such points as the need to mitigate "demographic momentum" and the obligation to meet "unmet need" for contraceptive services. But for reasons I detail, these new briefs for the old policy are no more convincing than the ones they were intended to replace.

To many observers, global hunger is taken as clear proof that there *is* a world "population problem," and that excessive birth rates and rates of natural increase are at the root of this problem. Serious malnutrition and famine, these observers note, are the lot of societies with high birth rates—not low ones.

But as I attempt to demonstrate in Chapter 9, "Starved for Ideas: Misconceptions that Hinder the Battle Against World Hunger," such reasoning stumbles through an elementary fallacy of composition. Although undernutrition is, indeed, generally more prevalent in higher-fertility settings, it does not necessarily follow that the incidence of hunger in these locales would be appreciably altered by changes in child-bearing patterns—even sudden and dramatic ones.

The phenomenon of modern-day famine, for its part, is quite unmistakably driven by the hand of state: more specifically, by killer regimes that have embraced and driven forward cruelly and predictably destructive policies with indifference to the suffering engendered. Demographic trends have only the most incidental bearing on the likelihood of such deliberately contrived and politically enforced disasters. Like a number of today's other purported "population problems," mass starvation is in essence actually a *moral* problem: a problem grounded not on human numbers or patterns of childbearing, but in the political treatment of human beings.

The prevailing view of "population problems" and the now-fashionable predisposition toward anti-natalism may perhaps be explained as a reaction to the overarching demographic phenomenon of our era: the "population explosion." Over the course of the twentieth century, human numbers are thought to have very nearly quadrupled to 6 billion persons. Nothing like that pace of growth—never mind absolute growth—had ever been witnessed previously.

Long-term demographic predictions are problematic in the extreme, since we lack any reliable methods for estimating the likely family size of the currently unborn. Nonetheless, accumulating evidence suggests that the global demographic trends that define the coming century population profiles will be very different from the ones familiar from living memory. If so, the prevailing conception of "population problems" seems certain to change—perhaps even to change drastically.

At the moment, the world's most populous region is Eastern Asia. One-third of the world's people now reside in the expanse that extends from Indonesia to China. Chapter 10, "Population Prospects for Eastern Asia to 2015," considers the political, economic, and social implications for this area of the demographic developments it is likely to experience over the next couple of decades. Barring utter catastrophe, we can already talk with some confidence about Eastern Asia's population profile some fifteen years hence: virtually everyone who will be in Eastern Asia's labor force, marriageable cohorts, or pension populations then is already alive today.

Over the past generation, Eastern Asia was swept by a great wave of population growth. Nothing like that is likely to happen again in the coming several decades. Current fertility patterns assure this much. Although fertility levels are hardly uniform in this vast region, the overall average is actually now slightly below replacement: continued into the future, that would presage an eventual population decline.

Some places in Eastern Asia—most importantly, Japan—may actually experience the onset of population decline in the years immediately ahead. But even in countries where population totals are still growing, demographic profiles will be changing portentously. For most of Eastern Asia, a rapid aging of populations looks to be immediately in store; for much of the region, a peaking of population of working ages would also appear to be just around the corner.

Whether these trends prove to be "population problems," of course, will depend upon many factors—the most important among these being how societies and governments respond to them. Population aging, recall, is the natural corollary of improved life expectancies; its implications are hardly unambiguously adverse. But another demographic trend on Eastern Asia's horizon may be rather more ominous, precisely because it is so unnatural. This is the gender imbalance now emerging in areas of Confucian heritage.

In China, Hong Kong, Taiwan, and South Korea, the conjuncture of subreplacement fertility, strong son preference, and the availability of sex-selective abortion, has resulted in an arresting imbalance between baby boys and baby girls. Today's imbalance between boys and girls will, inexorably, become tomorrow's imbalance between prospective brides and grooms.

Thus, an impending "bride shortage" has already been set into motion in East Asia. Its exact social and political ramifications are difficult to envision from our current vantage point—but they could be far-reaching. This prospective "population problem" can be attributed to a lack of respect for the life of human beings: in this case, female human beings.

The final chapter, "What If It's a World Population *Implosion*?," contemplates a contingency far removed from the preoccupations of current population policy: the prospect that global numbers might peak, and thereafter decline indefinitely. Conventional expectations—and concerns—presume the continuation of human population growth. But it is no longer fantastical to describe the demographic paths that would lead, by the middle of the coming century, to a peaking of world population—and thereafter, a steady drop. (Indeed, as I point out, these sorts of scenarios are already being sketched out by some of the world's leading demographers.) Such a prospect, one should emphasize, does *not* presuppose catastrophic upheavals: to the contrary, long-term global population decline could be entirely consonant with continuing, uninterrupted improvements in health conditions around the world.

In contemplating a world given over to orderly, progressive population decline, one is, of course, obliged to picture societies quite different from the ones with which we have to-date been familiar. These societies, for one thing, would be more elderly than any we have yet known: in a world of orderly population decline, there would likely be many countries where the *median* age was 50—or higher. Small children, of course, would be scarce—as novel, perhaps, as the elderly had been in preindustrial societies. That, too, would be quite different from today's circumstances—even for countries we currently consider "low-fertility." But perhaps the most mysterious of the implications of a world population decline would surround the structure and operation of actual families. As I show, for such a world, it is entirely possible that in some countries a majority of children would have no biological relatives except their ancestors—full siblings, cousins, uncles and aunts would have become a sort of social anomaly. Just how families, and societies, would function in those countries is very hard to conceive—at least today, from our present vantage point.

Would a world of orderly demographic decline be a world in the grip of serious "population problems?" Some readers today will surely think so. It is not self-evident to me, however, that this should necessarily be the case.

Population aging, as already mentioned, is the flip side of longer lifespans—and longer lifespans are no curse. With declining population, the pressures upon economies and governments would clearly change—but those demographic trends would by themselves neither forestall the spread of prosperity nor greatly complicate the task of protecting a citizenry's rights. The family patterns that could attend an orderly population decline might well look strange to a contemporary eye; to many contemporary eyes, perhaps troubling or unattractive as well. But even such seemingly radical transformations of demographic rhythms need not result in "population problems": with humane adjustments, new arrangements may help individuals and societies cope with a new and unfamiliar terrain.

Humane adjustments, indeed, would look to be the key here. For in such a possible future it is our very humanity that will serve as the first line of defense against potential "population problems"—just as it does today.

Notes

1. The situation in the other remaining communist state—North Korea—is unclear. It is widely presumed that death rates there have shot up in recent years due to a continuing, and officially acknowledged, food emergency. But the precise magnitude of this mortality crisis remains unknown—and Pyongyang's prospects for withstanding its mounting systemic troubles remains an open question.
2. See, for example, Martin Bobak et al., "Socioeconomic Factors, Perceived Control and Self-Reported Health in Russia: A Cross-Sectional Survey," *Social Science and Medicine*, vol. 47, no. 2 (1998).
3. Cf. Nicholas Eberstadt, "Russia: Too Sick to Matter?," *Policy Review*, no. 95 (1999).

Part I

Population Problems in the United States

1

Prosperous Paupers and Affluent Savages:
The New Challenges to Social Policy
in America

My assignment this morning is to discuss the problems of poverty and poverty alleviation in modern America. To appreciate the nature and context of a contemporary problem it is sometimes helpful to frame it in historical perspective. To understand the dilemmas we confront today, we would do well to consider how the struggle against deprivation and material poverty has changed in our country over the past sixty years.

Imagine with me that we find a time machine, which transports us back to the year 1935. We are in the midst of the Great Depression, near its depths. Imagine further that we somehow manage to buttonhole one of the men or women then in Washington busily formulating President Roosevelt's New Deal. (Lest anyone forget, there *were* women in the New Deal, and not merely as ornaments. F.D.R.'s Presidency, one might say, began the feminization of policy: Secretary of Labor Frances Perkins, for example, was instrumental in framing the Social Security system that endures to our day.)

Suppose we have a chance to tell this man or woman a few things about America sixty years hence—about a world he or she may not live to see, but is striving to influence through Depression-era reforms. Suppose we offer a glimpse of the future by revealing the following six key facts about it.

First, that the United States would enjoy a tremendous economic ascent in the decades ahead. Between 1935 and 1993, by the estimates of the Commerce Department's Bureau of Economic Analy-

13

sis, America's gross domestic product grew by about 650 percent in real terms after adjustments for inflation.[1] Over those same years, estimated per capita GDP rose by over 270 percent—nearly quadrupling, in other words. Even measured against the boom year of 1929, the U.S. 1993 GDP would be over six times as large, and per capita GDP nearly three times as great. The economy's long-term performance would significantly exceed the expectations of the best economists of our New Dealer's time. Joseph Schumpeter, for example, proposed that the long-term growth rate of the American economy might be as high as 2 percent a year, and its per capita growth rate as great as 1.4 percent a year, between 1928 and 1978—and these projections were intended to startle his audience for their optimism.[2] In the event, the American economy grew at an average estimated pace of nearly 3 percent a year between 1929 and 1993, and per capita output, at 1.7 percent per annum.

Second, that future generations would never again face anything like the unemployment crisis of the 1930s. In 1992, a relatively unfavorable "recession" year, the civilian unemployment rate would be only one-third of its 1934 level; for the nonfarm labor force, the unemployment rate in 1992 would be less than one-fourth the 1934 level.[3] During the 1992 recession, unlike the Depression, the median spell of unemployment for those out of work would be less than ten weeks.[4] Thanks in part to post-Depression insurance and income support programs for unemployed individuals, by the 1990s even long spells of joblessness would not typically raise the prospect of losing one's house, one's car, or the opportunity to send one's children to college.

Third, the mechanization of agriculture between the 1930s and the 1990s would, for all intents and purposes, bring a virtual end in the United States to the age-old burdens of field labor. In 1930, over 21 percent of U.S. workers toiled in the agricultural sector; by 1993, less than 3 percent of our workforce was employed in farm, forest, or fishery, and less than 1 percent of the U.S. workforce labored as farmhands.[5] This great transformation of employment patterns would be recognized as auspicious by our New Dealer for at least two reasons: because earlier Americans knew farm labor as poorly paying, physically demanding work, and because agricultural mechanization would permit a great movement of the people from the countryside into U.S. cities (which were, after all, our traditional centers of opportunity and learning).

Fourth, tremendous increases in life expectancy—a veritable explosion in health—together with changes in U.S. fertility patterns would very nearly bring an end to the tragedy of orphanhood in America. In 1920, by the estimate of researchers in the Social Security administration, something like 8.5 percent of America's children under the age of eighteen had lost their father; another 2 percent had lost both parents.[6] By 1965, the estimated share of paternal orphans among the nation's children had fallen by two-thirds, and only 0.1 percent—a tenth of a percent— were full orphans.[7] The numbers are lower still, we can be fairly sure, for the 1990s. A terrible and once-dread agent of family disruption—one that visited not only grief but also financial catastrophe upon the bereaved— threatens ever fewer children in modern America.

Fifth, we can let our New Deal reformer know that court decisions and legislative initiatives will finally put an end to legalized segregation and legalized discrimination on the basis of race. By the early 1990s, in fact, this grave stain on the fabric of U.S. society will have been removed for more than a generation; equality of opportunity—irrespective of race, creed, or color—will at last be the law of the land.

Finally, let us inform our New Dealer about the vast increases in expenditures for persons in financial need between the Depression and the early 1990s. By the early 1990s, state, local, and federal governments would be spending about a quarter of a *trillion* dollars a year explicitly and expressly on persons in financial need. In 1992, a recession year, the total of cash and non-cash public benefits for persons with low incomes reached $290 billion.[8] That total works out to over $5,600 for every man, woman, and child in the lowest fifth of the nation's income ladder—over $22,000 for a hypothetical family of four. Between the Depression and the 1990s, of course, the dollar lost a great deal of its value to inflation: twenty-two thousand dollars from 1992 were roughly equivalent in purchasing power to twenty-three hundred 1929 dollars. But in 1929, a family spending $2,300 a year was considered quite well-off: in that boom year, in fact, only about a fourth of all American families managed to consume at that level.[9]

These six revelations about the future would indeed inform our New Dealer about profound social and economic transformations that lie in store for America in the years ahead. But would they prepare our reformer for what awaits him (or her) in the early 1990s?

Let's use our time machine to bring our New Deal friend to the present for a moment. And now let's list six things our visitor from the past will quickly learn about the current condition of American society:

First of all, we would surely have to mention the failure, for a full generation, to achieve any appreciable reduction in the official index of poverty in America. In 1993, in fact, the officially measured poverty rate for the population as a whole was slightly higher than it had been in 1966, twenty-seven years earlier.[10] More ominously, the officially measured poverty rate for American families has registered a steady rise for over two decades. Most troubling of all, the official poverty rate for children in the early 1990s was reported to be nearly one-and-one-half times as high in the late 1960s, and distinctly higher than it had been in the mid-1960s, when the "War on Poverty" commenced.

Second, we would have to mention the progressive rise in the proportion of American children living in fatherless homes. In 1993, only 74 percent of America's families with children had both a mother and a father in the home—a lower proportion than in 1946, despite the disruption imposed and the casualties inflicted, by World War II.[11] By 1993, nearly a quarter of the nation's children under eighteen years of age would be living in a female-headed household. Over 40 percent of the country's children would be in families that did not include their biological father.[12]

Third, our visitor could hardly help but notice that hundreds of thousands of persons—persons often desperate and deranged—are now wandering homeless through the streets in America's cities.

Fourth, our New Deal reformer might be interested to learn that over a million persons, at any given time, were incarcerated in correctional facilities in America in the early 1990s—a figure which speaks to a huge increase in criminality since the Great Depression. In 1992, 1.3 million prisoners were being held at any given moment in local U.S. jails and state or federal prisons.[13] Over four times as many persons were serving time in prison in 1992 as in the early 1960s.[14] In 1992, nearly 12 million arrests were processed for criminal offenses—three times as many as thirty years before.[15] In 1990—the most recent year for which such figures are available—roughly one adult American in forty was under "correctional supervision": in jail, in prison, on probation, or on parole.[16] For men over eighteen years of age, that ratio was one in twenty-four; for African-American adults, one in thirteen; for black males over eighteen, roughly one in seven.[17]

Fifth, despite the overall improvement of health in modern America, our visitor would learn that health trends for vulnerable groups in modern America were much less favorable. The proportion of babies born with dangerously low birth weights, for example, was higher in 1993 than in 1980; the incidence of low birth weight over those years rose for both black and white infants.[18] In contrast to the Depression decade of the 1930s, during which time life expectancy at birth for non-whites increased fully by five years,[19] life expectancy for African Americans stagnated between 1982 and 1991.[20] Over those years life expectancy at birth for black males actually registered a slight decline.[21]

Sixth, and by no means least, our visitor from the past would learn that a higher fraction of Americans were on "relief"—or what we now call "means-tested public assistance"—in the early 1990s than had been in the depths of the Great Depression. The U.S. Census Bureau publishes an annual report on poverty in America; its estimates are instructive. For the nation as a whole in 1992, 24 percent of the population, almost a quarter, lived in households that received some form of means-tested assistance.[22] Among African Americans, the proportion of the population in households receiving some form of means-tested assistance was nearly 53 percent; over 28 percent were obtaining means-tested *cash* assistance.[23] By contrast, in January 1935, according to the National Resources Planning Board, an estimated 26 percent of the country's black Americans were on relief.[24] Lest one presume that the pattern is particular to African Americans, we can look at the trends for the white population. That same Depression-era report estimated that 16 percent of American whites were on relief in January 1935;[25] by 1992, according to the Census Bureau, nearly 20 percent of the country's whites were seeking and obtaining some kind of means-tested assistance.[26] In 1992, over 30 percent of America's white children under six years of age resided in households receiving at least one type of means-tested assistance; every seventh white child under the age of six lived in a household obtaining publicly provided, means-tested cash.[27]

Now what would our New Deal reformer make of these facts? How would he or she reconcile what we had told them about the future with these unpleasant, but unavoidable realities?

It is true, to be sure, that some rays of sunshine would greet our time traveler upon stepping out of the capsule and into modern America. He or she would learn, for example, about the near elimination of financial poverty among America's elderly: between 1959 and 1991, the official poverty rate for persons sixty-five and over dropped by two-thirds—or by as much as five-sixths, if one of the Census Bureau's alternative official measures is to be trusted.[28]

He or she would learn about dramatic increases in per capita income, after appropriate adjustments for inflation, for the country's African-

American population: between 1967 and 1993 alone, per capita income for black Americans increased by over 75 percent.[29]

And he or she would also learn about the equalization of incomes between black and white two-parent families: by 1990, to go by median earnings, African-American married couples in their late thirties or early forties were making 92 cents for every dollar earned by their white counterparts.[30] (Appropriate adjustments for differences in educational attainment, one may note, would narrow that earnings differential still further.)

But quite clearly, from the perspective of a New Deal reformer, there would be something very, very wrong with the picture of modern America. Despite tremendous material advances, revolutionary improvements in knowledge and technology, and a vast augmentation of national wealth, the country's domestic social problems have by no means been eliminated. Paradoxically, in the early 1990s, such problems as crime, dependency, and family breakdown were far more acute than they had been during the Great Depression—when general income levels, and general levels of schooling, were so much lower. For a reformer or an idealist from an earlier time, the social problems with which we must currently cope, I submit, would be especially troubling, because they would be so completely unexpected. Contemplating our social problems today, I suspect, a visitor from the past would be stricken with a severe bout of cognitive dissonance. It is precisely that dissonance that I wish to discuss.

How is the dissonance to be explained? I don't propose to explain its every aspect. There are a number of serious issues possibly bearing on the nature of our domestic problems today that I will not touch upon at all. The workings of the American labor market (especially with respect to low-pay employees), recent trends in economic inequality within our society, and the apparent slowdown in improvements in productivity in our economy since the early 1970s are all matters of legitimate concern. Despite the categorical pronouncements we occasionally hear about these three problems, they seem to me extremely complex—not yet adequately understood by objective, impartial researchers, despite the considerable attention they rightly receive.

My objective is more modest. I simply wish to suggest that part of the dissonance to which I have alluded can be explained by the fact that ours is now a nation whose social and economic problems are no longer familiar, nor in any real sense traditional. Modern America is a country inhabited by large numbers of prosperous paupers and affluent savages.

As mass phenomena, these are quite new. The patterns of mass behavior attendant upon these syndromes constitute major problems for our society today. It is precisely these patterns, I submit, that account for much of what would surprise or dismay earlier eyes on surveying our contemporary landscape.

Consider the poverty rate, since we all hear so very much about the poverty rate: in research studies, in the news, in speeches by our candidates running for office. The poverty rate is arguably the main statistical tool that our government uses to measure economic well being for our population as a whole. But it's a bad statistical tool. It is a fundamentally flawed indicator, because it can only offer a misleading indication of financial well being (to say nothing of material well being).

This tool has an interesting history. The "poverty rate" that we use today was put together thirty years ago, at the start of the Johnson administration's "War on Poverty," by a researcher in the Social Security administration. She was told to come up with an index of poverty in America, and to do it on the double—the War on Poverty was waiting. Assigned the administrative equivalent of an overnight term paper,[31] this researcher and her team understandably did a quick and dirty job: they jumped for data which happened to be readily available at the time, and cobbled it together to make their index. They could not have known at the time that their quick and dirty index would guide social and economic policy in the United States for decades to come.

What is the "poverty rate"? In essence, it is an estimate of the proportion of the population whose reported annual income falls below a stipulated "poverty threshold" (which is officially established and varies by household size and type). Over the years, many criticisms have been lodged against the poverty rate, including the charge that it fails to account for differences in living costs in different parts of the country; that it may be using inappropriate deflators when adjusting for changes in living costs over the years; that it does not report fully actual earnings accrued by families; that it does not take a proper measure of the value of means-tested benefits and other forms of assistance utilized by low-income households; that it does not include the value of the imputed rent that America's tens of millions of homeowners obtain from their houses. In greater or lesser degree, all of those criticisms are valid, and the Census Bureau, which is responsible for computing the official poverty rate, has attempted to respond to them. But in a broader sense, all of those criticisms miss a basic point.

The point is that material deprivation and material poverty are conditions defined by *consumption levels*: they relate directly to a household's purchasing power, to its ability to obtain goods and services. The so-called poverty rate, however, doesn't even look at consumption levels: it focuses instead on reported income levels. This is a mismatch—often a complete mismatch. The extent of the mismatch becomes clear when one takes a look at the Department of Labor's annual Consumer Expenditure Survey. In any given year, households at the bottom end of the American income spectrum report spending much more money than they report earning. In 1991, for example, the bottom fifth of the households in the survey reported an average pretax income of under $6,000, but average total expenditures of nearly $13,500.[32] For every dollar they reported taking in, they said they were spending two dollars and twenty-five cents.

This discrepancy is not a mystery, and it is not grounds for a major Internal Revenue Service investigation. The simple fact is household incomes can vary considerably from year to year. People have good years and bad years, and when people have bad years, they tend to try to prevent their levels of consumption from plunging. To maintain or stabilize their consumption levels, they can do many things: draw down their savings, sell assets, take out loans, get help from friends and family. All of these activities can permit households to spend more than they are taking in, entirely apart from any government benefits they may obtain. Under such circumstances, income can hardly help but be an unreliable indicator of actual consumption levels for the less well-off segments of our population.

The fact is that the level of expenditures for every stratum of our society has increased substantially over time. When poverty estimates are based on expenditures rather than income, one observes progressive and dramatic reductions over the postwar period. Calculations by Daniel T. Slesnick, an economist at the University of Texas, are instructive in this regard. Slesnick devised a poverty rate that compares estimated or actually reported household levels of income (including means-tested benefits) against a "poverty threshold," which is adjusted over time for inflation. One set of his results shows a "poverty rate" for America that begins at 31 percent of the population in 1949, falls to 13 percent by 1965, and then keeps on dropping more or less continuously until it hits 2 percent in 1989 (the last year for these computations).[33] One may, of course, challenge particular assumptions used in producing these alternative figures on the incidence of material poverty in modern America. There can be little doubt, however, that attention to consumption rather than income is more appropriate in approaching the problem of material poverty—and that such an approach creates a distinctly different picture of the problem in America today.

Clearly, though, we cannot stop here. It is not enough to say that the official poverty rate is a bad measure and close the discussion. We are well aware that troubling things are occurring in our society—things with very real and distinctly adverse implications for the material well being of our nation and our children.

Let me mention just one of these and its ramifications. Marxist utopians of the nineteenth and twentieth centuries have talked at great length about the withering away of the state. That withering away has not occurred in any of the societies for which this possibility was under discussion. But we *have* witnessed an amazing, perhaps even revolutionary, "withering away" of a central social institution in modern America: this is the withering away of the family. (That is to say, of the family as traditionally understood: a mother-father union with children. If one is sufficiently sophisticated or inventive, any household configuration including human beings can be defined as a "family," and a "crisis of the family" becomes a definitional impossibility.)

The trends of the past thirty-five years have been both striking and consequential. Around 1959, only about 10 percent of the children in the United States were living outside of two-parent families. By 1990, that proportion was over 27 percent[34]—a near tripling in only thirty years. Trends have been most extreme for African-American families, where something like a sea-change has been registered. In barely a generation, the two-parent family went from being the norm to the exception for our African-American population. By 1990, over half of all black children in America were living in mother-headed families. Less than 38 percent were living in two-parent families. By 1990, moreover, less than a quarter of the country's African-American children were living under the same roof as their biological mother and their biological father.

But trends for America's white population were only different in degree—not in direction. By 1990, less than two-thirds of America's white children were living with both their biological father and their biological mother. Ten years earlier, the corresponding fraction had been over three-fourths—that is to say, over ten points higher.[35]

Despite the tremendous improvements in survival chances for partners in a marriage between the Great Depression and the 1990s, the survival prospects for marriages themselves have been falling over time. With increasing frequency, marriages that have produced children are disrupted: not by death, but by divorce, separation, and desertion.

A recent Census Bureau study puts our proclivities toward family breakup in quantitative perspective. The results are arresting. Between 1985 and 1987, 7.4 percent of the white two-parent families with children under eighteen in the survey suffered "discontinuation"; for their African-American counterparts the corresponding "discontinuation" rate was 12.2 percent.[36] Projecting this two-year breakup rate forward, one produces figures suggesting that only half of the white babies and less than one-third of the black babies born to married parents can expect to reach adulthood in intact homes. For technical reasons, those unadjusted, aggregate projections overstate somewhat the actual odds of breakup for particular marital unions. But given the trends in family breakup that we have witnessed over the past forty years, it is by no means impossible that these rough numbers will finally *understate* the prevalence of broken homes among children born to married parents in the mid-1980s. It is strange: the richer and the more educated our country has been growing, the weaker our family units seem to become.

It is tempting, indeed, to speak of the *anomalization* of the marital union. African Americans are in the vanguard of this movement. In 1975, nearly 77 percent of black women in their late twenties had been married at some time in their lives.[37] By 1990, the corresponding figure was 45 percent—a drop of over thirty points in fifteen years! For black women in their early thirties, the falloff is almost as steep: a drop from 87 percent in 1975 to 61 percent in 1990, or over twenty-five points. If this pace of change continues for the rest of our decade, by the year 2000 less than a quarter of America's black women in their late twenties, and fewer than 45 percent of those in their early thirties, will ever have been married.

High rates of non-marriage, of course, can no longer be interpreted as signifying high rates of childlessness. Paralleling the breakup of two-parent families is the rise of families never fully formed. Over the past four decades our country has experienced a veritable explosion of out-of-wedlock births. Back in 1960, about 5 percent of the births in America were reportedly to unmarried mothers. By 1992, the proportion exceeded 30 percent.[38] When the figures are in for this year, we can expect the proportion to be higher still. And as these large fractions should indicate, out-of-wedlock birth is not only, or even predominantly, a black phenomenon in America these days.

To be sure, the situation is more extreme for our African-American population. By 1992, more than two out of three black babies were born out of wedlock. But black babies no longer comprise the majority of the infants born outside marriage in the United States. In 1992, 37 percent of the country's illegitimate births were black; 63 percent were *not*. The stereotype of the unwed mother as a black teenager, furthermore, is by now completely outdated: in 1992, that group accounted for less than one-eighth of the illegitimate births in America.

Illegitimacy has become a "white thing" over the past generation. In 1960, 2.3 percent of the country's babies were reportedly born out of wedlock. By 1992, 22.6 percent were born out of wedlock—a tenfold increase in thirty-two years. In recent decades, in fact, the fastest increase in out-of-wedlock births has been for white mothers: and not for white teenagers, but rather for mothers over the age of twenty-five. Between 1973 and 1992, the absolute number of illegitimate births to white teenagers rose by about 70 percent; for white women in their thirties, the total jumped by a factor of ten. (By contrast, the total number of illegitimate births to black teenagers increased by "only" 16 percent between 1973 and 1992).

By the 1960s, the plight of the black American family had become a topic of national policy discussion. All too seldom recognized today is the fact that illegitimacy ratios for America's white population are generally higher than were the country's black ratios at the time of the now-famous Moynihan report.[39] Consider: in 1960, roughly 42 percent of the babies born to non-white girls between the ages of fifteen and nineteen were reportedly illegitimate. In 1992, over 60 percent of the babies born to white girls of those same ages were reportedly out of wedlock. In 1970, the illegitimacy ratio for black babies born to mothers in their early twenties was 31 percent; in 1992, the corresponding white illegitimacy ratio was 32 percent. At the moment, it would seem as if illegitimacy ratios for white America are roughly one generation behind the trends established by black America.

What are the consequences of the now pervasive tendencies of family breakup, and failure of families to form, for the United States? Three come immediately to mind. The first, of course, is financial and economic hardship. Many studies have been done on the financial consequences of divorce for children and for mothers; none of them have shown economic improvement in the situation of the typical fatherless household. All of them have shown serious drops in income, although the estimates vary from one study to the next. A Census Bureau report on the problem may be the most comprehensive to date: By its estimates, in families with children where the father moves out, and where the mother does not reconcile or remarry, household income falls by an average of 40 percent in the first year, and per capita income drops by an average of 25 percent.[40] The financial situation is even harder for the families of unwed mothers. The Census Bureau does not make a practice of disaggregating the income levels of various types of single-mother families, but my colleague Douglas Besharov has taken that extra step in some of his research. For 1990, he found a fateful difference between the incomes of never-married mothers with children and divorced mothers with children. For blacks and whites alike, the median incomes of these never-married single-mother households were lower by 40 percent, or more.[41]

Breakup of families, or failure of families to form, has also resulted in a great rise in dependence upon government assistance programs. In 1992, according to the Census Bureau, over 70 percent of those living in female-headed families with children were seeking and getting means-tested benefits; 44 percent of this population was using means-tested public cash. Among black female-headed families with children, reliance upon means-tested public benefits is now the norm: 86 percent of such households obtained at least one form of means-tested assistance in 1992, and 56 percent were getting means-tested public cash. But participation in government aid programs is fast becoming the norm for white single mothers, too: in fact, by 1992 over two-thirds of this group was drawing upon at least one form of means-tested aid, and nearly 43 percent were spending means-tested government money.[42] Long-term dependence upon public assistance programs is a very real prospect for the single-mother family. Recent research suggests that 14 percent of the country's divorced mothers with children had spent over ten years on the Aid to Families with Dependent Children (AFDC) program; among never-married mothers, roughly 40 percent had been on AFDC for a decade or more.[43] Those rates, of course, were calculated on the basis of past patterns. We have every reason to expect that the likelihood of long-term dependence would be higher for a single mother starting out today.

Finally, family breakup and illegitimacy are associated with the rise in crime in our nation. In modern America, the relationship between family breakdown and crime is not just strong: it is *very* strong. I could quote any number of studies to this effect, but here is Barbara Defoe Whitehead, from her widely read *Atlantic Monthly* article of April 1993:

> The relationship [between single parent families and crime] is so strong that controlling for family configuration erases the relationship between race and crime and between low income and crime. This conclusion shows up time and again in the literature. The nation's mayors, as well as police officers, social workers, probation officers, and court officials, consistently point to family breakup as the most important source of rising rates of crime.[44]

There is a good deal of discussion these days about health problems in our country. Some of the disturbing health trends in our country today relate directly to the problems of the modern American family. As I noted earlier, the incidence of low birth weight among America's newborns has been rising for a decade or more. Why should this be so in our increasingly affluent, educated, and technologically advanced society? One possible explanation relates to parental behaviors and practices. Simply put, there are many ways parents-to-be can predictably expose their babies to risk: these include (but are by no means limited to) heavy smoking, heavy drinking, illicit drug use, and neglect of prenatal medical treatment. Infants born out of wedlock are much more likely to face these hazards than babies born to married couples—even after taking race and educational differences of legitimate and illegitimate births into account. Indeed, the difference in health prospects is so stark that in the early 1980s black and white babies alike were less likely to survive the first year of life born to an unmarried college graduate than to a married high school dropout.[45] Like so many revolutions before it, our revolution in life-styles is eating its young.

Dangerous adult behavior, however, does not just threaten the health of our infants. I mentioned earlier the stagnation and decline in life expectancy for African Americans between the early 1980s and the early 1990s. How are these adverse trends to be explained? Statisticians at the National Center for Health Statistics (NCHS) have broken them down by component causes of death. Between 1984 and 1989, they found, black Americans enjoyed distinct reductions in mortality from heart disease, stroke, cancer, and other causes. But these improvements were overpowered by two other, extremely negative trends. One was a rise in deaths from homicide and what is called "legal interventions." The other was the sharp rise in deaths from HIV infection: AIDS death. Between 1984 and 1989 (the years covered by the NCHS study), worsening homicide and HIV mortality caused an overall decline in life expectancy at birth for both black men and black women, and accounted fully for those declines.[46] Both homicide and HIV are, as we know, behavior-related phenomena for which, at the moment, no medical cure exists.

To talk of the erosion of the traditional American family structure and of the rise of public social welfare programs is, inescapably, to beg the question of the connection between these two overarching twentieth-century trends. If we want to examine the role of social welfare programs in the ongoing fragmentation of American family patterns, we should perhaps begin by taking a look at AFDC. The AFDC program is only a tiny component of the modern American welfare state: in 1990, for example, AFDC expenditures accounted for barely 10 percent of all government means-tested outlays.[47] But AFDC is one of the federal government's longest-standing "family support" programs, reaching back as it does nearly sixty years. It is also one of the country's best known and most controversial social welfare policies.

In the 1930s, during the New Deal, the Social Security program now known as AFDC was called ADC—Aid to Dependent Children. The purpose of that program was outlined very clearly: it was a fund for widows and orphans—for survivors of deceased or incapacitated breadwinners. (This was the logic behind including ADC within the Social Security structure, which was ostensibly an arrangement for workers' insurance.) There were some criticisms of ADC at the time: worries voiced, for example, that this program might be used to support out-of-wedlock childbearing. Such criticisms, however, were peripheral. After all, when ADC got underway, over 70 percent of the children awarded benefits were the sons and daughters of dead or incapacitated fathers.[48] Less than 3 percent of the children accepted into the program qualified because their mother was not married to their father.

In the nearly sixty years since this program began, there has been a complete and utter transformation in its workings. Whereas less than 3 percent of the young beneficiaries of the program in the late 1930s were the children of unmarried women, by the early 1990s less than 3 percent were orphans: in the year between October 1991 and September 1992, only 1.6 percent of the children on AFDC qualified because a parent was deceased.[49] Over half of the children on the program (53 percent in the aforementioned year) qualified because their mother was not married to their father. In 1961, fewer than half a million children of never-married mothers were on AFDC.[50] By 1991-92, over five million such children were being supported in part by AFDC.[51] Indeed, by the early 1990s, every thirteenth American child under eighteen years of age was both living with an unmarried mother and living on means-tested public cash.

Contemplating these ominous developments, many people in the United States have wondered whether perverse incentives embedded in our social welfare programs might not be driving the adverse changes in family patterns over the last generation or two. The impact of our antipoverty policies on the country's family structure is a question of the utmost importance. Unfortunately, as a social science researcher I must report to you that it is extremely difficult to test for this impact, much less to quantify it, because the changes we would wish to consider are complex and intertwined. This may help to explain why there seem to be so many contradictory studies in this area,[52] although obviously it cannot explain why the conclusions from such studies are so often presented with such stridency.

I cannot resolve the disputes in what has become a large body of literature. I can, however, offer two observations. First, as I have already noted, by 1992 over half the children on AFDC were illegitimate. Furthermore, by 1992 rather more than half the children of never-married mothers in America were on AFDC.[53] Judged purely by its performance specifications, AFDC can therefore be accurately described as a policy instrument for financing illegitimacy in contemporary America. By extension, depending upon their particulars, other government social support programs can be seen, in greater or lesser degree, as vehicles for financing the out-of-wedlock life-style in modern America. To observe that such programs underwrite out-of-wedlock or single-parent life-styles is not to judge whether they create the syndromes they support, but simply to recognize what they do.

The second observation can be offered as a sort of "thought experiment." Imagine that all of the incentives—or if you will, disincentives—embedded in today's U.S. social welfare programs were suddenly transported back in time—not to our New Deal reformer's time, but back to Salem, Massachusetts, around 1660 or 1670. Now let us wonder: how many additional out-of-wedlock births might have occurred in Salem, Massachusetts, in the midst of the Puritan era, in the face of all the perverse incentives of the modern welfare state? Like all thought experiments, this one can't be answered conclusively. But my guess would be very few. The reasoning behind my guess is that most people in Salem, Massachusetts, in those years thought that engaging in what we now sometimes term "disorganized life-styles" would lead them to Hell. And there were a lot of people in Salem, Massachusetts, around 1660 and 1670 who believed in Hell.

To sum up: today's antipoverty efforts confront problems that were not faced by the New Dealers—and may not even have been imagined by them. (These problems, on the other hand, *were* imagined by the Puritans—although it is doubtful that many Puritans would have predicted such problems would ever be so rampant in their City on a Hill.) The problems to which I refer devolve from predictably injurious patterns of individual and parental behavior. These injurious patterns do not explain all of the social problems that we confront in our nation today. But they may account for a great fraction of the domestic problems we confront.

A revolution in personal behavior and personal attitudes has taken place in the United States since the New Deal. That revolution has coincided with a great surge in policy experimentation, as we have attempted to apply the techniques of problem-solving governance to an increasingly ambitious agenda of social concerns. For better or worse, we have been living through interesting years.

We have learned, to our sorrow, that the state is a limited and highly imperfect father for the family. If ambitious plans for restructuring our health care system (such as those widely entertained in 1993 and 1994) are eventually implemented, I fear that we will learn that the state is also a limited and highly imperfect mother for the family. No matter how expertly devised the policy, no matter how dedicated the civil servants, no matter how generously funded the initiatives, antipoverty and social policy programs will be judged a failure in any confrontation against the perverse patterns of behavior that characterize so much of what troubles us about modern American life.

The reassertion of individual and familial responsibilities, I believe, is central to the revitalization of our society. It is also central, I believe, to dealing with the dysfunctions that sadden and dismay us most about our national condition. But how such a resurgence is to be accomplished generally and effectively—much less how our governmental institutions are to abet such a resurgence—is far from clear to me.

Notes

*This paper is based upon a lecture delivered at St. Vincent's College in Latrobe, Pennsylvania, on September 14, 1994.

1. Derived from U.S. Bureau of the Census, *Statistical Abstract of the United States* (Washington, DC: Government Printing Office), 1993 edition: p. 445; 1994 edition: pp. 16, 451; idem., *Historical Statistics of the United States, Colonial Times to 1970* (Washington, DC: Government Printing Office, 1975), p. 10.
2. Joseph A. Schumpeter, *Capitalism, Socialism and Democracy* (London: George Allen and Unwin, 1943), pp. 64-65.
3. Derived from *Statistical Abstract of the United States 1994*, p. 417, and *Historical Statistics of the United States*, p. 126.
4. *Statistical Abstract of the United States 1994*, p. 416.
5. Derived from *Historical Statistics of the United States*, p. 138; *Statistical Abstract of the United States 1994*, pp. 407, 409.
6. Louis O. Shudde and Lenore A. Epstein, "Orphanhood—A Diminishing Problem," *Social Security Bulletin*, vol. 18, no. 3 (March 1955), p. 18.
7. Lenore A. Epstein and Alfred M. Skolnik, "Social Security Protection After Thirty Years," *Social Security Bulletin*, vol. 28, no. 8 (August 1965), p. 16.
8. *Statistical Abstract of the United States 1994*, p. 373.
9. Derived from *Statistical Abstract of the United States 1994*, p. 451, and *Historical Statistics of the United States*, p. 327.
10. Jason DeParle, "Census Sees Falling Income and More Poor," *New York Times*, October 7, 1994, A16; U.S. Bureau of the Census, *Poverty in the United States: 1992*, series P 60-185, p. 2.
11. Derived from *Statistical Abstract of the United States*: 1994 edition, p. 66; 1947 edition, p. 51. Postwar figures are for 1946.
12. Derived from *Statistical Abstract of the United States 1994*, pp. 16, 66-67.
13. *Statistical Abstract of the United States 1994*, p. 215.
14. Derived from *Statistical Abstract of the United States 1994*, p. 215, and *Historical Statistics of the United States*, p. 420.
15. Derived from *Historical Statistics of the United States*, p. 415; *Statistical Abstract of the United States 1994*, p. 206.
16. Bureau of Justice Statistics, *Correctional Populations in the United States, 1990* (Washington, DC: U.S. Department of Justice, 1992), p. 6.
17. Idem., pp. 6, 9, 24, 49-50, 121-22; *Statistical Abstract of the United States 1994*, p. 21. Estimates for the ratio of black male adults under correctional supervision are for non-Hispanic blacks, and are computed under the assumption that the proportion of male and female offenders is the same among African Americans as for the population as a whole.
18. National Center for Health Statistics, *Health: United States, 1993* (Hyattsville, MD: Public Health Service, 1994), p. 69. "Low birth weight" is defined as less than 2500 grams (about 5 1/2 pounds); "very low birth weight" is set at under 1500 grams (about 3 1/3 pounds). The incidence of both low and very low birth weights has been rising for both black and white babies in recent years.
19. *Historical Statistics of the United States*, p. 55.
20. *Health: United States, 1993*, p. 91.
21. Ibid.
22. *Poverty in the United States: 1992*, p. 31.
23. Ibid., p. 35.

24. Bobbie Green Turner, *Federal/State Aid to Dependent Children Program and Its Benefits to Black Children in America, 1935-1985* (New York: Garland Publishing, Inc., 1993), p. 95.
25. Ibid.
26. *Poverty in the United States: 1992*, p. 33.
27. Ibid.
28. *Poverty in the United States, 1992*, p. 4; U.S. Bureau of the Census, *Measuring the Effect of Benefits and Taxes on Income and Poverty: 1979 To 1991*, series P-60, no. 182-RD, p. 100.
29. Unpublished data, U.S. Bureau of the Census, provided to the author, October 26, 1994.
30. U.S. Bureau of the Census, *Money Income Of Households, Farms, and Persons in the United States*, series P-60, no. 174, pp. 68, 72.
31. This effort is described vividly in a retrospective by the principal creator of the "poverty rate." See Mollie Orshanksy, "The Poverty Rate: A Comment," *Social Security Bulletin*, vol. 31, no. 10 (October 1988).
32. *Statistical Abstract of the United States 1993*, p. 454.
33. Daniel T. Slesnick, "Gaining Ground: Poverty in the Postwar United States," *Journal Of Political Economy*, vol. 101, no. 1 (February 1993).
34. Arthur J. Norton and Louisa F. Miller, *Marriage, Divorce and Remarriage in the 1990s*, U.S. Bureau of the Census Special Report, series P-23-180 (October 1992), p. 11.
35. Derived from Ibid.
36. Donald J. Hernandez, *Studies in Household and Family Formation*, U.S. Bureau of the Census series P-23, no. 179 (September 1992), p. 9.
37. Figures derived from *Marriage, Divorce and Remarriage in the 1990s*, p. 3.
38. National Center for Health Statistics, *Monthly Vital Statistics Report*, vol. 43, no. 5 (S) (October 25, 1994), p. 48.
39. For further discussion of that report, see chapter 3.
40. Suzanne Bianchi and Edith McArthur, *Family Disruption and Economic Hardship: The Short-Run Picture for Children*, U.S. Bureau of the Census series P-70, no. 23 (January 1991), p. 10.
41. Douglas J. Besharov, "Not All Single Mothers Are Created Equal," *The American Enterprise*, vol. 3, no. 2 (September/October 1992), p. 15.
42. *Poverty in the United States: 1992*, pp. 31, 35, 33.
43. "Not All Mothers Are Created Equal", p. 17.
44. Barbara Defoe Whitehead, "Dan Quayle Was Right," *Atlantic Monthly*, April 1993, p. 72, cited in Michael Tanner, "Ending Welfare As We Know It," *Cato Institute Policy Analysis*, no. 212 (July 7, 1994), p. 14.
45. Nicholas Eberstadt, "America's Infant Mortality Puzzle," *The Public Interest*, no. 105, p. 37.
46. Kenneth D. Kochanek, Jeffrey D. Maurer, and Harry M. Rosenberg, *Causes of Death Contributing to Changes in Life Expectancy: United States, 1984-1989*, National Center for Health Statistics, series 20, no. 23 (1994), pp. 11-12.
47. Derived from *Statistical Abstract of the United States 1993*, p. 371.
48. Bureau of Public Assistance, "Changes in the Types of Families Accepted for Aid to Dependent Children," *Social Security Bulletin*, vol. 5, no. 6 (June 1943); figures are for 1937-38.
49. U.S. Department of Health And Human Services, *Characteristics and Financial Circumstances of AFDC Recipients: FY 1992* (Washington, DC: USDHHS Administration for Children and Families, 1994), p. 34.

50. Derived from Robert M. Mugge, "Aid to Families with Dependent Children: Initial Findings of the 1961 Report on Characteristics of Recipients," *Social Security Bulletin*, vol. 25, no. 3 (March 1963), and U.S. Bureau of the Census, *Household and Family Characteristics: March 1961*, series P-20, no. 116.
51. *Characteristics and Financial Circumstances of AFDC Recipients: FY 1992*, p. 34.
52. For a review of some of these contradictory findings, see Charles Murray, "Welfare and the Family: The U.S. Experience," *Journal of Labor Economics*, vol. 11, no. 1, part 2 (1993), especially pp. S234-S238.
53. Derived from ibid. and U.S. Bureau of the Census, *Marital Status and Living Arrangements, March 1992*, series P-20, no. 468, p. 29. In comparison with estimates of the nation's March 1992 population totals, the 1991-92 figure for children of unmarried women receiving AFDC payments was equal to 93 percent of the children living with never-married mothers; it was equal to 59 percent of the children living with "separated" or never-married mothers.

References

Besharov, Douglas J. "Not All Single Mothers Are Created Equal." *American Enterprise*, vol. 3, no. 2 (September/October 1992).

Bianchi, Suzanne and Edith McArthur. *Family Disruption and Economic Hardship: The Short-Run Picture for Children*. U.S. Bureau of the Census, series P-70, no. 23 (January 1991).

Bureau of Justice Statistics. *Correctional Populations in the United States, 1990*. (Washington, DC: U.S. Department of Justice, 1992).

DeParle, Jason. "Census Sees Falling Income and More Poor." *New York Times*, October 7, 1994, p. A16.

Eberstadt, Nicholas. "America's Infant Mortality Puzzle." *Public Interest*, no. 105.

Epstein, Lenore A. and Alfred M. Skolnik. "Social Security Protection after Thirty Years." *Social Security Bulletin*, vol. 28, no. 8 (August 1965).

Hernandez, Donald J. *Studies in Household and Family Formation*. U.S. Bureau of the Census, series P-23, no. 179 (September 1992).

Kochanek, Kenneth D., Jeffrey D. Maurer, and Harry M. Rosenberg. *Causes of Death Contributing to Changes in Life Expectancy: United States, 1984-1989*. National Center for Health Statistics, series 20, no. 23 (1994).

Mugge, Robert M. "Aid to Families with Dependent Children: Initial Findings of the 1961 Report on Characteristics of Recipients." *Social Security Bulletin*, vol. 25, no. 3 (March 1963).

Murray, Charles. "Welfare and the Family: The U.S. Experience." *Journal of Labor Economics*, vol. 11, no. 1, part 2 (1993).

National Center for Health Statistics. *Health: United States, 1993*. (Hyattsville, MD: Public Health Services, 1994).

———. *Monthly Vital Statistics Report*, vol. 43, no. 5 (S) (October 25, 1994).

Norton, Arthur J. and Louisa F. Miller. *Marriage, Divorce and Remarriage in the 1990s*. U.S. Bureau of the Census Special Report, series P-23-180 (October 1992).

Orshanksy, Mollie. "The Poverty Rate: A Comment." *Social Security Bulletin*, vol. 31, no. 10 (October 1988).

Schumpeter, Joseph A. *Capitalism, Socialism and Democracy*. London: George Allen and Unwin, 1943.

Shudde, Louise O. and Lenore A. Epstein. "Orphanhood–A Diminishing Problem." *Social Security Bulletin*, vol. 18, no. 3 (March 1955).

Slesnick, Daniel T. "Gaining Ground: Poverty in the Postwar United States." *Journal of Political Economy*, vol. 101, no. 1 (February 1993).

Turner, Bobbie Green. *Federal/State Aid to Dependent Children Program and Its Benefits to Black Children in America, 1935-1985*. (New York: Garland Publishing, Inc., 1993).

U.S. Bureau of Public Assistance. "Changes in the Types of Families Accepted for Aid to Dependent Children." *Social Security Bulletin*, vol. 5, no. 6 (June 1943).

U.S. Bureau of the Census. *Household and Family Characteristics: March 1961*. Series P-20, no. 116.

——. *Historical Statistics of the United States, Colonial Times to 1970*. (Washington, DC: Government Printing Office, 1975).

——. *Measuring the Effect of Benefits and Taxes on Income and Poverty: 1979 to 1991*. Series P-60, no. 182-RD.

——. *Poverty in the United States: 1992*. Series P 60-185.

——. *Marital Status and Living Arrangements, March 1992*. Series P-2-, no. 468.

——. *Statistical Abstract of the United States*. Washington, DC: Government Printing Office, 1993 and 1994 editions.

——. Unpublished data provided to the author October 26, 1994.

——. *Money Income of Households, Farms, and Persons in the United States*. Series P-60, no. 174.

U.S. Department of Health and Human Services. *Characteristics and Financial Circumstances of AFDC Recipients: FY 1992*. (Washington, DC: USDHHS Administration for Children and Families, 1994).

Whitehead, Barbara Defoe. "Dan Quayle Was Right." *Atlantic Monthly*, April 1993. In "Ending Welfare As We Know It" by Michael Tanner. *Cato Institute Policy Analysis*, no. 212 (July 7, 1994).

2

Why Babies Die in D.C.

Across the country and around the world, Washington is notorious as the "murder capital of America"—the city with the highest homicide rate of any major U.S. urban center.[1] Less publicized, but no less scandalous, is another D.C. distinction involving needless loss of life. The District of Columbia is also the "infant mortality capital of America"— the population center in which a baby is most likely to die during his or her first year of life.

Statistics from the Centers for Disease Control and Prevention (CDC) tell the story.[2] In 1991, the District's infant mortality rate stood at 21 per 1,000 live births. This was more than 2 1/3 times the national average, and over 75 percent higher than the infant mortality rate for the next worst federal area (the state of Delaware). Furthermore, whereas infant mortality in the rest of America has progressively and predictably declined over time, the death rate for babies born in the nation's capital was actually rising during the 1980s.

In 1989, for example, D.C.'s infant mortality rate was higher than it had been a decade earlier.[3] Washington's infant mortality rate has subsequently declined: even so, provisional figures indicate a slightly higher level for the city in 1992 than in 1983.[4]

What is it that ails babies born in the District? Try as they may, concerned citizens are unlikely to get a straight answer from elected officials. Nor will they fare much better if they try to wade through the blizzard of medical papers that are produced each year on the infant mortality problem in America. In political circles, and even within the U.S. public health community, inquiries about the causes and correlates of this tragic D.C. syndrome are all too often deflected, or answered as if by rote.

FIGURE 2.1

Health and Wealth in Black America: Black U.S. vs. Black D.C., c. 1989

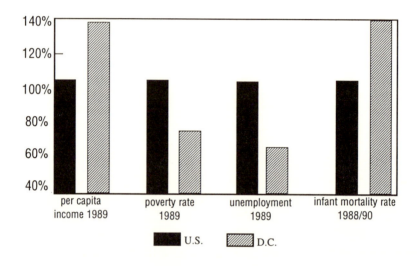

Sources: Census Bureau, Bureau of Labor Statistics, Centers for Disease Control and Prevention

The subtext to this unseemly reticence, apparently, is race. The District, of course, is the only contemporary U.S. state or would-be state with an African-American majority. And everyone knows that African Americans today generally suffer poorer health than U.S. whites. That, it would seem, is that: syllogism completed—discussion closed. Given the hypersensitivity within intellectual circles about any matter that may bear upon our country's racial problems, one can perhaps see why it is that investigations of the infant mortality crisis in our nation's capital have not been pursued more vigorously.

Has it actually become necessary to argue that the health of our children should not be sacrificed to prevailing intellectual fashions and prejudices? Apparently so. For even a cursory examination of available data reveals three important points about infant mortality in Washington that to date have somehow eluded our view:

- First, far from being representative of the condition of black America as a whole, the infant mortality situation within the District's African-American community is anomalous and distinct.
- Second, the traditional public health and public policy explanations for high levels of infant mortality are almost completely inadequate in explaining the District's strikingly poor performance.
- Third, the factors most strongly associated with the D.C. infant health problem—to wit, risks resulting from parental life-styles and adult behavior patterns—increasingly threaten children of all races all over the country.

To appreciate just how anomalous the District of Columbia's infant mortality situation is, compare it with Detroit's. By any variety of measures, after all, blighted Detroit is a vastly poorer city than Washington. Detroit's child poverty rate, according to the 1990 census, was very nearly twice as high as Washington's.[5] Per capita income was nearly 40 percent higher for African Americans in the nation's capital than for those in the Motor City.[6] The unemployment rate around 1990 for black Detroiters was well over twice that for black Washingtonians.[7] Despite all this, African-American infant mortality rates were actually higher in Washington than in Detroit in 1990.[8]

The contrast between wealth and infant health evidenced by Detroit and Washington is indicative of a broader paradox. While the black infant mortality rate for America has steadily fallen over the past generation, the black infant mortality rate in D.C. charted a much more troubling course. A generation ago, the city's black infant mortality rate was distinctly lower than the nation's; by the 1980s, it was distinctly higher.[9] In recent years, in fact, the black infant mortality rate has been higher for the District than for any state in the nation. According to the CDC's National Center for Health Statistics (NCHS), for example, Washington's black infant mortality rate in the years 1988-90 was roughly 40 percent higher than the national level for black Americans.[10] Yet the District of Columbia does not demarcate an area of extreme impoverishment within black America. Quite the contrary, as figure 2.1 demonstrates.

Per capita income for black Washingtonians is much higher than the African-American average nationwide: indeed, it is higher than the white per capita incomes of such states as Utah and Idaho.[11] The poverty rate for black Washington, according to the U.S. Census Bureau, is distinctly lower than for black America.[12] So is the unemployment rate.[13] As for education, the proportion of adults twenty-five or older with college degrees is distinctly higher for blacks in the District than for those in the country as a whole.[14] All in all, to judge by the sorts of yardsticks conventionally used for such measurements, the District of Columbia would appear to be an unusually affluent region of black America— possibly even the most prosperous population center in which black Americans gather.

That a most prosperous area should also experience a population's very worst infant mortality rates, needless to say, flies in the face of what is conventionally taught and thought about public health in modern America. Yet the contradiction between public health "models" and D.C.'s realities extends through an array of subsidiary detail. For many of the noneconomic indicators traditionally examined by public health specialists similarly fail to explain the District's terrible infant mortality problem.

Teenage mothers, for example, are commonly taken to be an epicenter of "high risk" births—yet, as of 1990, the fraction of babies born to teen mothers was lower among blacks in Washington than for blacks nationwide (21 percent vs. 23 percent).[15] By the same token, abortion procedures are sometimes said to be an instrument for dealing with "high risk" pregnancies; if so, women in Washington should be well-protected against adverse outcomes, for the D.C. abortion ratio consistently runs at roughly twice the national average for the non-white population of the United States.[16]

Finally, it is widely argued that access to medical care is often the decisive factor in health results for individual patients. The concept of "health care access" is more slippery than one might at first suppose: even so, there is no compelling evidence to suggest that the availability of health services is more limited for black Washingtonians than for other black Americans.

Unlike the rural counties of the South (whose black infant mortality rates, incidentally, compare quite favorably today with the District's), Washington is a medical mecca. Even after discounting the capital's many federal physicians and highly specialized internists, the level of public health service provision is very high. In 1990, according to the CDC, Washington's ratio of population to non-federal doctors engaged in primary care was nearly twice the national average.[17] So was its ratio of community hospital beds to population.[18]

Recent estimates by the U.S. Department of Health and Human Services (HHS), as well as D.C. government figures provided by District delegate Eleanor Holmes Norton's office, suggest that the per capita expenditure on health services for the District's resident population was as much as 60 percent higher than the national average around 1991-92.[19]

Estimates of D.C.'s population without health insurance, for their part, are far from precise. This is because Census Bureau figures on health insurance coverage are not broken down by race; moreover, the D.C. numbers are subject to a high margin of error (owing to the small size of the sample). The District's overall percentage of persons without health insurance in the early 1990s is estimated to have been one of the very highest in America. But U.S. blacks were far more likely to lack such coverage than U.S. whites in those years, and D.C.'s overall rate of coverage (through private health insurance and Medicaid combined) was about what one would expect to see in a random selection of whites and blacks from around the country, corresponding to D.C.'s racial composition. It is possible, in other words, that the prevalence of health insurance coverage might be lower for black Washingtonians than for the rest of black America—but it is also possible that it may be higher.[20]

In any case, several other states seem to have had levels of health insurance coverage as low as Washington's in the early 1990s. Yet their infant mortality rates for blacks and whites alike were far lower than the District's. In 1990, for example, the prevalence of health insurance coverage was about the same in Oklahoma as in the District of Columbia—but Oklahoma's black infant mortality rate was only about half as high as the District's.[21]

What then accounts for D.C.'s extraordinary infant death toll? The proximate answer is straightforward: It lies in the incidence of low birth weight babies born in the District. For entirely biological reasons, tiny babies are much less likely to survive infancy, no matter what their race. An American baby weighing less than 5 $1/2$ pounds at birth (the customary delineation of "low birth weight") is roughly twenty times as likely to die in its first year of life as one weighing more than 5 $1/2$ pounds. "Very low birth weight" babies (defined as less than 3 $1/3$ pounds at birth) are almost 100 times more likely to perish during infancy.[22]

The District of Columbia is, far and away, the low birth weight capital of America. In 1988-90, according to the CDC, over 15 percent of the babies born to D.C. residents were of low birth weight. This was over twice the national incidence, and nearly two-thirds above the level in the next highest federal jurisdiction (the state of Mississippi).[23]

It is well known that black babies in America are much more likely to suffer a low birth weight than white ones (although the reasons for this disparity are not yet fully understood). D.C.'s peculiar disposition toward low birth weight, however, cannot be explained by race alone. For the incidence of low birth weight is higher for black Washingtonians than for blacks from any state in the nation. In the years 1988-90, for example, a black American baby was nearly one-third more likely to be of low birth weight if born in the District (17.7 percent vs. 13.3 percent in the rest of the United States).[24] The risk of very low birth weight was over 50 percent higher in black Washington than for the rest of black America (4.5 vs. 2.9 percent).[25] Moreover, the incidence of low birth weight for blacks has risen steadily—and steeply—in Washington over the past two decades; far more so than in the rest of black America (see figure 2.2). Over the course of the 1980s, the proportion of black babies born at super-vulnerable, very low birth weights increased by more than half in Washington.[26] Despite some evidence of a decline since the late 1980s, preliminary figures for 1992 indicate that the incidence of low birth weight for black babies in Washington is higher than it was twenty or even twenty-five years earlier.[27]

Why is the District so fearfully efficient at turning out vulnerable and endangered babies? Less information is available than one might expect. Despite its infant mortality crisis, the D.C. municipal government has not yet gotten around to publishing vital statistics compendia that include data beyond the year 1986.[28] (Some would say that this fact itself is revealing about the nature of that crisis.) Unpublished figures drawn from Washington's birth certificates, however, point to a strong association between low birth weight and inadequate prenatal medical care. According to unpublished numbers for 1989, for example, a D.C. baby receiving no prenatal medical care whatsoever was nearly three times as likely to end up with low birth weight as one whose care began in the first three months of pregnancy.[29]

This fateful disparity is not solely due to the salutary properties of modern medicine. Mothers who do not get medical care for their babies during pregnancy are likely to endanger their fetuses in other ways as well. According to unpublished birth data for Washington for 1991, for example, black mothers who obtained no prenatal care during pregnancy were over twice as likely to say they smoked during gestation, and over three times as likely to say they drank, as those whose prenatal care began in the first trimester.[30] (Hard data are not available on illicit drug use, but it seems reasonable to guess this followed a similar pattern.)

FIGURE 2.2

Black Low Birth Weight: U.S. vs. D.C., 1970-91

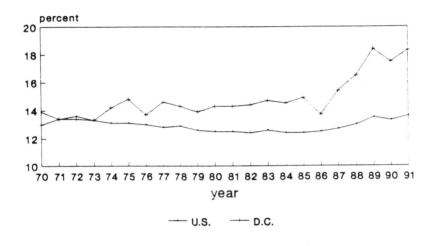

year

⎯⎯ U.S.   ⎯+⎯ D.C.

Source: Centers for Disease Control and Prevention

The District may be one of black America's most prosperous areas, but it is also has one of its worst rates of prenatal care utilization. In 1991, according to the CDC, about 62 percent of black America's mothers began their prenatal care during the first trimester of pregnancy; the corresponding figures for black mothers in the District were over eleven points lower.[31] The proportion of black mothers obtaining prenatal care for their babies only in the third trimester, or not at all, is over two-thirds higher in the District than in America as a whole (18.4 vs. 10.7 percent).[32]

FIGURE 2.3

**Percentage of Black Births with Inadequate Prenatal Care:
U.S. vs. D.C. 1991**

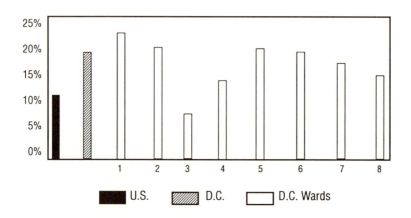

Sources: Centers for Disease Control and Prevention, D.C. Department of Human Services (unpublished data)

By this particular measure of inadequacy, in fact, the prenatal care situation for black babies in Washington was worse for virtually every ward in the city than for black Americans in the country at large (see figure 2.3). (Ward 3 is the exception to this generalization, and only a partial one at that: it accounted for less than fifty of the more than 9,000 black births to D.C. residents in 1991, and is thus basically irrelevant to overall patterns within the District.) One may note, incidentally, that these prenatal care patterns do not fit neatly within the conventional "socioeconomic" schema: Ward 8, for example, perennially has the worst poverty rate in the city, yet it also has one of the city's better levels of prenatal care utilization.[33]

If we could identify the parental characteristics associated with the District's very high incidence of low birth weight and its very poor utilization of prenatal medical care, we would be much closer to understanding the underlying causes of its infant mortality problem. By serendipity, a little-known compendium assembled by the D.C. Office of Planning permits us to take a step in that direction.[34] This compilation breaks down the District into about 170 neighborhoods ("census tracts"), providing economic, educational, and other information for these areas compiled by the 1990 census. It also offers data by census tract on items the census does not address. It tabulates, for example, the incidence of low birth weight, the illegitimacy ratio, the extent of participation in one means-tested public assistance program (food stamps), and the rate of violent crime by census tract. It also calculates the proportion of births within each census tract in 1989 and 1990 that received inadequate prenatal care according to the widely used "Showstack index,"[35] which plots the number of prenatal health care visits against the length of gestation.

For a number of somewhat technical (but commonsense) reasons, these census-tract figures are not ideal for exploring the relationship between low birth weight or poor prenatal care and the factors that might be behind them. To begin with, they do not provide breakdowns by race, even though the racial composition of the city's census tracts varies dramatically—and though there is reason to expect differences in these variables according to race. Even if racial breakdowns were available, moreover, a comparison of differences at the census tract level raises the risk of what statisticians call "ecological bias": that is to say, the danger of confounding general attributes of a neighborhood with the specific and possibly different attributes of the households within these neighborhoods into which babies are actually being born.

From a statistical standpoint, such intrinsic limitations are obvious. But what is also obvious is that one must work with what one can get, and the fact of the matter is that the U.S. statistical system does not regularly collect the sorts of data that would permit a detailed examination of the socioeconomic, behavioral, and environmental correlates of infant mortality. Birth and death certificates in our country provide no information on a mother's income level, much less the crime level in her neighborhood. The Census Bureau and the CDC collect enormous amounts of socioeconomic and health data, respectively, but they do not coordinate their research. And while the CDC does conduct a "National Mortality Followback Survey," which obtains financial data about decedents, it is specifically designed to "follow back" on adult deaths alone. D.C.'s census tract compendium may offer nothing more than a first look at the correlates of infant mortality in the nation's capital. But an interesting look—and for good or ill, a better look is unlikely to be available anytime soon.

Results from an examination of this compendium may seem in some respects counterintuitive. Washington is a city of great contrasts in poverty and wealth: at the census tract level, the official poverty rate ranged from less than 3 percent to over 60 percent. Despite such wide variations, however, the poverty rate appears to share only a weak association with differences in the incidence of low birth weight throughout the city. Such factors as educational levels and median household income correspond more strongly with low birth weight; yet the impact of even these factors is reduced to utter insignificance if illegitimacy is added to the equation. No other factors are so closely associated with differences in low birth weight among D.C.'s neighborhoods as their ratios of out-of-wedlock births and single-parent families.

Why does illegitimacy relate so strongly to low birth weight in Washington? In large part, it would seem, it is because of behavioral differences between married and unmarried parents. The out-of-wedlock birth ratio, for example, is an extremely powerful predictor of inadequate prenatal care among the District's diverse census tracts (see figure 2.4). This is true even if one controls for such things as the poverty rate and the fraction of births to teen mothers. Within Washington around 1990, it would seem, a 10-point difference in a neighborhood's illegitimacy ratio was associated with about a 5-point difference in the share of mothers who did not obtain adequate prenatal care over the course of their pregnancy.

Relatively prosperous as it may be, black Washington has one of the highest illegitimacy ratios of any black population in contemporary America. In 1991, according to the CDC, over 77 percent of the District's black infants were born to unmarried women. This is a ratio nearly 10 points higher than the black American average, and one exceeded in only three states (Illinois, Pennsylvania, and Wisconsin).[36] For a time in the early 1970s, the out-of-wedlock birth ratios for blacks in D.C. and the nation as a whole were roughly similar, but the subsequent pace of increase in the District proved to be more rapid than in the rest of the country.

The relentless rise of births outside of marriage has completely transformed patterns of childbearing in the District over the past generation. Between 1966 and 1991, for example, the ratio of out-of-wedlock births

FIGURE 2.4

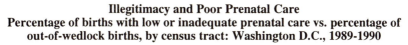

Illegitimacy and Poor Prenatal Care
Percentage of births with low or inadequate prenatal care vs. percentage of
out-of-wedlock births, by census tract: Washington D.C., 1989-1990

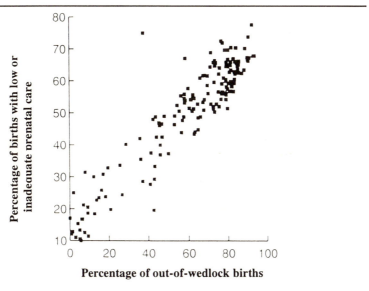

Source: D.C. Government Office of Planning

jumped by over 43 points (see figure 2.5). The chances that a baby would be born to an unmarried woman rose for mothers of virtually every age. So dramatically have the norms of family formation changed over these years that the illegitimacy ratios for black mothers in Washington are now about the same for women in their early thirties as they were for the city's teenagers in the mid-1960s.

This revolution in life-styles constituted an explosion of risk for the city's black newborns. One cannot assume that the relationship between illegitimacy and the risk of low birth weight in D.C. neighborhoods today has remained exact and steady over time. But if D.C.'s black illegitimacy ratio today were only as low as it had been during the Great Society era, our census tract correlations would lead us to expect an incidence of low birth weight nearly a third lower—and an infant mortality rate roughly one-fourth lower—than the ones that characterized the District in the early 1990s.

FIGURE 2.5

Age-Specific Illegitimacy Ratios for D.C.: 1966 vs. 1991

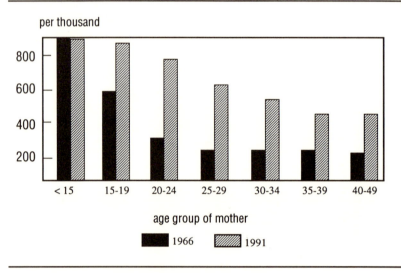

Source: Centers for Disease Control and Prevention

    There are other parental practices that appear to expose infants in the District to deadly risks as well. Within the boundaries of the city, differences in means-tested program participation rates track significantly with differences in rate of low birth weight. One may object that this is matching apples with oranges: After all, persons on such public benefit programs by definition are supposed to be poor. It is therefore somewhat surprising to find that after controlling for a neighborhood's poverty rate, higher levels of food stamp recipience still relate closely with higher rates of low birth weight.

    Other things being equal, a supply of food stamps should reduce the health risks facing newborns by improving a needy family's nutritional opportunities. But, evidently, other things are not equal. For within Washington, higher food stamp recipience closely corresponds with lower usage of prenatal medical services, even after such factors as poverty and educational levels are taken into account.

And then there is violent crime. This may seem an improbable indicator of health risk to the newborn, insofar as violent criminals are not generally capable of getting pregnant. Nevertheless, even after controlling for poverty and education, differences in reported rates of violent crime track with differences in rates of low birth weight in the city's diverse neighborhoods. The same is true for violent crime and poor prenatal care: that relationship holds up even when such things as median household income, poverty rates, educational levels, and teen motherhood are taken into account.

What explains the association between violent crime and low birth weight in Washington? At the moment, unfortunately, we can only guess. It may be that neighborhoods in which violent crime is out of control are also afflicted by a breakdown of norms that have traditionally served to protect the life chances of the newborn. Perhaps there are alternative or independent reasons for this striking relationship—such possibilities cannot be ruled out. At the very least, however, this statistical correspondence should prompt us to wonder whether Washington's concurrent status as "murder capital" and "infant mortality capital" might be the result of something other than pure coincidence.

To summarize: D.C.'s ongoing infant mortality crisis can indeed be understood—if we are willing to face what we see. Understanding the crisis, however, compels us to recognize new realities. Impersonal "social forces"—material deprivation, joblessness, economic insecurity—cannot explain why one of the very richest black populations in America suffers from black America's very worst infant mortality rates. This perverse situation can, however, be explained in terms of dysfunctional or even pathological behavior by parents and adults—including parents and adults who happen to be neither poor nor poorly educated. Illegitimacy, welfare dependence, and the environment of violent crime mark out a vector of deadly risks to infants in Washington, D.C.

But not in Washington, D.C. alone—and not just for black Americans. Over the past three decades, crime, illegitimacy, and welfare dependence have all been moving from the periphery of the American scene to the center. In the process, these syndromes also appear, in varying degrees, to have been getting "whiter." Between 1960 and 1991, the annual number of white persons arrested in America more than tripled.[37] From 1961 to 1991, the estimated U.S. white illegitimacy ratio octupled.[38] By 1992, according to the Bureau of the Census, over a quarter of the country's white families with children under six years of age accepted some form of means-tested public assistance; in the early 1990s every seventh white family with young children was taking cash aid from the state.[39] By a strange twist of fate, this is almost exactly the same fraction that one would have found for non-white children in America some thirty years ago.[40]

And there is another thing. The incidence of very low birth weight babies in white America started rising in 1978; it has been going up ever since.[41]

The District of Columbia may thus offer a glimpse of the sorts of infant health problems that the nation as a whole will know in the years to come. In the District, however, the future has already arrived. By all indications, we are woefully unprepared.

Notes

1. For the period 1985-1994, the homicide rate for Washington, DC, was higher than for any other American city with a population of 200,000 persons or more. For the years 1988-1992, Washington had the highest annual murder rate of any major metropolitan center. See Pamela K. Lattimore et al., *Homicide in Eight U.S. Cities: Trends, Context and Policy Implications* (Washington, DC: U.S. Department of Justice, National Institute of Justice Research Report NCJ 167262, December 1997).
2. CDC National Center for Health Statistics, *Monthly Vital Statistics Report*, vol. 42, no. 2 (S), August 31, 1993, p. 53.
3. Fern Johnson and Olive Shisana, "Infant Mortality in the District of Columbia: Reasons for No Statistically Significant Change," Washington, DC: Government of the District of Columbia Office of Policy and Planning, Research and Statistics Division, Statistical Note #91, January 1991, p. 26; *Vital Statistics of the District of Columbia 1986* (Washington, DC: District of Columbia Office of Policy and Planning, n.d.), p. 31.
4. *Vital Statistics of the District of Columbia 1986*, p. 31; "Births, Infant Deaths and Infant Mortality Rates (IMR*) by Ward (1990-1992)," District of Columbia Commission on Public Health, Office of Maternal and Child Health, April 1993 (unpublished).
5. U.S. Bureau of the Census, *Statistical Abstract of the United States 1993* (Washington, DC: Government Printing Office, 1993), p. 472.
6. Ibid., p. 468.
7. See U.S. Bureau of Labor Statistics' annual publication, *Geographic Profile of Employment and Unemployment*. In 1989, the black unemployment rate in Washington, DC was 6.7 percent, versus Detroit's 17.7 percent; in 1991, the corresponding percentages were 10.3 and 23.2, respectively.
8. "Live births, infant deaths, and infant mortality rates by race of mother and race of child for twenty-two cities of 500,000 population or more in 1980: 1990," unpublished data prepared by the CDC National Center for Health Statistics Mortality Division (dated September 27, 1993).
9. In 1967-69, for example, the black infant mortality rate for the United States was 36.1 per 1000 and 29.3 per thousand for the District of Columbia. For the years

1988-90, the infant mortality rate for African-American babies was 18.4 for the United States as a whole, but 25.7 for D.C. [National Center for Health Statistics, *Health: United States* (Hyattsville, MD: U.S. Public Health Service): 1982 edition, p. 55; 1992 edition, p. 37.] Over the course of those two decades, Washington, DC's black infant mortality rate, which had been nearly 20 percent below the national average, ended up almost 40 percent above it.

10. Cf. note 9.
11. *Statistical Abstract of the United States 1993*, p. 468.
12. In 1989, the official poverty rate for African Americans was 29.5 percent nationwide, and 20.2 in the District of Columbia. (*Statistical Abstract of the United States 1993*, p. 471.)
13. In 1989, the black unemployment rate was 11.4 percent countrywide, and 6.7 percent in the District of Columbia; in 1991, the respective percentage rates were 12.4 and 10.3. (U.S. Bureau of Labor Statistics, *Geographical Profile of Employment and Unemployment, 1989*, Bulletin 2361, May 1990, p. 105; idem, *Geographical Profile of Employment and Unemployment, 1991*, Bulletin 2410, August 1992, p. 110.)
14. In 1990, 11.3 percent of all black Americans twenty-five years of age or older were estimated to have completed four years or more of college. In Washington, DC, in 1989, 15.3 percent of the black population twenty-five and older had attained bachelor's degrees or some graduate or professional degrees. Derived from *Statistical Abstract of the United States 1993*, p. 154, and U.S. Bureau of the Census, *1990 Census of Population: Social and Economic Characteristics, District of Columbia 1990 CP-1-10* (Washington, DC: Government Printing Office, 1993), p. 200.
15. Derived from National Center for Health Statistics, *Vital Statistics of the United States 1990* (Hyattsville, MD: U.S. Public Health Service, 1994), vol. 1, Table I-60.
16. For the years 1980-89, for example, the abortion ratio (abortions per 100 live births) was 54 for non-whites nationwide, and 111 for D.C. births of all races. Derived from *Health: United States*, 1992 edition, p. 28; "Infant Mortality in the District of Columbia: Reasons for No Statistically Significant Change," Table 2; and Sara T. Glendinning, "Statistical Note: Induced Terminations of Pregnancy (Abortions) in the District of Columbia: 1992," District of Columbia Commission on Public Health, Research and Statistics Division, August 1993.
17. *Health: United States*, 1992 edition, p. 141.
18. Ibid., p. 156.
19. In 1991, per capita health care expenditures for the United States as a whole averaged an estimated $2,518. In FY 1992, expenditures for health care services and supplies for D.C. residents totaled an estimated $2,486.4 million. Since D.C.'s estimated population in 1990 was 607,000, estimated per capita health expenditures averaged roughly $4,100. Derived from *Health: United States*, 1992 edition, p. 169; *Statistical Abstract of the United States 1993*, p. 36; and unpublished data from congressional delegate Eleanor Holmes Norton's office, transmitted January 26, 1994.

Figures on per capita health care expenditures in Washington, DC, may be biased upwards due to the fact that medical facilities for the Veteran's Administration and other organizations ministering to a countrywide clientele happen to be located in the nation's capital. Estimates of health expenditures for D.C. *residents* should, in principle, not be subject to that bias. Even if it did not, however, per capita expenditures would still be substantially higher for Washington than for the country as a whole. Limiting health care expenditures to private house-holds, local businesses, and the major public sources (Medicare, Medicaid, the D.C. Commission on Public Health, the D.C. Commission on Mental Health, and D.C. General Hospital) would imply a FY health spending total of just over $2 billion—or about $3,350 per capita. That would still be roughly one-third higher than the national level of per capita health care spending in 1991.

20. Analysis based upon special data request to U.S. Census Bureau, Income Statistics Branch; processed March 10, 1994.

21. Derived from note 20 and *Statistical Abstract of the United States 1993*, p. 90.

22. Derived from *Health: United States*, 1992 edition, pp. 22, 34.

23. Ibid., p. 26.

24. Ibid.

25. Ibid., p. 27.

26. Ibid.

27. Provisional figures for 1992 indicate that the incidence of low birth weight (LBW) for D.C. babies *of all races* was 14.9 percent. By contrast: the incidence of LBW for *black* babies in D.C. was 13.4 percent in 1971, and 12.9 percent in 1969. "Births, Infant Deaths and Infant Mortality Rates (IMR*) by Ward (1990-1992)," loc. cit.; "Vital Statistics of the District of Columbia 1986," loc. cit., p. 28; Government of the District of Columbia, *Vital Statistics Summary 1969* (Washington, DC: Department of Human Resources, Research and Statistics Division, n.d.), pp. 27, 28.

28. This essay was written and published in 1994. At that juncture, it was the most "up-to-date" volume of *Vital Statistics of the District of Columbia*. Over the intervening five years, the situation has become, if anything, even more anomalous and extreme.

As of 1999, apparently the only data on infant mortality published by the D.C. Government were in the Office of Policy and Evaluation's *Indices: A Statistical Index to District of Columbia Services*. That volume, however, appeared only biennially—and contained no more than six pages of information pertaining to vital trends! Some data on D.C. vital trends have been available, since late 1998, at a private website <http://www.dcstats.org>. Unfortunately, the data available on this website to date are minimal: a total of six simple summary tables on births and deaths in the District of Columbia in the year 1996.

To appreciate the contrast with an earlier period, one may simply note that the 1983 edition of *Vital Statistics of the District of Columbia* was a 132-page volume.

29. "Infant Mortality in the District of Columbia: Reasons for No Statistically Significant Change," loc. cit., appendix 19.

30. Unpublished data, D.C. Government Department of Human Services; run-date October 1, 1992.

31. *Health: United States*, 1992 edition, p. 23; unpublished data, D.C. Government Department of Human Services, run-date October 1, 1992.

32. Ibid.

33. Poverty rates by Ward for 1990 available from *Indices: A Statistical Index to District of Columbia Services* (Washington, DC: Office of Policy and Evaluation, December 1992). Data on prenatal health care utilization by Ward from unpublished D.C. Government Department of Human Services datafile, run-date October 1, 1992.

34. D.C. Government Office of Planning, *District of Columbia Socio-Economic Indicators by Census Tract* (Washington, DC: D.C. Government, 1992). I am in-

debted to Herbert Bixhorn for bringing this source to my attention.

35. Showstack, J. A., et al, "Factors Associated with Birthweight: An Exploration of the Roles of Prenatal Care and Length of Gestation," *American Journal of Public Health*, vol. 74, no. 9 (1984), pp. 1003-1008.

36. *Vital Statistics of the United States*, 1991 edition, vol. 1, Table 1-83.

37. U.S. Bureau of the Census, *Historical Statistics of the United States: Colonial Times to 1970* (Washington, DC: Government Printing Office, 1975), part 1, p. 415; *Statistical Abstract of the United States 1993*, p. 198.

38. *Vital Statistics of the United States*, 1991 edition, vol. 1, Table 1-76.

39. Derived from U.S. Bureau of the Census, *Poverty in the United States: 1992*, Series P60-185, September 1993, Table 7.

40. Derived from U.S. Department of Health, Education and Welfare, "Characteristics of Families Receiving Aid to Families with Dependent Children, November-December 1961," (Washington, DC: H.E.W. Welfare Administration, Bureau of Family Services, Division of Program Statistics and Analyses, April 1963).

41. In 1978-80, the incidence of very low birth weight was 0.91 percent for white American babies. By 1993-95—fifteen years later—it was 1.03 percent. In 1996—the most recent year for which such data are available—it was 1.10 percent. *Health: United States*, 1992 edition, p. 27; 1996-97 edition, p. 92; 1996 incidence derived from *Monthly Vital Statistics Report,* vol. 46, no 12 (S), August 27, 1998, p. 10.

References

CDC National Center for Health Statistics. *Monthly Vital Statistics Report*, vol. 42, no. 2 (S), August 31, 1993.

CDC National Center for Health Statistics Mortality Division. Unpublished data (dated September 27, 1993).

District of Columbia Commission on Public Health, Office of Maternal and Child Health. "Births, Infant Deaths and Infant Mortality Rates (IMR*) by Ward (1990-1992)." April 1993 (unpublished).

District of Columbia Office of Policy and Planning. *Vital Statistics of the District of Columbia 1986* (Washington, DC: District of Columbia Office of Policy and Planning, n.d.).

——. *District of Columbia Socio-Economic Indicators by Census Tract* (Washington, DC: D.C. Government, 1992).

Glendinning, Sara T. "Statistical Note: Induced Terminations of Pregnancy (Abortions) in the District of Columbia: 1992." District of Columbia Commission on Public Health, Research and Statistics Division, August 1993.

Johnson, Fern and Olive Shisana. "Infant Mortality in the District of Columbia: Reasons for No Statistically Significant Change." Washington, DC: Government of the District of Columbia Office of Policy and Planning, Research and Statistics Division, Statistical Note #91, January 1991.

Lattimore, Pamela K. et al. *Homicide in Eight U.S. Cities: Trends, Context and Policy Implications* (Washington, DC: U.S. Department of Justice, National Institute of Justice Research Report NCJ 167262, December 1997).

National Center for Health Statistics. *Health: United States* (Hyattsville, MD: U.S. Public Health Service), 1982 and 1992 editions.

——. *Vital Statistics of the United States 1990* (Hyattsville, MD: U.S. Public Health Service, 1994), vol. 1.

Office of Policy and Evaluation. *Indices: A Statistical Index to District of Columbia Services* (Washington, DC: Office of Policy and Evaluation, December 1992).

Showstack, J. A., et al. "Factors Associated with Birthweight: An Exploration of the Roles of Prenatal Care and Length of Gestation." *American Journal of Public Health*, vol. 74, no. 9 (1984), pp. 1003-1008.

U.S. Bureau of the Census. *Historical Statistics of the United States: Colonial Times to 1970* (Washington, DC: Government Printing Office, 1975), part 1.

——. *Statistical Abstract of the United States 1991* (Washington, DC: Government Printing Office, 1991).

——. *Poverty in the United States: 1992*, Series P60-185, September 1993.

——. *1990 Census of Population: Social and Economic Characteristics, District of Columbia 1990 CP-1-10* (Washington, DC: Government Printing Office, 1993).

——. *Statistical Abstract of the United States 1993* (Washington, DC: Government Printing Office, 1993).

U.S. Bureau of Labor Statistics. *Geographical Profile of Employment and Unemployment, 1989.* Bulletin 2361, May 1990.

——. *Geographical Profile of Employment and Unemployment, 1991.* Bulletin 2410, August 1992.

U.S. Department of Health, Education and Welfare. "Characteristics of Families Receiving Aid to Families with Dependent Children, November-December 1961." (Washington, DC: H.E.W. Welfare Administration, Bureau of Family Services, Division of Program Statistics and Analyses, 1962).

3

Daniel Patrick Moynihan, Epidemiologist

Daniel Patrick Moynihan, it seems safe to say, ranks today as America's most eminent public policy intellectual. Now beginning his third decade of service in the United States Senate, and currently embarked upon his fifth decade of life within the public arena, Moynihan has established himself as a learned, penetrating, and often provocative analyst on a panoply of problems pertaining to what is sometimes called "the public interest." Moynihan, moreover, never seems to have trouble committing his thoughts to paper. In between his other activities, Moynihan is constantly writing or editing books. *Miles to Go: A Personal History of Social Policy* (Cambridge, MA: Harvard University Press, 1996) is the seventeenth of these—and most likely not the last.

Anyone even vaguely familiar with his work will already know that Daniel Patrick Moynihan is a polymath. Indeed, this sometime political adviser, sub-Cabinet member, special assistant to the President, Harvard professor, diplomat, and senator has occupied himself as an established expert, if not a preeminent authority, in an unnerving multiplicity of intellectual disciplines and academic fields: among them, American history, architectural criticism, arms control, educational policy, ethnology, incomes policy, international law, public finance, public policy research and evaluation, the sociology of the family, and urban planning. It should come as no surprise that the intellectual ambit of this evidently incorrigible trespasser among fields of specialized learning has taken him into many other areas not enumerated above. What may, nonetheless, surprise readers is that Daniel Patrick Moynihan's writings—including this recent book—show him to be a formidable student of epidemiology.

51

Epidemiology, in the careful but inelegant definition of a recent dictionary devoted to the topic, is the "study of the distribution and determinants of health-related states or events in specified populations, and the application of this study to control of health problems" (Last 1988: 42). In Dr. Ian Rockett's somewhat more lucid explanation, epidemiologists investigate "why disease and injury afflict some people more than others, and why they occur more frequently in some locations and times than at others—knowledge necessary for finding the most effective ways to treat and prevent health problems" (Rockett 1994: 2). In the epidemiological approach to public health problems, "the primary units of concerns are groups of persons, not individuals" (Friedman 1974: 1), and the method, in the classic formulation of Dr. W.H. Frost, "includes [the] orderly arrangement of [established facts] into chains of inference which extend more or less beyond the bounds of direct observation" (Frost 1936: 9). From these specifics, it will be apparent that Daniel Patrick Moynihan has demonstrated an epidemiological inclination, and displayed an epidemiological virtuosity, in his nearly forty years of study of three contemporary American social issues: traffic safety, crime, and drugs. *Miles to Go*, while also covering a number of more familiar Moynihan policy concerns, provides us with some update on his abiding interest in these three public health questions.

Violent crime, illicit drug use, and traffic hazards are of course more than just public health questions. But public health questions they most assuredly are. And when considered as health problems, there is a characteristic similarity between them. Indeed, the International Classification of Diseases (ICD), the standard taxonomy against which doctors issue diagnoses and coroners fill out death certificates, groups the adverse consequences of these three ills together under a single broader heading: "Injury and Poisoning." Although relatively few non-epidemiologists might recognize this to be the case, "Injury and Poisoning" have posed a major, and, by some indices, a mounting threat to the nation's health over the postwar period—that is to say, during an era in which the United States not only has enjoyed an unsurpassed and still-growing affluence, but also suffered demographically negligible losses and injuries due to military conflict.[1] Yet even as the U.S. lifespan has steadily lengthened, deaths due to "external causes" (unintentional injuries, including motor vehicle crashes; suicide; and what is termed "homicide and legal intervention") have assumed a troubling prominence in the modern American mortality structure.

In 1960, according the National Center for Health Statistics (NCHS), deaths from "external causes" accounted for 8.6 percent of all deaths in the American population; in 1993, the fraction had risen to 10.4 percent (derived from NCHS 1996: 110-11). (These figures are age-standardized and thus unaffected by intervening shifts in the country's demographic composition; no less tellingly, the ominous upward trend is evident for every major sub-population, from black males to white females.) Trends are even more dramatic when cast in terms of "years of potential life lost" (YPLL), a measure of premature mortality among those under sixty-five years of age. In 1970, deaths due to "external causes" were calculated to comprise 24.7 percent of total YPLL; by 1993, they comprised 28.9 percent—a higher fraction for the general American population than had been characteristic for black males just twenty-three years earlier (derived from NCHS 1996: 112-113). In 1993, the toll in YPLL from "unintentional injuries" (principally, motor vehicle crashes) was greater than from all types of cancer ("neoplasms") combined; by the same measure, "homicide and legal intervention" that year resulted in more premature loss of life than did heart attacks ("ischemic heart disease"). Despite continuing and dramatic improvements in emergency-room and paramedic intervention capabilities, moreover, the age-standardized death rate in America due to "homicide and legal intervention"—injuries that were crimes in themselves, or caused by crime—more than doubled between 1960 and 1993.[2] Of all the deadly risks in postwar American daily life, perhaps only the AIDS epidemic has proved more stubbornly resistant to the diverse public and private therapies that have been applied in the attempt to subdue it.

The phenomenon of violent injury in modern American life is in some sense similar to a number of other public policy challenges with which Moynihan's name has become associated: it is a problem (or set of interrelated problems) with major consequences for the nation's well being, surprisingly poorly understood even by specialists, and seemingly unsubmissive in the face of sustained policy intervention. Moynihan, the epidemiologist, did not discover cures to the afflictions he analyzed. In epidemiology, there usually are no "cures." A good epidemiologist, instead, can help to reduce the burden upon a population from given health risks by devising strategies based upon an informed assessment of the "etiology" (what social scientists might call "dynamics") of the hazard in question. American policymakers today understand the "etiology" of traffic injury, crime, and drugs more clearly, thanks to Moynihan's insights.

Traffic Safety

Miles to Go only glances upon the topic of auto safety, observing that

In the 1960s the morbidity and mortality associated with automobile crashes was arguably a major public health problem; the public health strategy arguably brought the problem under a measure of control (p. 155).

Yet this aside fails to convey either the consequence of the policy interventions in question, or Moynihan's own role in shaping them. A little background is necessary here.

Moynihan has been a student of automobile safety since the late 1950s, when he worked on highway safety policy (among other things) for New York Governor Averell Harriman. His most important analytical contribution to the study of vehicular injury, however, was his essay, "Traffic Safety and the Body Politic," which appeared originally in *The Public Interest* in the spring of 1966.[3] This is, quite simply, an extraordinary piece of work. Even thirty years after its publication, the reader cannot help but be impressed by the originality and the intellectual power of its exposition. In fewer than 10,000 words, Moynihan revolutionized the American approach to auto safety, transforming the then-deadly-dull topic of "road safety" into an intriguing (and researchable) area of policy inquiry, and outlining the directions by which private and collective action could progressively reduce the human toll exacted by the driving machine. Since this remarkable article is less widely known than it should be, it deserves special attention here.

The central insight in "Traffic Safety and the Body Politic" derived directly from epidemiological teaching: namely, that there was nothing accidental about traffic "accidents." In any given episode, a car crash or a collision with a pedestrian might seem a random and inexplicable tragedy. But when viewed in the aggregate (remember that the epidemiological method examines "groups of persons, not individuals"), quite predictable overall patterns of risk could be discerned: there was a regular structure to, or an "etiology" of, motor vehicle injury. Yet neither policymakers nor the public seemed to be aware of this. "Just as classical forms of disease were in general treated by magic until perhaps two centuries ago," wrote Moynihan, "accidents have until this moment been thought of as somehow wild' occurrences which do not conform to the sequential chain of causal events that define the way things in general take place" (Moynihan 1973: 98).

Because interventions at the individual, corporate, or governmental level could alter the various risk schedules associated with driving, Moynihan reasoned, it should correspondingly be possible to contain and diminish the human cost of motorized travel: "there is a considerable body of empirical evidence," he argued, "that automobile accidents can be reduced without substantially compromising the essential transportation system by which they are generated" (ibid.: 81).

In Moynihan's diagnosis, the central impediment to a more effective traffic policy was that government authorities had embraced an approach to enhancing public safety completely inadequate to the task. For peculiar historical reasons, America was applying the wrong "paradigm" to auto injury prevention. As he explained,

> The entire pattern of State Police management of the automobile complex is derived directly from the model of prevention, detection, and punishment—of crime....This involves intense concentration on the guilt of individuals, as measured by the conformance to statutes, and the belief in the efficacy of punishment, either threatened or carried out, as a means of social regulation. There is not much evidence that this works.
>
> [T]here is no evidence [for example] that drivers who are arrested for speeding, or similar offenses, or that they act differently thereafter....[W]e must live for the moment with the probability that most "convicted speeders" are little more than innocent victims of the Poisson distribution. (Ibid.: 93-94)

By contrast with the existing juridical framework for auto injury control, an epidemiological approach to the dangers of motor travel (what Moynihan called "Federal concern with automobile transportation, properly conceived") would not only offer the possibility of substantially reducing vehicular casualties, but would

> as much as possible put an end to the present idiocies of armed police arresting and often imprisoning hordes of citizens who are then hauled before courts incompetent to judge a problem that in any event is almost impossible to define in legal terms. (Ibid.: 99)

"Traffic Safety and the Body Politic" identified three key syndromes that were, in Moynihan's estimate, exposing the public to unnecessarily high risk of auto injury: "the venality of the automobile industry," "the psychological role of the automobile" in daily life, and "the failure of government" (ibid.: 82, 88, 89).

American automakers, as he explained in painful and convincing detail, in those days were defiantly indifferent to issues of design safety in their product. "I have come to the conclusion," commented an exasperated Moynihan, "that for brute greed and moral imbecility the American automobile industry has no peer"(ibid.: 83).

The public, for its part, was "ambivalent on the question of traffic safety," for the automobile constituted "a prime agent of risk-taking in a society that still values risk-taking, but does not provide many outlets" (ibid.: 89, 88). As Moynihan observed tartly,"the largest reason we have not done anything to tame the automobile is that we have not much wanted to" (ibid.: 88).

Then there was the government. Not only had federal, state and local authorities opted for the wrong tools for the job, but they did not even collect the sorts of information that would permit an evaluation of performance:

> Directly related to the absence of facts about safety design is the absence of facts about the whole subject....[T]here are in fact no standard national statistics about traffic safety. The United States government does not collect them.

> The only moderately reliable statistic that exists is the number of persons killed... a dependable but meaningless number, in the sense that it provides no guide to action of any sort.

> It is hardly a complicated matter to conceive what basic national data ought to be collected....Most of the data could be gathered by standard sampling techniques. (Ibid.: 91-92)

Legislation then just introduced—the Highway Safety Act of 1966— had "the potential," Moynihan noted, for redirecting auto safety policy toward more promising strategies. "The issue now," he mused, "is whether the forthcoming legislation will evoke the sustained and responsible concern of those who have so neglected the subject in the past" (ibid.: 99). It did; and in the following decades, the dangers of road travel were dramatically reduced.

Mortality statistics convey some impression of the transformation in risk schedules. Between 1950 and 1970, America's age-standardized death rate from motor vehicle crashes had risen by almost one-fifth; between 1970 and 1991-93, on the other hand, it declined by over two-fifths (derived from NCHS 1996: 146). All the while, however, Americans were spending more time in the car and on the road; thus mortality rates per se understated the gains against the deadly risks of driving as an activity. In 1965, the U.S. traffic death rate per 100 million vehicle miles was 5.3; in 1994, this figure had fallen by two-thirds, to 1.7 (see figure 3.1).

FIGURE 3.1

Rate of Fatalities per 100 Million Miles of Vehicle Travel: United States, 1965-94

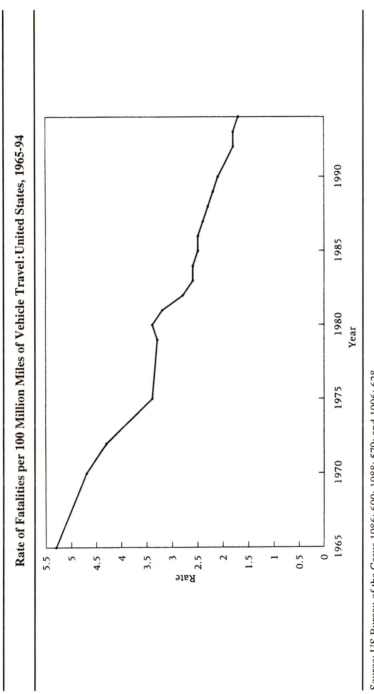

Source: US Bureau of the Cesus 1986: 600; 1988: 579; and 1996: 628.

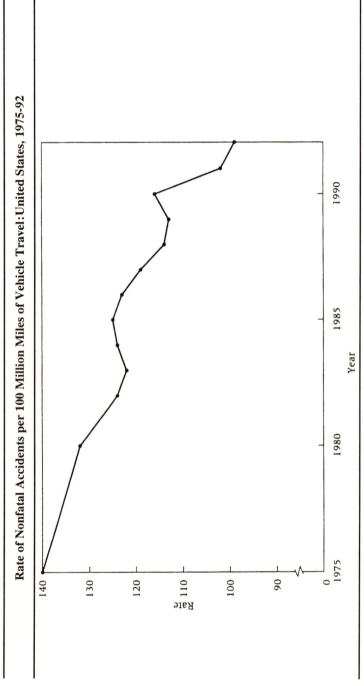

FIGURE 3.2

Rate of Nonfatal Accidents per 100 Million Miles of Vehicle Travel: United States, 1975-92

Source: US Bureau of the Census 1988: 580; 1996: 629.

In 1966, Moynihan was not persuaded that such statistics conveyed meaningful information about underlying public health risks: trends derived from them, he warned, could be biased or even dominated by the secular advance of modern medicine, which steadily increased the survival chances for crash victims (Moynihan 1973: 91). Yet other data can now corroborate the general trends indicated by motor vehicle mortality figures. National data on auto injuries, for example, are available from 1975 onwards: between 1975 and 1992, nonfatal injuries per 100 million passenger miles dropped by almost 30 percent (see figure 3.2). "In 1960," Moynihan wrote, "I made some tentative calculations that something like a third of the automobiles manufactured in Detroit ended up with blood on them" (ibid.: 83); for the early 1990s, a comparably tentative computation would suggest that the odds for domestically purchased cars and light trucks had dropped to about one in 4.5, or less.[4]

How, exactly, are these improvements to be explained? In quantitative terms, it is not possible to allocate the change among the various contributing factors. Nevertheless, it is clear that the overall trend was influenced by generally auspicious responses by each of the three sets of independent actors Moynihan had identified: the auto industry, the motorist, and the government.

In the early 1960s, it is fair to say that Detroit did not take auto safety terribly seriously; in the 1990s, on the other hand, the entire auto industry had completely internalized the concept of design safety into its corporate cultures, assigning it a high and enthusiastic priority. This was a more mature attitude for a more mature industry; it could be explained almost in terms of "life passages." At a point between the early 1960s and the early 1990s, the American auto industry had faced its own version of a "near-death experience." Suddenly confronted by increasingly restrictive regulation, expensive tort litigation, disenchanted consumers, and adept foreign competitors, three major American auto manufacturers could no longer take their survival for granted: for some time, in fact, it seemed to be seriously in doubt. The now-international auto industry that has developed in the wake of that corporate trauma is firmly committed to "selling safety." Demographics has probably played a role here. At one end of the business, the auto industry's ancien régime has been replaced by a younger generation of decision makers to whom safety issues were profit issues; for another, the "feminization" of the auto market—the growing importance of mothers and other women in

FIGURE 3.3

Trends in Drivers' Use of Safety Belts: United States, 1982-91

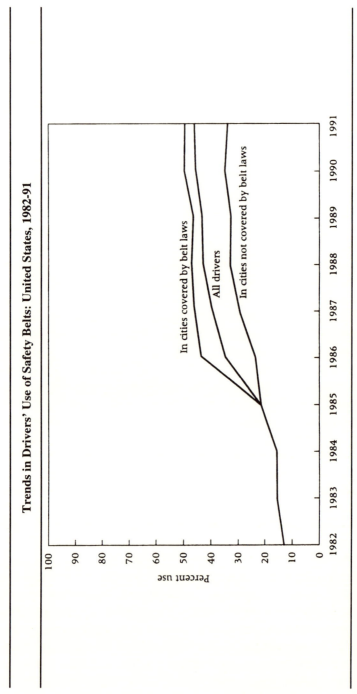

Notes: Estimates based on data for 19 US cities. The percent shown for 1982 includes some 1981 data. Data for 1989 and later were computed somewhat differently than earlier data.

Source: GAO 1992: 8–9

FIGURE 3.4

Percent of Drivers in Fatal Crashes with Blood Alcohol Concentration of 0.10 or Higher: United States, 1982-94

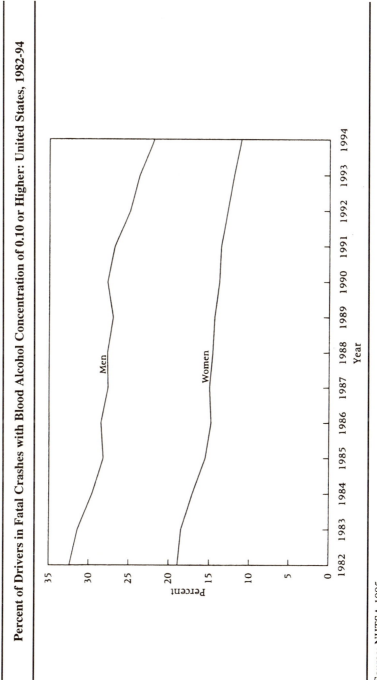

Source: NHTSA 1995.

the selection and purchase process—has rewarded the orientation toward design safety, reinforcing its new standing within corporate strategy.

Demographics alone, however, do not explain the shift in American driving habits. If safety-consciousness is a feminine trait, all American motorists have become more "feminized"—men and women alike. Americans may be no more likely today than in the past to observe the strict letter of the law when it comes to speed limits, but they are much more likely to buckle up, and considerably less likely to drive drunk. Significant changes in behavior have occurred over relatively short periods of time. The National Highway Traffic Safety Administration (NHTSA), for example, estimates that between 1982 and 1991, seatbelt use increased from about 11 percent of all American auto passengers to about 50 percent (GAO 1992: 8-9). (See figure 3.3.) At much the same time, the proportion of fatal crashes in which the driver's blood alcohol concentration measured 0.10 or above dropped sharply: from 30 percent in 1982 to under 20 percent in 1994. This drop in blood alcohol concentrations, incidentally, was totally pervasive: it showed up among men and women (see figure 3.4), the young and the old, and for drivers of trucks, cars, and motorcycles alike, and irrespective of the time of day (or night) of the crash.

Legislation and enforcement may have played some part in these shifts, but much more can probably be credited to "public education," broadly construed. In an increasingly affluent and healthy nation, the public tends to place a progressively higher value on its time, and on its life; information that reliably augments or preserves these quantities tends to result in behavior modification. To be sure, a tolerance for risk—even a taste for it—is reflected in some driving behavior, as Moynihan pointed out in 1966. In response to safety improvements, some drivers may choose to take greater risks than before.[5] But such instances appear to be anomalous. On the whole, recent American driving habits suggest that tolerance for these sorts of risks has been far from immutable, much less perverse. In this particular respect, Moynihan may have underestimated the scope for traffic safety enhancement.

The impact of government interventions on achieved traffic safety has hardly been unidirectional. Micromanagerial stipulations on the "corporate average fuel economy" of the manufactured "fleets" (CAFE), for example, have been pure epidemiological idiocy: the enforced heterogeneity in highway vehicle size dictated by this "environmental" ukase have predictably consigned hundreds, perhaps thousands, of

Americans to violent death each year since, ceteris paribus, people in the smaller car are more likely to be hurt in a collision.[6] New safety regulations, moreover, cannot automatically take credit for saving lives: as Sam Peltzman's econometrics persuasively attested over twenty years ago, the same demand for and use of life-saving seatbelts would likely have been witnessed for American auto buyers of their own free will as was legislated into new autos after the Highway Safety Act (Peltzman 1975). Yet when all is said and done, governmental attention to traffic safety post-Moynihan incontestably saved vastly more lives than it cost (although its financial cost-effectiveness may be another story). Government's concern with auto safety and control of construction purse-strings resulted in better and less hazardous highways and roads. Government's hectoring of the U.S. auto industry about design safety almost certainly accelerated life-saving innovations, at least in the early phase of that regulated relationship. And introduction of the data-gathering and evaluation systems that Moynihan had advised provided far-ranging guidance for corrections and new directions in auto safety for the public, the individual driver, and the corporate sector.

The complaint has, at times, been lodged that auto safety policies have made no difference whatsoever to the well being of the American driver: that reductions in fatalities per 100 million miles driven, for example, follow an almost smooth trajectory, unaffected over time by changing policy interventions or regimens. This is true, at least as far as past mortality trajectories are concerned; but from the standpoint of the safety policymaker, this is beside the point. For safety innovation does not occur spontaneously, any more than new highways design and build themselves. In a rational and risk-averse population, increases in income, education, and information will be expected to lower the incidence and cost of transportation-related injury. But how it does so at different junctures, and by how much, is not preordained. The spread and gradual inculcation of epidemiological reasoning over the past generation and a half was partly responsible for the specific auto safety improvements that were actually achieved over that period, and Daniel Patrick Moynihan was a prominent vector in this process.

Violent Crime

Although the orders of magnitude for injuries and deaths from driving and crime happen to be similar in America today, the etiologies obviously are not. Driving is not axiomatically a social pathology; criminal activity is. Unlike criminal assault, physical or emotional injury of other persons is not a necessary consequence of every trip in a car. And while the risks of both road hazard and crime derive in large measure from concentrated subpopulations, crime—unlike reckless driving—often is a way of life for its practitioners: a profession, a pastime, simply an attractive challenge.

Given the characteristic differences between the agents of auto injury and the agents of criminal injury, it should be no surprise that public policy has been markedly more successful in controlling the former than the latter. Indeed, the virtual explosion of crime and the attendant spread of criminality within the American population over the past three and a half decades arguably demarcates one of the greatest social—and policy—failures in modern American history. Epidemiologists can claim no special credit for helping to quell this still raging epidemic. Nevertheless, Moynihan has offered us valuable observations and intriguing hypotheses about the epidemiology of contemporary American crime.

Demography is a regular tool for the epidemiologist. In his study of domestic criminal violence, Moynihan, the epidemiologist, collaborated closely with Moynihan, the demographer. One product of this partnership was an essay titled "'Peace,'" first published in his collection, *Coping*, in 1973. Addressing the question of "peace at home," Moynihan ventured that

> most of the events that tore American society almost apart, or so it seemed in the 1960s, arose from conditions unique to the decade in which they occurred. They had not existed before. They will not exist again. They involve the interaction of demographic and political-cultural changes.

> [T]he 1960s saw a profound demographic change occur in American society which was a one-time change, a growth in population vaster than any that had ever occurred before or any that will ever occur again, with respect to a particular population subgroup, namely those persons fourteen to twenty-four years of age. (Moynihan 1973: 422-423)

Moynihan went on to explain that the "people who cause most of the trouble in a society, as you probably know, are people fourteen to twenty-four.... Societies, no matter where they are, are mostly organized around the problem of how to get people from fourteen to twenty-four" (ibid.: 423). Because the baby boom of the 1950s resulted in an unprecedented increase in the absolute number of infants, there was an unprecedented increase in the absolute number of adolescents and very young adults a decade and a half later; and because America was already heading to-

FIGURE 3.5

Number of Persons Aged 15-24 Compared with Total Arrests for All Ages: United States, 1960-95

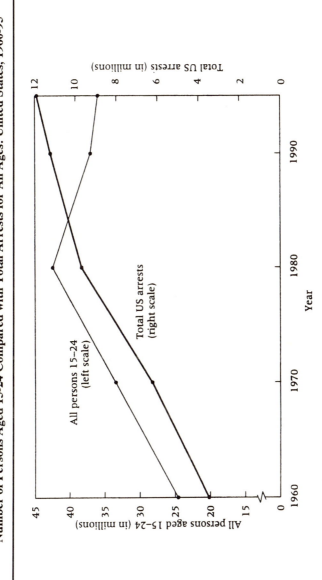

Source: US Bureau of the Census, Historical Statistics of the United States, Colonial Times to 1970, Vol. 1, pp. 50, 415 (Washington, D.C.: Government Printing Office, 1975); US Bureau of the Census 1982/83: 28, 181; 1992: 14, 187; 1996: 21, 209.

FIGURE 3.6

Death Rates for Homicide and Legal Intervention for Persons Aged 15-24 and 25-34: United States, 1950-89 (per 100,000 resident population)

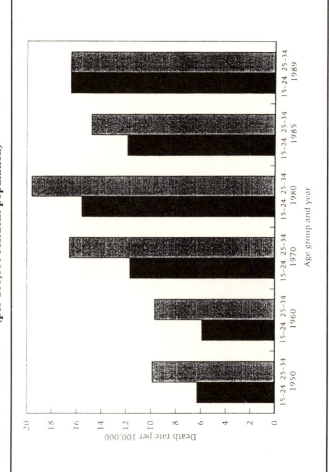

ward sub-replacement fertility by the late 1960s, there were no repeat performances on the horizon. Thus, in the coming decades, Moynihan predicted, "We shall have peace, but it will in some respects be a peace of exhaustion" (ibid.: 428).

"'Peace,'" it should be emphasized, addressed the prospects for domestic social disturbance in general, rather than crime in particular. The demographic reasoning undergirding the analysis, moreover, was eminently sound. Even so, we now know that events subsequently unfolded in a manner that Moynihan's audience in 1973 would have been poorly prepared to anticipate. In the late 1970s, the absolute number of Americans aged fifteen to twenty-four finally peaked and commenced a steady decline—but the number of Americans "getting into trouble" continued to rise seemingly inexorably. From the late 1970s to the mid-1990s, the trends for total youth population in America and total arrests in America were heading in opposite directions (see figure 3.5). Like the famous "scissors" in the 1965 "Moynihan Report," which depicted caseloads for persons receiving Aid to Families with Dependent Children rising even as nonwhite male unemployment rates were falling (U.S. Department of Labor 1965: 12), this was an ominous and unexpected divergence.

In retrospect, it may be that the fifteen-to-twenty-four-year-old population is a less suitable "risk group" to track for violent crime than for other social disturbances. Despite all the attention to the "young offender" in social work and criminology, after all, the fact of the matter is that most delinquents in America today are not chronologically juvenile. To judge by homicide mortality rates, for example, the prime risk cohort in America between 1950 and 1989 was the twenty-five-to-thirty-four-year-old male.[7] (Rates for these age groups are shown in figure 3.6.) Twenty-five-to-thirty-four-year-olds also record higher arrest rates and higher proportions of alcohol-related driver fatalities than younger cohorts. The actual existing crime problem in contemporary America, it would seem, can largely be defined in terms of adult predators and "problem-case" grownups at large in a graying, child-scarce society.

The crime problems of tomorrow are surely affected not only by the absolute size of today's rising cohorts, but by their composition. Moynihan pointed this out over thirty years ago, and has been reminding us of this central fact ever since. In 1965, in his essay, "The Case for a Family Policy,"[8] Moynihan warned that there is one unmistakable lesson in American history: a community that allows a large number of young men to grow up in broken families, dominated by women, never acquiring any stable relationship to male authority, never acquiring any set of rational expectations about the future—that community asks for and gets chaos. Crime, violence, unrest, unrestrained lashing out at the whole social structure—that is not only to be expected; it is very near to inevitable. (Moynihan 1973:76)

Not even Moynihan, though, could have guessed in 1965 how characteristic the broken home and the fatherless family would become for America over the next thirty years. By the early 1990s, the fraction of white families that were fatherless, and the ratio of out-of-wedlock births among whites, were about the same as they had been for nonwhites in the early 1960s[9]—conditions Moynihan had then judged sufficiently alarming to warrant his 1965 "Negro Family" report and his *America* essay.

The trend of young males raised in fatherless homes has proved to be a fearsomely good predictor of overall trends for violent crime over the past generation. By this indicator, pressures for future crime epidemics continue to mount. How are we to cope with this coming onslaught?

In early 1993, in *The American Scholar*, Moynihan described how we *were* coping: by "Defining Deviancy Down." That essay, augmented by additional commentary, stands as the third chapter of *Miles to Go.* "In offering the thesis," writes Moynihan,

that over the past generation... the amount of deviant behavior in American society has increased beyond the levels the community can "afford to recognize" and that accordingly we have been redefining deviancy so as to exempt much conduct previously stigmatized, and also quietly raising the "normal" level in categories where behavior is abnormal by any earlier standard. (p. 144)

The public reaction to steadily rising incidences of crime, Moynihan continued, "is curiously passive." "James Q. Wilson comments that Los Angeles has a St. Valentine's Day Massacre every weekend. Even the most ghastly reenactments produce only moderate responses" (p.153). Having described the new "denial" mechanisms in discomfiting detail, Moynihan admonished that

we are getting used to a lot of behavior that is not good for us.... If our analysis wins general acceptance—if, for example, more of us came to share Judge Torres' genuine alarm at "the trivialization of the lunatic crime rate" in his city (and mine)—we might surprise ourselves how well we respond to the manifest decline of the American civic order. Might. (p.157)

"Defining Deviancy Down" is a masterful essay—in social psychology, not epidemiology. Strikingly, though Moynihan invokes the need for epidemiological reasoning in addressing the crime problem in this study (pp. 155-56), he refrains from broadly describing the shape such an approach would take. He does propose a particular intervention— federal regulation of the domestic supply of handgun bullets—that might well affect current homicide rates if enacted; but surely bullet rationing would only be a small component of an overall epidemiologically grounded anticrime strategy.

Generally speaking, epidemiology addresses public health problems from two directions: prevention and control. If the supply of violent criminals in the nation is closely related to the supply of fatherless younger men, prevention is problematic, insofar as we have yet to devise a workable way to purposely halt, much less reverse, this rising tide of fatherlessness. On the other hand, we may understand more about control than is always apparent. As recent experience in New York City suggests, moreover, we are learning—or relearning—things about crime control from time to time.[10]

One sure fact about crime control is that jailed criminals do not prey upon the public. Over the past thirty years, an explosion of incarceration has accompanied the explosion in crime. By 1994, nearly 1.5 million Americans were jailed or imprisoned on any given day: nearly every hundredth white adult male and every fifteenth black adult male (derived from Brown et al. 1996: 7). This is, incontestably, a disturbing development and a sorry commentary on America today. But what is its epidemiological significance?

Studying the crime epidemic unleashed since the 1960s, an epidemiologist might well conclude that we are currently undersupplied with prisons; that incarceration rates in America are presently too low; and that public policy is devoting too few resources to punishment: that we are not, in other words, adequately availing ourselves of the one sure avenue of crime control we know to work. Daniel Patrick Moynihan's epidemiological writings, however, have not directly indicated his own view on this troubling question.

Drugs

Although there is considerable overlap today between the public health problems posed by crime and illicit drugs, the etiologies of the two syndromes can be distinguished from one another. In 1993, Moynihan published a probing assessment of America's drug problem in *The American Scholar* under the title "Iatrogenic Government."[11] "Iatrogenic," one may dimly recall, is a medical term of art referring to illnesses caused or exacerbated by the physician's own interventions. As one may surmise from that title, Moynihan's estimate of governmental efforts to mitigate the drug problem were less than sanguine.

In the expanded version of the essay published as chapter 5 of *Miles to Go*, Moynihan put his thesis and his critique, bluntly:

> There are discernible rhythms in drug epidemiology. They appear to burn themselves out as the initial enthusiasts succumb to the effects of the drug, or to lateral afflictions (HIV/AIDS, in the case of the 1960s heroin cohort), or disappear into prison. Their behavior has become aversive; fewer recruits are attracted, and the episode subsides. No thanks, or little thanks, to the federal government, and here is the point…. The problem of drug abuse in the United States today—which is to say, the use of illicit drugs—is the direct, unambiguous consequence of federal law prohibiting their licit use. (p. 193)

Heroin, cocaine, and now crack, Moynihan reminds us, are only the latest in a long series of powerful intoxicants made possible by technological advance. In eighteenth-century England and early-nineteenth-century America, the advent of high-proof distilled spirits resulted in enormous social and public health problems; for a time, he observes, gin may even have exerted something like a Malthusian check on the growth of the population of the city of London (pp. 197-98).

In the United States, as in England before it, a religiously based temperance movement helped to reduce alcohol consumption dramatically. But Americans then attempted to eliminate alcohol use through a national legislative prohibition—the Eighteenth Amendment, enacted in 1920, repealed in 1933. As Moynihan recounts, "Alcohol prohibition was a convulsive event that, among other things, led to the creation of a criminal underworld of exceptional influence and durability" (p. 199). Extending the analogy, Moynihan wryly comments that

> in dealing with drugs [today] we are required to choose between a crime problem and a public health problem. In choosing to prohibit drugs, we choose to have a more or less localized—but ultimately devastating—crime problem rather than a general health problem…. It is essential that we understand that by choosing to prohibit drugs we are choosing to have an intense crime problem concentrated among minorities. (pp. 200, 206)

Moynihan's criticism of government policy is stinging:

Clearly the federal drug policy is responsible for a degree of social regression for which there does not appear to be any equivalent in our history. The number of inmates imprisoned for drug offenses now exceeds those in prison for property crimes. (p. 207)

But he also has harsh words for the American medical profession, which, he asserts, "finds drug research aversive behavior" (p. 202). In the final analysis, he concludes, "only the development of a blocking or neutralizing agent will have any real effect, given the setting in which our drug problem now occurs"; "interdiction and 'drug busts' are probably necessary symbolic acts, but nothing more" (p. 208).

Though "Iatrogenic Government" stands as a foray into epidemiology, one would not describe it as an essay of clinical detachment. There is a tone of resignation—some would say pessimism—out of keeping with a usual Moynihan study. Reading his analysis, one suspects that Moynihan judges the current drug problem in America to be beyond positive strategies for solution—or rather, to be amenable to solution by long-term demographic trends, as the high-risk subgroups destroy themselves or inoculate themselves, and are replaced.

Such a grim prognosis may ultimately prove accurate; Moynihan's predictive record, as we all know, has been amazingly good over the years. Yet other readings of the epidemiological evidence at hand can also be suggested. The possibilities for prevention, for example, may be greater than Moynihan believes, as well as somewhat different from those he outlines.

The great distilled-alcohol epidemic in the English-speaking world, after all, was tamed by religious temperance movements. These were not constructs of government—they arose from civil society itself—but they seemed to prove considerably more effective in their time than today's government-sponsored programs for drug "treatment on request." Successful anti-intoxicant movements, moreover, continue to spring up from society itself, unsummoned by the state: think of Alcoholics Anonymous and Mothers Against Drunk Driving.

Flawed as they may arguably be, existing control policies, for their part, may also have their virtues. Current drug laws, after all, are used for more than just drug control: like the income tax statutes that eventually snared Al Capone, they are now routinely used against violent criminals by law enforcement officials lacking evidentiary basis for prosecution on other offenses. The prisons have, indeed, swelled with felons convicted of drug offenses: between 1980 and 1994, those ranks increased by over 180,000 (Brown et al. 1996: 10). But the number of prisoners convicted of violent offenses rose even more dramatically over those same years—by over a quarter million—and some fraction of the "drug" offenders, in reality, were themselves wanted for such offenses. Given this state of affairs—"set and setting," so to speak—an epidemiologist might entertain the possibility that a relaxation of current controls on illicit drugs could lead, for some period of time, to a worsening of both the crime problem and the public health problem.

Concluding Observations

It is sometimes supposed that rigorous policy research requires that the analyst be value-neutral. But as Daniel Patrick Moynihan has proved by long and honorable personal example, this is not the case. Indeed, there is distinct hazard when policy research becomes unmoored from ethical norms or inured to moral distinctions. As Moynihan notes in *Miles to Go*, the same holds for epidemiology:

> Epidemiologists have powerful insights that can contribute to lessening the medical trauma, but they must be wary of normalizing the social pathology that leads to such trauma. (p. 156)

Within epidemiology, that risk is greatest with respect to injuries and deaths due to "external causes." The great figures of epidemiology have long recognized this to be so. As Dr. H. O. Lancaster has written,

> the one unifying feature of many of these deaths, which include suicides, homicides, accidental poisonings, and external violence, is a lowered appreciation of the sanctity of human life. Therefore, ultimately the prevention of a proportion of these deaths is a moral problem. (Lancaster 1990: 341)

In his writings on auto safety, crime, and drugs—to mention only the three topics discussed above—the moral element of the epidemiological problem has always been obvious and inescapable to Moynihan. For others, sad to say, this has not always been true.

In recent years, for example, New York City's public health authorities have made it their enlightened practice to get the government into the business of supplying drug users with clean needles. Does it seem farfetched to imagine that there may be unanticipated public health consequences from such seeming official support for dangerous drug use? By the same token, do the "chains of inference which extend more or less beyond the bounds of direct observation" suggest it is pure coincidence that teenage drug use in the United States, which had, according to survey data, been dropping for a decade, began to rise with the inauguration of a president who offered only lawyerly and unrepentant answers to questions about his own youthful drug use?

America's foremost political epidemiologist has never been one to shrink from the hard questions, or one to neglect their moral dimension. That is a legacy to be ignored only at considerable risk to the health of the nation, and of its people.

Notes

1. *Demographically* negligible, that is. Between 1947 and 1997, over 90 million deaths were recorded in the United States. Of these, less than 90,000 were battle deaths. Derived from *U.S. Bureau of the Census*, 1996 edition, pp. 74, 360.
2. NCHS 1996: 110. For some subgroups in some periods, the impact of trends in "external cause" mortality have been not only adverse, but dominant. For black males during the years 1984-1989, for example, the losses in life expectancy at birth due to homicide and unintentional injury were of sufficient magnitude to cancel out all the longevity improvements that would otherwise have accrued from progress against heart disease (Kochanek, Maurer, and Rosenberg 1994: 11).
3. Initially titled "The War Against the Automobile," *The Public Interest*, no. 3 (1966), pp. 10-26; retitled "Traffic Safety and the Body Politic," in Moynihan 1973: 79-99.
4. Derived from U.S. Bureau of the Census, 1981 edition, p. 622; 1995 edition, pp. 632, 638. This crude computation recalibrates Moynihan's original estimate according to the proportional change in reported traffic injuries and in registered vehicles between 1960 and 1993. Note that this method likely *understates* intervening improvements, insofar as injuries were more likely to be underreported in 1960 than in 1993, and injuries sustained in 1993 were less likely to draw blood than in 1960.
5. For two of the studies that appear to document this effect, see Garbacz 1992 and Risa 1994.
6. One careful econometric study, for example, predicted that CAFE regulations would be responsible for 2,200 to 3,900 additional fatalities in America over a ten-year period from 1989 model year autos alone! (Crandall and Graham 1989).
7. This pattern, however, appears to be changing in the 1990s. For 1991-93, according to the NCHS, mortality rates for homicide and legal intervention were higher for the fifteen to twenty-four group than the twenty-five to thirty-four group.
8. Originally titled "A Family Policy for the Nation," *America*, vol. 113, no. 12 (September 18, 1965), pp. 280-83; reprinted in Moynihan 1973: 69-78.
9. Derived from U.S. Bureau of the Census, 1996 edition: 63,78; U.S. Department of Labor 1965: 59, 61.
10. For details and preliminary analysis, see DiIulio 1995 and Krauss 1996.
11. Daniel Patrick Moynihan, "Iatrogenic Government," *The American Scholar*, summer 1993, pp. 351-62.

References

Brown, Jodi M., et.al. *Correctional Populations in the United States, 1994.* Washington, DC: U.S. Department of Justice, Bureau of Justice Statistics, 1996.

Crandall, Robert W., and John D. Graham. "The Effects of Fuel Economy Standards on Automobile Safety." *Journal of Law and Economics*, vol. 32, no. 1 (1989), pp. 97-118.

DiIulio, John J. Jr. "Arresting Ideas: Tougher Law Enforcement Is Driving Down Urban Crime." *Policy Review*, fall 1995, pp. 12-16.

Friedman, Gary D. *Primer of Epidemiology.* New York: McGraw-Hill Book Company, 1974.

Frost, W.H. *Snow on Cholera.* New York: Commonwealth Fund, 1936.

Garbacz, Christopher. "Do Front-Seat Belt Laws Put Rear-Seat Passengers at Risk?" *Population Research and Policy Review*, vol. 11, no. 2 (1992), pp. 157-68.

Kochanek, Kenneth D., Jeffrey D. Maurer, and Harry M. Rosenberg. "Causes of Death Contributing to Changes in Life Expectancy: United States, 1984-89." *Vital and Health Statistics*, series 20, no. 23 (1994).

Krauss, Clifford. "Bratton Hailed as Pioneer of New Style of Policing." *New York Times*, March 27, 1996, B5.

Last, John M., ed. *A Dictionary of Epidemiology.* New York: Oxford University Press, 1988.

Lancaster, H. O. *Expectations of Life: A Study in the Demography, Statistics, and History of World Mortality.* New York: Springer-Verlag, 1990.

Moynihan, Daniel Patrick. *Coping: Essays on the Practice of Government.* New York: Random House, 1973.

Peltzman, Sam. "The Effects of Automobile Safety Regulation." *Journal of Political Economy*, vol. 83, no. 4 (1975), pp. 677-725.

Risa, Alf Erling. "Adverse Incentives from Improved Technology: Traffic Safety Regulation in Norway." *Southern Economic Journal*, vol. 60, no. 4 (1994), pp. 844-57.

Rockett, Ian R.H. "Population and Health: An Introduction to Epidemiology." *Population Bulletin*, vol. 49, no. 3 (1994).

U.S. Bureau of the Census. *Statistical Abstract of the United States.* Washington, DC: Government Printing Office, various editions.

U.S. Department of Labor. *The Negro Family: The Case for National Action.* Washington, DC: Department of Labor, Office of Policy Planning and Research, March 1965.

U.S. General Accounting Office (GAO). *Highway Safety: Safety Belts Save Lives and Reduce Costs to Society.* Report GAO/RCED-92-106, July 1992.

U.S. National Center for Health Statistics. *Health, United States, 1995.* Hyattsvillle, MD: NCHS, 1996.

Part II

Population Problems Under Communism

4

Mortality and the Fate of Communist States

The crisis and collapse of communist rule in Eastern Europe and the Soviet Union between 1989 and 1991 was, arguably, one of the defining moments of modern history. It has also proved to be a moment of truth for the large and established community of Western specialists—within government, the academy, and private institutes—who have made it their purpose to study the Soviet bloc countries. For with a sudden flash, the weaknesses and shortcomings of a generation of extensive studies were exposed and glaringly illuminated.

One may begin with what did *not* happen. Students of the Warsaw Pact region provided virtually no forewarning of the convulsions that were coming to the states they studied. Quite the contrary: the demise of Warsaw Pact communism seemed to take the field as a whole by almost complete surprise. Though a sizeable literature on the Warsaw Pact states was published in the generation before the "revolutions of 1989," one would be hard pressed to locate more than a handful of items that would seem to anticipate the fact (much less the timing) of this dramatic political departure from the Eurasian stage.[1]

Prediction of political outcomes, it must be said, remains rather more of an art than a science. Premonitions about impending political changes may speak more to intuition than to positive analysis; it may be unreasonable to fault a specific discipline for failing to announce an advent almost no one was expecting. More troubling, from a methodological standpoint, than the unpredicted collapse of Soviet bloc communism itself has been the light this collapse has newly thrown on Western studies of the quantitative performance of those economies.

Of course, the closed nature of those societies, and the peculiar nature of their economic organization, posed obvious and formidable obstacles to any effort at measuring true patterns of production, consumption, and growth under central planning. But it is equally true that Western researchers devoted formidable resources to developing just such measurements. In fact, by such criteria as expense, duration, or technical manpower absorbed, the U.S. intelligence community's postwar quest to describe and model the Soviet economy was in all likelihood the largest social science research project ever undertaken.

With the crumbling of the Berlin Wall and the "end of the Cold War," it now seems virtually incontestable that this corpus of quantitative studies, for all their apparent rigor, was for the most part off the mark. As late as 1987, for example, the U.S. Central Intelligence Agency (CIA 1987) was estimating per capita GNP to be somewhat higher in East Germany than in West Germany. As every German taxpayer is today all too aware, the actual level of per capita output in what have become the "New Federal States" was in reality vastly lower than in the rest of Germany on the eve of that nation's reunification.[2] This signal misreading of communist economic performance was by no means an isolated incident. Comparable overestimates of economic performance by the CIA may be adduced for every other country in the Soviet bloc. And the CIA was hardly alone in overestimating productivity, living standards, and economic growth within the Soviet bloc during the "Cold War." In a defense of his analysts, the Bush administration's Director of Central Intelligence pointedly (and correctly) observed that many independent scholars and specialists had taken the CIA's old estimates to task for purportedly underestimating the economic performance of Warsaw Pact countries (Gates 1992).

My purpose in reciting these particulars is not to criticize the work of those in the West who strove so diligently to understand the workings of a system, and a way of life, with which they were fundamentally unfamiliar. It is rather to suggest, with all the benefits of hindsight, that our understanding of the Soviet bloc might have been significantly enhanced if students of those countries had paid a little more attention to their demographic trends. More specifically, I wish to suggest that valuable and telling insights into the social, economic, and even political circumstances of these countries could have been gleaned from analysis of their death rates: their schedules of mortality, and their reported patterns of cause of death.

Such an application of demographic technique, one hopes, would have been gratifying to Roger Revelle. It responds, after all, to an invitation he extended a quarter of a century ago. In offering the results of that now-classic project on "Historical Population Studies" to the reader in 1968, Revelle also framed an agenda for future research. "The new science of historical demography," he observed, "has devoted almost all of its efforts to the determinants of population change, and very few to an examination of its consequences." Among the specifics that "we do not understand," in his enumeration, were "the consequences of greater longevity on allocation of resources and the distribution of political power" (Revelle 1968, p. 362).

What we have witnessed in the Soviet bloc since 1968, however, is an unprecedented demographic phenomenon that could scarcely be imagined at the time: long-term stagnation—even decline—in life expectancy among a group of industrialized societies that were not at war. This was a major and highly visible event, rife with consequence and implication. Some of those consequences and implications will be explored in this essay.

This chapter proceeds through four sections. The first reviews the anomalous history of mortality trends in Eastern Europe and the USSR between the end of the Second World War and the "end of the Cold War." The second draws inferences about economic performance in those countries from their mortality trends. The third examines some characteristic differences in mortality trends between those areas in which communist rule has recently collapsed and those in which it continues, and speculates about the significance of the distinction. The final section discusses the significance of current mortality trends for postcommunist societies, especially as they pertain to the prospective transition to a stable economic and political order.

I

For the Soviet Union and the Eastern European countries over which it gained mastery during and immediately after World War II, the "Cold War" began with an explosion of health progress. Improvements in mortality, of course, had been underway in these areas before the advent of Marxist-Leninist rule, and had proceeded even during the crisis years for interwar capitalism: between 1929/32 and 1937, for example, Czechoslovakia's life tables recorded an increase in expectation of life at birth of about three years for males and three and a half for females (United Nations Demographic Yearbook 1968). Nevertheless, the pace of mortality decline under Red Army Socialism was noteworthy. Even after recovery to prewar levels had been attained, the tempo continued to be brisk. It was not idle conceit to assert during those years, as the Soviet bloc governments did, that they were outperforming their capitalist rivals in the field of public health.

A few summary figures can lay out the contrast. Between the early 1950s and the early 1960s, according to recent United Nations Population Division estimates, infant mortality dropped by nearly half in Warsaw Pact Europe, and by over half in the USSR (United Nations 1991). This was a much more rapid pace of progress than in Western Europe as a whole, or even in Western Europe's Mediterranean regions (which were arguably more comparable to the Balkans or Ukraine than Switzerland or Sweden would have been). Over that same decade, life expectancy at birth in Warsaw Pact Europe is estimated to have risen by over five years for males, and by nearly six and a half for females; in the USSR the corresponding increments are estimated at five and a half and four and a half years, respectively. Improvements in "imperialist countries" were not nearly so dramatic. In West Germany, for example, the overall increase in life expectancy at birth between 1950/55 and 1960/ 65 was about two and a half years; in the United States, it was barely one year. Among the OECD countries, Japan could claim to match the average of Warsaw Pact Europe's increments, but her performance was exceptional for a grouping in which she was clearly an atypical member (ibid.).

By the mid-1960s, mortality levels in the Warsaw Pact region were very nearly as low as those of the advanced capitalist countries. By the U.N.'s estimate, less than a year separated overall levels of life expectancy at birth in the U.S. and the USSR; the differential between OECD Europe and Eastern Europe was apparently only very slightly greater. If trends were extrapolated only a few years into the future, the Soviet bloc could be seen catching up with, and then surpassing, advanced Western countries by this important, and politically significant, measure.

That general crossover point, of course, was never reached. Instead, the Warsaw Pact countries collectively, and most unexpectedly, entered a new era: one of stagnation, and deterioration, in overall health conditions. The sudden slow-down is highlighted by the official life tables of the countries in question. (Despite the problems with some of these life tables, largely attendant upon underreporting of infant deaths; their results are informative.) According to its life tables, life expectancy at birth in Poland rose by less than 2 years between the mid-1960s and the late 1980s—and this apparently was the region's star performer. Overall increases of less than one year over this same generation were estimated by Bulgaria, Czechoslovakia, and Romania; Hungary's life expectancy was basically stationary over the period as a whole; and life expectancy at birth is officially reported to have fallen in the USSR. Worse still was the situation for men: according to these life tables, East Germany enjoyed an increase in life expectancy at birth for males of about one year over these decades, and this was the best of the group. Czechoslovakia's male life expectancy in 1988 is placed at the same level as in 1964, while Bulgaria, Hungary, Poland, Romania, and the USSR all report long-term declines. The USSR also reports a slight long-term decline in female life expectancy at birth.[3] Strikingly, the slowdown, and reversal, of health progress within the Soviet bloc coincided with an acceleration in OECD countries. Between the mid-1960s and the late 1980s, according to the latest U.N. estimates, life expectancy for both sexes rose by an average of about four years in Western Europe, and by about five years in the United States (United Nations 1992).

How is the virtual cessation of overall health progress within the Soviet bloc to be explained? The phenomenon may be better understood by examining component parts. In most of the Warsaw Pact region, infant mortality rates apparently continued their declines through the 1960s, 1970s, and 1980s, although at a slower pace than in the early postwar period. (There are strong indications that Soviet infant mortality actually increased over some portion of the past generation; owing to the poor state of the relevant Soviet data, however, the debate about this possibility has not yet been settled.)[4]

Mortality data tend to be more comprehensive and reliable for those over the age of one than for infants. They are worth examining, not least for this reason. Table 4.1 presents official life table estimates of life expectation at age one for the Soviet bloc countries for the mid-1960s and the late 1980s. A striking pattern emerges from these data. In five of the seven countries, combined male and female life expectancy for the non-infant population registers at least a slight decline. The situation is even starker by age thirty: in six of the seven countries, life expectancy for adults fell over these decades, slight increases in female life expectancy being more than offset by the fall in life expectancy for males. In less than a quarter of a century, Bulgarian and Polish life

TABLE 4.1

Expectation of Life at Age One and Age 30: Warsaw Pact Region, c. 1965-c. 1989

Country	Life Expectation at One Year of Age (years)		Life Expectation at Age 30 (years)	
	Male	Female	Male	Female
Bulgaria				
1965/67	70.28	73.81	43.06	45.99
1987/89	68.42	74.64	40.87	46.53
- increment	-1.86	+0.83	-2.19	+0.54
Czechoslovakia				
1964	68.44	73.96	41.15	45.84
1988	67.70	75.07	39.73	46.62
- increment	-0.74	+1.11	-1.42	+0.78
East Germany				
1967-68	69.77	74.70	42.46	46.70
1987-88	69.53	75.46	41.67	47.08
- increment	-0.24	+0.76	-0.79	+0.38
Hungary				
1964	69.08	73.45	41.74	45.45
1989	65.58	73.86	37.84	45.55
- increment	-3.50	+0.41	-3.90	+0.10
Poland				
1965/66	68.98	74.43	41.68	46.46
1988	67.37	75.70	39.60	47.29
- increment	-1.61	+1.27	-2.08	+0.83
Romania				
1963	69.36	72.96	42.66	45.65
1987/89	67.53	73.13	40.55	45.56
- increment	-1.83	+0.17	-2.11	-0.09
Soviet Union				
1965/66	— 68[1,2] —		— 45[1] —	
1986/87	— 67.2[1,2] —		— 43.5[1] —	
- increment	negative		at least one year	
1958/59	65.62	73.07	39.51	46.13
1989/90	65.29	74.43	38.62	46.78
- increment	-0.33	+1.36	-0.89	+0.65

Notes: [1] = life expectancy for both sexes
         [2] = life expectancy at age 5

Sources: For USSR 1958/59 and 1986/87 = USSR State Statistical Committee, *Tablitsy Smertnosti i Ozhidaemoy Prodalzhitel'nosti Zhizni Naseleniya* (Moscow: Goskomstat, 1989). All others, United Nations, *Demographic Yearbook* (New York: U.N. Department of International Economic and Social Affairs), various issues.

expectancy for men at age thirty dropped by more than two years; in Hungary the drop was closer to four years. The Soviet Union, for its part, never released any life tables for its population for the mid-1960s. Official tables for the late 1950s and the late 1980s, however, report male life expectancy at age one, and life expectancy at age thirty for the two sexes together, to have been lower in 1989/90 than they were over thirty years earlier!

Age-specific death rates can cast further light on the deterioration of adult health within the Soviet bloc (see table 4.2). Between the mid-1960s and the late 1980s, all seven countries reported rising death rates for at least some of their adult male cohorts. Some of these increases were little short of astonishing: in Hungary, for example, death rates for men in their forties doubled between 1966 and 1989. In most of these countries, women in various adult cohorts experienced at least some slight declines in age-specific mortality, although broad increases in female mortality were evident in both Hungary and the Soviet Union. Although health trends were, by this measure, arguably unfavorable in all these countries for all adult cohorts, they were especially bad for persons in their forties and fifties.

The health situation—call it a health crisis—in the Soviet bloc countries during their last generation under communism was without historical precedent or contemporary parallel. Mortality decline in Western countries, it is true, has been neither smooth nor uninterrupted; various countries—including the Netherlands, Sweden, and the United States—have reported drops in life expectancy at birth for their male population at some juncture during the postwar period. These drops, however, have been slight and temporary, whereas the rise in death rates for broad groups within Warsaw Pact countries has been major, and sustained over the course of decades.

What accounts for these extraordinary trends? A fully satisfactory answer to this question must await further interdisciplinary study. Some preliminary indications, however, may be drawn from data on reported cause of death in these countries. These data must be used with care, for they are shaped by an unavoidable element of subjectivity under the best of conditions, and the best of conditions did not obtain in the statistical offices of Warsaw Pact states. Cause-of-death data, nevertheless, can speak directly to the proximate reasons for reduced life expectation, and may be broadly suggestive of the underlying factors driving the decline.

The World Health Organization (WHO) has prepared age-standard-ized breakdowns of mortality rates by reported cause of death for all of its corresponding member states for the period extending from the early 1950s to the present. It offers breakdowns for the 1965/69-1989 period for four of the seven countries in the Warsaw Pact: Bulgaria, Czecho-slovakia, Hungary, and Poland. Some of the trends highlighted are in-triguing. Levels of mortality attributed to accident and injury, for example,

TABLE 4.2

Changes in Age-Specific Death Rates for Cohorts Aged 30-69:
Warsaw Pact Region, c. 1965-c.1989 (percent)

Country and Sex							Cohort Age	
Males	30/34	35/39	40/44	45/49	50/54	55/59	60/64	65/69
Bulgaria (1966-89)	+19	+32	+62	+70	+56	+47	-16	+14
Czechoslovakia (1965-89)	- 5	+ 8	+19	+40	+33	+29	+15	+ 6
East Germany (1965-88)	- 5	- 8	- 5	+ 7	+ 3	+ 1	-15	-17
Hungary (1966-89)	+67	+96	+100	+131	+93	+69	+46	+25
Poland (1966-88)	+ 9	+17	+36	+51	+47	+38	+23	+ 6
Romania (1966-89)	+32	+36	+43	+61	+44	+32	+35	+15
Soviet Union (1965/66-89)	- 5	0	+21	+25	+24	+25	+20	+25
Unweighted average:	+17	+26	+39	+55	+43	+34	+15	+ 8
Females								
Bulgaria (1966-89)	-11	-15	-10	+ 4	- 4	- 4	- 7	- 6
Czechoslovakia (1965-89)	-13	-23	-14	- 9	-10	0	- 3	- 9
East Germany (1965-88)	-12	-15	-14	-12	-12	-10	-16	-17
Hungary (1966-89)	+33	+26	+26	+33	+23	+22	+ 7	- 2
Poland (1965-88)	-27	-25	- 9	- 9	- 2	- 1	- 3	-14
Romania (1966-89)	- 8	+13	+ 4	- 3	0	- 2	- 3	- 3
Soviet Union (1965/66-89)	-21	-17	- 4	- 3	+ 2	+11	+ 4	+19
Unweighted average	- 8	- 8	- 3	0	- 1	+ 2	- 3	- 5

Note: All changes rounded to the nearest percentage point. Percentages derived from sources.
Sources: For Soviet Union 1965/66: John Dutton, Jr., "Changes in Soviet Mortality Pat-terns, 1959-77," *Population and Development Review*, vol. 5, no. 2 (1979), pp. 276-77. All other data: United Nations, *Demographic Yearbook* (New York: U.N. Department of International Economic and Social Affairs), various issues.

are consistently high among these states; Hungary—the country of the four with perhaps the best cause-of-death data—reports that age-standardized mortality from cirrhosis and chronic liver disease was, by 1987, higher for women than it had been for men only seventeen years earlier. But mortality ascribed to these causes does not trend upward with any consistency in these countries, and in any case cannot account for much of the overall increment in age-standardized death rates. It is, instead, deaths attributed to cardiovascular disease (CVD) that appear to have shaped these countries' age-standardized mortality trends. In all four countries, deaths attributed to CVD accounted for more than half of all age-standardized mortality by the late 1980s. Moreover, all four countries are reported to have suffered huge rises in CVD mortality levels between the late 1960s and the late 1980s. Whereas mortality ascribed to CVD has declined substantially in recent decades throughout the Western industrialized world, Bulgaria reported a 52 percent increase in age-standardized CVD mortality for males between 1965/69 and 1989. Over the same period, CVD mortality seems to have risen dramatically for East bloc women as well: by over 16 percent in Bulgaria and 20 percent in Poland, to select two of the more arresting examples. In proximate terms, the explosive rise in CVD-attributed mortality seems to account fully for the rise in age-standardized mortality in these Soviet bloc countries.[5] Diverging levels of CVD mortality, moreover, seem to account for most of the divergence in overall age-standardized mortality rates over the past generation between Western and Eastern European countries.

The underlying factors contributing to this rise, of course, are more difficult to identify than the proximate ones. Deaths from cardiovascular disease are commonly associated with a variety of specific behavioral or life-style characteristics, including heavy smoking, heavy drinking, poor diet, lack of exercise, and psychological stress or emotional strain.[6] There is ample evidence to suggest that Warsaw Pact populations may have been increasingly exposed to such "risk factors" as the era of "detente" progressed.

But such behavioral indications, in a sense, beg the question, for they skirt an obvious etiological issue: not only is the phenomenon of secular increases in mortality in industrialized societies at peace a new one, the patterns accounting for this rise are also unprecedented. Higher levels of general mortality are typically associated with higher levels of death from infectious and parasitic disease, whereas the Warsaw Pact group's path back to higher mortality was paved by increases in deaths attributed to chronic, noncommunicable causes. The rise, and its pattern, was unique to populations living under Warsaw Pact communism, and indeed apparently common to all of them, despite their manifest differences in language, culture, and levels of material attainment. By these forensics, one might surely be drawn to inquire whether the health problems evidenced by the Warsaw Pact countries were not, in some fundamental sense, systemic. Moreover, in an age when health progress is all but taken for granted, and when scientific, technical, and administrative advances have made it possible to attain given levels of mortality at ever lower income levels, an inability of a particular set of governments to prevent severe long-term declines in health conditions for broad segments of its populations is surely suggestive of a systemic crisis.

II

During the Cold War decades, Western efforts to assess the Soviet bloc economies and to measure their performance were hampered not only by secrecy and mutual mistrust, but by features characteristic of Soviet-style command planning.

For one thing, the incentive structure in the Soviet-type planning rewarded overstatement of results at all levels, including the very highest. As Jan Winiecki (1986) once aptly observed, the "law of equal cheating" does not obtain in such a milieu. Even figures for physical output were routinely padded and exaggerated, albeit by varying margins across countries, industries, and time.

Yet even if perfectly accurate time series data had been available for all items of physical output, Western analysts would still have faced a second problem: valuing the goods and services produced in a way that would make them comparable with output from a market-oriented economy. Ingenious attempts to translate a price structure set by the state into one reflecting scarcity costs were devised: most importantly, the "adjusted factor cost" method pioneered by Abram Bergson and his colleagues in the 1950s.[7] But the problem of finding a common valuation process for systems that allocated resources by such fundamentally different principles could neither be finessed, nor ultimately solved.

For all these difficulties, economic estimates for the Warsaw Pact group were produced, and internally consistent time series were developed to trace their performance. The most authoritative of these time series, published by the CIA, did indicate a fairly steady slowdown in the tempo of economic growth for the region as a whole between the mid-1960s and the late 1980s. At the same time, it suggested quite considerable economic progress. For the twenty-four-year span, 1966-1989, for example, the CIA estimated per capita output in Warsaw Pact Europe to have risen by over half; per capita growth for the period as a whole was said to average 1.8 percent a year. By this reading, the region's growth rate would have been lower than the European Community's (2.4 percent for those same years), but the ostensible gap was not dramatic. Specific comparisons, moreover, painted a more favorable picture of the Warsaw Pact's performance against its rivals. The CIA's estimates of per capita growth for the U.S. and the USSR for these years, for example, were virtually identical (1.9 percent per annum), and East Germany's per capita growth rate was placed slightly ahead of West Germany's (2.7 vs. 2.6 percent). On the eve of the "revolutions of 1989," furthermore, CIA estimates indicated that the Warsaw Pact economies had attained fairly high levels of productivity. For 1988, per capita output for the USSR was placed at over three-fifths of the West German level. Per capita output in Czechoslovakia was placed at 78 percent of the level for the Netherlands, and per capita output in East Germany was estimated to be virtually the same as for the European Community as a whole (CIA 1988).

Plausible as such numbers may have seemed when juxtaposed solely against one another, they would seem suspicious—indeed anomalous— if held next to mortality data. Mortality statistics, for example, would immediately seem to call into question the proposition that per capita output in Eastern Germany had reached the level of Western Europe's by the late 1980s. After all, in 1989, WHO's age-standardized death rate for males was 26 percent higher for East Germany than for the countries of Western Europe. For females, East Germany's age-standardized death rate was fully 32 percent higher than Western Europe's. Indeed, by this measure of mortality, death rates in Eastern Germany were actually higher than in such places as Argentina, Chile, Uruguay, or Venezuela! (WHO 1991).

Such discrepancies in mortality levels are pertinent to economic performance in a number of respects. General levels of mortality bear more than a passing relation to labor productivity, which, in turn, establishes constraints on a population's level of per capita output. Mortality levels, moreover, are directly related to a population's living standards, which are, in turn, related to its level of per capita consumption.[8]

The relationship between mortality and economic performance, of course, is neither tight nor entirely mechanistic. A country's level of per capita output is determined by more than just its supply of "human capital." Human capital, for its part, is a complex fabric of many strands, of which health is but one, and for which mortality rates may not always provide a satisfactory proxy.[9] Finally, the very fact that fairly low levels of mortality can today be purchased in some low-income countries (such as Sri Lanka or China) should qualify generalizations about the relationship between overall levels of per capita consumption and overall levels of mortality. With such caveats in mind, we may nonetheless be able to read an economic significance from the exceptional mortality trends of the Warsaw Pact region.

Consider once more the comparison of *fin de régime* East Germany with the countries of the European Community on the one hand, and with selected Latin American countries on the other. Is it conceivable that a country with general levels of mortality so much higher than the EC's average could manage to attain the EC's level of per capita output? In theory, yes: but only under three specific, and highly restrictive, conditions.[10] Equivalent levels of output could coincide with such different mortality levels if: (1) the process of resource allocation were markedly more efficient in the high mortality society; (2) the high mortality society enjoyed a markedly superior endowment of such factors of production as capital or technology; and/or (3) the high mortality society mobilized its labor force in a way that allowed it to evince vastly greater hours of work from its typical resident.[11]

Were these conditions satisfied by East Germany in the period leading up to unification? Soviet-type economies may be good at various tasks, but allocative efficiency was never one of these.[12] Thus, Condition 1 does not obtain. The same may be said for Condition 2: even during the "Cold War," it was no secret that East bloc industry lagged considerably behind the EC in most fields of production with respect to deployed technology and capital stocks.[13] What about Condition 3? Soviet-style systems do seem to be effective in achieving high rates of labor-force participation: census data, for example, indicated that over 54 percent of East Germany's population was economically active in the 1980s, as against West Germany's 48 percent.[14] But East Germany's extensive employment strategy entailed the induction of more marginal laborers into the workforce; consequently, the average number of hours worked per week was reportedly lower than in West Germany (under thirty-six vs. over forty in 1988 in the nonagricultural sectors) (International Labor Office 1991). Total hours worked per year, on a population-equivalent basis, appears to have been only slightly higher in East Germany than in West Germany (or by extension in other Western European countries). Insofar as none of the conditions adduced appears actually to have obtained, one would conclude from these mortality differentials, in the absence of other evidence to the contrary, that per capita output in East Germany was actually substantially lower than within the EC countries in the years immediately before reunification.

What of the comparison between East Germany and, say, Argentina? Is it plausible that levels of per capita consumption would be higher for the society with the higher general mortality level? Once again, the answer is: in theory, yes, but only under specific conditions. Such a paradox might be explained by peculiarities of the income distributions of the countries in question; by differences in the reach and scope of health care policies; or by differences in the availability and incidence of other "public consumption" goods and services, such as rationed staples, medical care, or education. Yet by any of these criteria one would expect mortality levels to be lower in an Eastern European socialist economy than in a Latin American economy characterized by equivalent levels of per capita consumption. In the absence of other evidence, therefore, mortality levels would appear to indicate that East Germany's level of per capita consumption was rather more like a Latin American country's than that of a Western European country—and that it may actually have been lower than per capita consumption levels in some parts of Latin America. By way of perspective, one may note that the World Bank's "purchasing power parity" adjustments give Argentina a level of per capita output roughly one-third that of West Germany for 1985 (World Bank 1985).

This approach to mortality analysis can be extended to render a more general impression of the performance of Soviet-type economies in the generation before their demise. One instructive comparison comes from matching estimates of change in per capita output with changes in age-standardized mortality (WHO "European Model") for males over roughly the same period. That particular measure of mortality would seem appropriate as an alternate aperture on economic progress for two reasons. First, though it is a summary measure of mortality for all age groups, the model age-structure upon which it rests is heavily weighted toward persons of working ages, and is therefore sensitive to their mortality trends. Second, despite doctrinally stipulated equality of the sexes, labor force participation rates within the Soviet bloc were always higher for men than for women; moreover, Soviet bloc men tended to be disproportionately represented in higher-pay sectors. For these reasons, Soviet bloc output might be expected to be affected more by changes in male mortality than changes in female mortality.

Table 4.3 presents a match-up of CIA and WHO estimates for Soviet bloc countries and selected states from Western Europe. In all of the Soviet bloc countries, rising male mortality levels coincide with what are calculated to be substantial gains in per capita output. The situation in these four countries is contrasted with four of Western Europe's "slow growers": the Netherlands, Sweden, Switzerland, and the United Kingdom. Over the past generation, faster-growing Western European economies have also been characterized by a somewhat faster pace of change in age-standardized mortality; mortality change in the slow growers is less than the Western European average. Even so, these four countries exhibit an entirely different pattern of mortality change from the four Warsaw Pact countries, despite purportedly similar magnitudes of per capita growth. Where the Warsaw Pact group's mortality rates all rise, Western Europe's "slow growers" all register declines. In view of this radical difference, is it really possible that the Eastern and Western European countries in table 3 would actually have experienced similar per capita growth rates over the generation in question? Under certain conditions, possibly so—if, for example, the Soviet bloc had enjoyed a clear and overriding advantage with regard to technological innovation. But as has been noted, no such advantage was in evidence then, or can be seen in retrospect.

As a final comparison, one may match CIA (per GNP capita) and WHO (age-standardized mortality) estimates for the Soviet bloc and for Latin America for the year 1989 (see table 4.4). According to the CIA's assessment, none of these Soviet bloc countries had a level of per capita output nearly so low as the most affluent of these Latin American nations; as a group, their level of per capita GNP was said to be over three times as high as those Latin American countries listed. Those same Latin American societies, however, reported substantially lower levels of age-standardized mortality. Of the entire Warsaw Pact grouping in 1989, in fact, only East Germany could have passed for an advanced Latin American society on the basis of its age-standardized mortality figures. These mortality data do not offer a precisely cali-

TABLE 4.3

CIA Estimates of Changes in Per Capita GNP vs. WHO Estimates of
Changes in Age-Standardized Male Mortality: Selected Warsaw
Pact and Western European Countries, c. 1965-c. 1989

Country	Estimated Changes in Per Capita GNP 1966-89 (percent)	Estimated Changes in Age-Standardized Male Mortality, 1965/69-89 (percent)
Bulgaria	+ 61.2	+ 13.4
Czechoslovakia	+ 62.7	+ 1.8
Hungary	+ 57.3	+ 12.5
Poland	+ 62.3	+ 7.9
unweighted average	+ 60.9	+ 8.9
Netherlands	+ 63.4	- 11.5
Sweden[1]	+ 61.1	- 13.3
Switzerland	+ 51.6	- 27.1
United Kingdom	+ 63.0	- 25.1
unweighted average	+ 59.8	- 19.4

Notes: WHO age standardization is for its "European Model" population. [1] = 1988
Sources: Derived from U.S. Central Intelligence Agency, *Handbook of Economic Statistics*, 1980 edition, p. 29; 1990 edition, p. 44; World Health Organization, *World Health Statistics Annual*, 1988 edition, table 12; 1990 edition, table 10; 1991 edition, table 11.

brated adjustment of official Western estimates of Soviet bloc economic performance, but they appear to provide a strong implicit challenge to such figures, and thereby may be seen as serving something of a corrective function.

Even among market-oriented societies, international economic comparisons remain a complex and exacting business, for reasons both practical and theoretical. It should be no surprise that opportunities for mismeasurement were greater still when surveying the economies of the Soviet bloc. It may have been too much to hope for a single, unambiguous statistical account of the performance of economies so very different from our own.

Even so, the simple device of inspecting mortality rates might have indicated a great deal about economic performance in these countries.

TABLE 4.4

CIA Estimates of Per Capita GNP vs. WHO Estimates of Total
Age-Standardized Mortality: Warsaw Pact Countries and Selected
Latin American Countries, c. 1989

Country	GNP ($1989)	Age-Standardized Mortality, 1989 (deaths per 100,000)
Bulgaria	5690	1141.0
Czechoslovakia	7900	1158.0
East Germany	9670	1014.7
Hungary	6090	1229.6
Poland	4560	1118.7
Romania	3440	1240.5[1]
Soviet Union	9230	1159.9[1]
- unweighted average	6654	1151.8
Argentina	2250	1043.7[2]
Chile	1880	969.0[2]
Mexico	2340	1026.3[3]
Venezuela	2100	1003.8
- unweighted average	2143	1010.7
Ratio of unweighted averages (Latin America = 100)	310	114

Notes: WHO age-standardization is for "European Model" population [1] = 1988; [2] = 1987; [3] = 1986
Sources: Derived from U.S. Central Intelligence Agency, *Handbook of Economic Statistics,* 1990 edition, pp. 30-34; *World Health Statistics Annual,* 1990 edition, table 10; 1991 edition, table 11.

In the absence of countervailing evidence, they would have suggested that long-term per capita growth was negligible, if indeed positive, between the mid-1960s and the late 1980s; that per capita output was closer to the Latin American than the Western European level at the time of Soviet communism's collapse; and that levels of per capita consumption in the Soviet bloc might approximate those of Latin America as well. With the benefit of hindsight, and a largely unforeseen revolution, it may now be said that such a reading would not look too far off the mark.

III

Though communist rule has collapsed in the Warsaw Pact region, it continues in other lands: China, Cuba, North Korea, and Vietnam among them. This partial collapse of a once-global political and economic system poses an obvious question: why did some Marxist-Leninist regimes shake and fall in 1989-91, whereas others managed to weather the storm? The question may seem most appropriate for the historian or the student of international affairs, but it can also be framed in demographic terms. For one may wonder: is it entirely a coincidence that the governments that vanished during this crisis of international communism had all witnessed long-term health reversals among broad segments of the populations under their control, while all the governments that endured had supervised populations characterized by general and continuing mortality improvements?

The contrast in mortality trends of now-defunct and still surviving communist governments could hardly be more vivid. Comparison of these trends, however, is not a straightforward proposition. Vital registration data, for the most part, are rather less comprehensive in these surviving states than they were within the Warsaw Pact. (Cuba is the exception to this generalization, although even there questions remain as to the quality of its infant mortality data [Hill 1983]). For China, North Korea, and Vietnam, demographic trends had to be reconstructed on the basis of census returns and/or incomplete registration system data; such reconstructions do not permit more exacting or specific analyses of mortality conditions (e.g., year-to-year changes in age-specific death rates). They do, however, provide reasonably reliable estimates of long-term changes in general mortality levels. In particular, it is possible to estimate changes in life expectancy at birth over the past generation for these three countries (see table 4.5).

In all four countries, gains in life expectancy are quite substantial. Whereas life expectancy for males stagnated, or declined, in the Warsaw Pact countries between the 1960s and the 1980s, it is reported to have increased in Cuba by over eight years, and is estimated to have risen by nearly fourteen years in North Korea. China and Vietnam appear to have enjoyed gains in life expectancy at birth of nearly a decade for both males and females over the course of that same generation. By any historical measure, progress in reducing mortality in all these countries over the past decades would arguably qualify as rapid.

TABLE 4.5

Officially Claimed or Independently Reconstructed Changes
in Life Expectancy at Birth: Surviving Communist Regimes, c. 1965-c.1989

Country and Year	Life Expectancy at Birth for Males (years)	Life Expectancy at Birth for Females (years)
Cuba		
1965	65.4	67.2
1983/84	72.7	76.1
- increment	+ 7.3	+ 8.9
China		
1965	56.6	57.9
1989	66.2	67.0
- increment	+ 9.6	+ 9.1
North Korea		
1965	51.0	57.1
1987	64.7	71.0
- increment	+ 13.7	+ 13.9
Vietnam		
1965	49.7	57.0
1989	62.0	65.9
- increment	+ 12.3	+ 8.9

Notes: Cuban data taken from official life tables. Estimates for China, North Korea, and Vietnam are reconstructions based on census and/or registration data.
Sources: Cuba: United Nations, *Levels and Trends in Mortality Since 1950* (New York: U.N. Department of International Economic Aid and Social Affairs, 1982), p. 174; *Demographic Yearbook 1990* (New York: U.N. Department of International Economic and Social Affairs, 1992), p. 490; China and Vietnam: unpublished estimates, U.S. Bureau of the Census, Center for International Research. North Korea: Nicholas Eberstadt and Judith Banister, *The Population of North Korea* (Berkeley, CA: University of California, Institute of East Asian Studies, 1992), pp. 108-9.

This is not to say that health progress in the surviving communist states has been steady and consistent. China's "Great Leap Forward" (1957-58) brought on a demographic catastrophe, in which tens of millions perished and life expectancy plummeted. More recently, Beijing's anti-natal population policies have been associated with infanticide, and rising mortality, for baby girls; by some estimates these increases were for a while sufficiently consequential to reduce life expectancy at birth for females (Banister 1987). Such reversals, however, were tied to specific political campaigns. With the relaxation or reversal of the afflicting policy, mortality reductions in both cases resumed their downward trend under the same standing government.

Is there a political significance to this broad distinction in mortality trends within the former communist world? I believe there may well be, and that the distinction may be useful to understanding the very different fates of these two sets of regimes.

Let me be clear. I do not propose to replace the Marxist notion of historical materialism with determinism of a demographic variety, or to deny the significance of individual actions and discrete decisions within the great play of history. The collapse of Soviet bloc communism can be traced through a progression of specific events that was in no sense "historically inevitable": the accession of Mikhail Gorbachev; Moscow's decision to abide by the results of Poland's 1989 elections; Budapest's announcement later that year that it would permit East German "vacationers" to use Hungary as a transit stop on the way to West Germany; the failed coup in Moscow in August 1991. I wish instead to underscore the fact that, in our era at least, long-term rises in mortality are fraught with an unavoidable political significance. Whatever else they may portend, secular increases in mortality may today be read as an indicator of fragility for a regime, or an entire system.

The systemic political significance of the Warsaw Pact region's long-term health trends may be better appreciated by comparing their circumstances with the experiences of the Latin American and Caribbean region during the 1980s. For that area, after all, the 1980s were a decade of economic crisis and social reversals; of debt default and "structural adjustment." Whatever the inexactitudes of the calculations, the World Bank now estimates per capita output in the region as a whole to have been lower in real terms in 1990 than it had been in 1980; in countries such as Argentina, Panama, Peru, and Venezuela, corresponding estimates suggest that per capita GNP was over 15 percent lower at the end of the decade than at its start (World Bank 1992). Local austerity measures typically targeted public consumption—the "social safety net"—and most countries in the region could point to cutbacks in public expenditures on income support, education, and health. (Even before these cutbacks, Latin America's "social safety nets" were not considered famously sturdy.)

Despite these various shocks and setbacks, there is to date no evidence of pervasive increases in mortality in the Latin American and Caribbean region. To be sure: the vital registration systems in many of

these countries—including some of the ones apparently hardest hit—
were poorly developed, and would not have been capable of providing
an immediate representation of mortality reversals. Nevertheless, demographers who have examined mortality trends in the region since the
advent of "structural adjustment" have concluded—sometimes to their
own admitted surprise—that there is as yet no reason to believe that the
direction or even the tempo of mortality change has been affected by
this great depression.[15]

To judge by their mortality trends, the population of the Warsaw Pact
region, in the generation leading up to the fall of their communist regimes, was suffering through a much more drastic crisis than the one
that jolted Latin America in the 1980s. We may lack a compass adequate to the task of charting economic change in these communist
societies; even so, we know that governments in other parts of the world
and in other times have been able to forestall mortality reversal during
severe economic downturns and dislocations. Why were these Warsaw
Pact regimes not up to the challenge?

The very fact of secular mortality increase is evidence of a serious
failure in health policy. But it is suggestive of much more. Mortality
conditions are affected by a constellation of social, economic, and environmental factors. Education, housing conditions, and environmental
quality are but a few of the areas bearing upon health in which virtually
all modern governments routinely intervene. In centrally planned economies, where government arrogates a more far-reaching authority over the
social and economic rhythms of life, the correspondence between mortality
trends and government performance is presumably all the more comprehensive and direct. For the Warsaw Pact governments, the secular rises in
mortality in the populations under their supervision may have been suggestive of an inability to cope—of uncorrectable policy, administrative
incapacity, or even of the erosion of the governing power of the state.

In the event, those Marxist-Leninist regimes that outlasted Warsaw
Pact communism may (individually or collectively) be overturned in
the near future, or instead may prove able to hold onto power for many
more years. If they fall, moreover, their demise (individual or collective) may be preceded by secular mortality decline. After all, most coups
and revolutions in our century have been preceded (and followed) by
periods of general improvement in local public health conditions. Broad
rises in mortality over long periods of time are neither a necessary nor
sufficient condition for the collapse of a country's government, or its

political system. Such rises, however, do signify the existence of extraordinary social, economic, and even political stresses. As such, they serve as markers denoting risk for the regime in question. Thus, while it was in no sense preordained that the Warsaw Pact states would be the first of the communist governments to collapse, neither should it be surprising that things happened to turn out this way.

IV

As postcommunist societies in Europe and the former Soviet Union contemplate the course before them, they know they will be traveling in unexplored terrain. What Janos Kornai (1990) has called "the road to economic freedom" is, in fact, a desired destination, not a route map. Open societies, inviolable civil liberties, established and liberal legal systems, and functioning market economies may be widely desired in the postcommunist region, but in general remain distant objectives. Traversing the no-man's land between Leninist order and a secure market order confronts would-be reformers with a monumental task. Addressing the issue of privatization, Jan Winiecki (1991) has written that the challenge is to "find a way...that is both economically efficient and politically acceptable"; the same may be said for the entire process of transition.

Students of politics and economics have been kept busy by the almost daily changes in these areas since the end of communism. Political and economic plans or recommendations have proliferated; political and economic analyses of local and regional prospects are now something of a cottage industry. But in looking toward this uncertain future, the student of demography may have something to contribute, too. Once again, much of this contribution can draw from the examination of mortality trends.

In transitional economies, mortality trends can be seen as imposing a variety of constraints on the realm of the possible. Mortality levels and trends, for example, will have a direct bearing on the potential productivity of labor, thus on potential economic efficiency and growth. Mortality trends also bear directly upon a household's well being, albeit in a way that does not always show up in conventional income accounts. Dan Usher (1997) and Sherwin Rosen (1988), among others, have made the argument that consumers and individuals are likely to place considerable economic value on the improvement in their own life expectancy (and similar arguments could be extended to cover other aspects of their health status). Conversely, deterioration of health status or life expectancy represents a self-evident reduction in well being and living standards. While mortality decline may not be invested with political significance in the modern era, continued mortality rises, as we have seen, may betoken regime fragility. In transitional situations, one would interpret secular increases in mortality to presage reduced economic potential and administrative incapacity; one might further expect the phenomenon to generate populist pressures that could translate into the political realm.

With these considerations in mind, let us examine the initial indications about mortality trends in postcommunist territories.

Eastern Germany

In a way, Eastern Germany may constitute the best of all possible postcommunist worlds. Before its demise, the GDR was widely viewed as the most efficient and productive of the communist economies. By virtue of their incorporation into the existing Federal Republic of Germany, moreover, the territories of Eastern Germany almost instantly secured established frameworks for civil and commercial law, and were subsumed into a stable and successful political economy. Eastern Germans, furthermore, have had their transition pains eased by subsidies of a magnitude unimaginable for any other postcommunist population: due to the favorable terms upon which monetary union was concluded, and the guarantees now available through the Federal Republic's welfare state, Eastern Germans have been receiving non-investment transfers amounting (even after PPP adjustments) to about $4,000 per person per year since the end of 1989.[16] Finally, Eastern Germany enjoyed the best health conditions of any country in the Warsaw Pact; its infant mortality rate, in fact, compares quite favorably with that of the white American population.

Auspicious as such soundings may be, the contrast between health conditions in Eastern and Western Germany on the eve of unification was stark (see table 4.6). By the measure of age-standardized mortality, Eastern Germany's male death rate was 22 percent higher than Western Germany's in 1989; for females the gap was 31 percent. By this measure, Eastern Germany joined Western Europe with the distinction of being its least healthy member; age-standardized mortality rates in Ireland, heretofore the highest in the EC or EFTA, were 8 percent lower for males and 6 percent lower for females than were the GDR's in 1989 (WHO 1990). The mortality differences between East and West Germany in 1989, one may note, were greatest for the cohorts of working age—not exactly an ideal circumstance for equalizing productivity across this expanse.

Nor do preliminary figures for 1990 provide occasion for satisfaction (see table 4.7). By these data, age-specific mortality rates would appear to have risen for most cohorts in East Germany between 1989 and 1990. These apparent rises were recorded despite the magnitude, and broad incidence, of hard currency transfers from the Federal Republic to Eastern Germany households, and despite the opportunity to avail of Western German health care. It is possible that some portion of this rise is a statistical artifact, attributable to improved coverage under the Federal Statistical Office, but the GDR's mortality data (if not its cause of death data) had been reasonably good. The apparent broad rise in mortality in Eastern Germany, one must note, would actually mark a reversal of the trend for the area. Between 1985 and 1989, age-standardized mortality had declined by about 6 percent for males and about 8 percent for females.

TABLE 4.6

Mortality Differentials in Germany, 1989: Eastern German Death Rates as a Ratio of Western German Death Rates

(Western Germany = 100)		
Age Group	Males	Females
0	105	97
1-4	98	112
5-14	131	103
15-24	115	122
25-34	126	126
35-44	135	109
45-54	130	123
55-64	123	132
65-74	122	140
75 +	120	126
Age-standardized	122	131

Note: Age-standardization refers to WHO "European Model" population.
Source: Derived from World Health Organization, *World Health Statistics Annual 1990* (Geneva: WHO, 1991), pp. 226, 228, 380.

TABLE 4.7

After "Die Wende": Reported Changes in Age-Specific Death Rates
Eastern Germany, 1989-1990 (percent)

	0	1/4	5/9	10/14	15/19	20/24	25/29	30/34	35/39	40/44
Male	- 2	+ 48	+ 11	+ 68	+ 44	+ 37	+ 26	+ 24	+ 24	+ 4
Female	+ 6	+ 23	+ 63	+118	+ 18	+ 12	+ 23	- 3	+ 17	- 2

	45/49	50/54	55/59	60/64	65/69	70/74	75/79	80/84	85/89	90+
Male	+ 36	+ 8	+ 3	0	+ 4	-15	+ 16	+ 6	+ 2	+ 7
Female	+ 18	0	+ 1	+ 5	+ 2	-18	+ 10	- 2	- 2	+ 2

Note: Changes rounded to the nearest percentage point.
Sources: Statistiches Bundesamt, *Statistiches Jahrbach 1991 Fuer Das Vereinte Deutschland* (Wiesbaden: Metzler Poeschel Verlag, 1991), p. 87; unpublished data, Statistiches Bundesamt.

Eastern Europe

1990 was the first year of the political and economic transition from communism in Bulgaria, Czechoslovakia, Hungary, and Poland. The details of their reform programs differed, as do the estimates of their respective performance. It is generally agreed that the economies of all these countries contracted dramatically during their first year of post-communist rule, although the significance of their output declines is an issue of debate among observers.

Less open to debate are their recorded mortality trends (see table 4.8). According to these figures, age-standardized mortality for males rose in all four of these countries, and overall age-standardized mortality rose in three of them. Age-standardized mortality for females rose in one of them as well: Hungary. However one interprets these numbers, it cannot be reassuring that "adjustment" and "restructuring," in contrast with the Latin American experience, seem here to be coinciding with at least an initial increase in death rates for broad population groups. One may further ponder on the coincidence that Hungary, the country of the four with the worst recorded deterioration in mortality conditions between 1989 and 1990, is also widely viewed by international investors as the country in Eastern Europe most receptive to foreign capital, and moving fastest in the transition to a market economy.

TABLE 4.8

"After the Revolution": Age-Standardized Mortality in Eastern Europe, 1989-1990 (deaths per 1000,000 population)

Country and Sex	1989	1990	% change
Bulgaria			
Males	1396.6	1397.3	+ 0.1
Females	917.8	913.5	- 0.5
Czechoslovakia			
Males	1522.8	1552.1	+ 1.9
Females	888.4	874.1	- 1.6
Hungary			
Males	1624.9	1670.6	+ 2.9
Females	933.4	955.0	+ 2.3
Poland			
Males	1498.0	1670.6	+ 1.2
Females	838.5	833.0	- 0.7

Note: Age-standardization is for WHO "European Model" population.
Sources: World Health Organization, *World Health Statistics Annual* (Geneva: WHO), 1990 edition, table 10; 1991 edition, table 11.

These initial upticks, of course, may in the event be followed by sustained and rapid mortality declines. At the very least, however, it is apparent that the "environment" of policy and social or economic conditions that would bring mortality rates down is not yet in place; liberation from communist rule in and of itself, evidently, is not a sufficient condition. Moreover, even if a rapid and sustained mortality decline could immediately be arranged for these postcommunist regions, they would not reach the levels characteristic of Western Europe today for many years. If one posited a rate of decline of 2 percent a year (an exceptionally rapid rate, equivalent to that which Chile has enjoyed over the past generation), overall age-standardized mortality rates in Eastern Germany would not match today's Western German rates for another twelve years; Hungary would not reach today's Austrian level for twenty-three years; and Ukraine would not reach today's Swiss level for twenty-four years. For obvious reasons, actual convergence might be expected to take much longer.

Reflection upon mortality conditions, in sum, emphasizes the enormity of the challenges, and potential tribulations, that lie in store for postcommunist populations. Marxist-Leninist rule may or may not ultimately be viewed as an enormous historical detour. Those acquainted with mortality statistics for the postcommunist regions, however, will appreciate that repair of the damage experienced under communism's tenure, and attainment of Western European levels of performance, should probably be viewed as an historical process: one that may take decades, or even generations to complete.

Notes

1. This was not the first time big events had gone unanticipated. Leopold Labedz, longtime editor of the former *Survey of Soviet Studies*, has written that the only Western journal to predict Khrushchev's ouster in 1964 was *Old Moore's Almanac*—an astrological guide. See his "Small Change for Big Brother," *Survey* (1984): 120, p. 3. For a systematic assessment of the performance of the social sciences in this field, see Seymour Martin Lipset and Gyorgy Bence, "Anticipation of the Failure of Communism," *Theory and Society,* vol. 23 (1994).
2. The German Federal Statistical Office, for example, estimates per capita GDP in the second half of 1990 in the "new Federal States" to have been at 30.6 percent of the Western level. Statistisches Bundesamt, *Zur wirtschaftlichen und sozialen Lage in der neuen Bundeslaendern*, Special Edition, April 1993, p. 127.

   That precise figure, however, should not necessarily be retrofitted to the communist period. The collapse of communism was attended by a massive reallocation of factors of production—and also by a drop in their utilization. But inexactitudes notwithstanding, it is clear now that per capita production was far lower in East than in West Germany in the last days of *Ostpolitik*.
3. Figures are drawn from various issues of the U.N. *Demographic Yearbook*.
4. For one recent view of this controversy, see Barbara A. Anderson and Brian D. Silver, "Trends in Mortality in the Soviet Population," *Soviet Economy* 6 (1990):2, pp. 191-252.
5. For a more detailed assessment, see Nicholas Eberstadt, "Health and Mortality in Eastern Europe, 1965-85," *Communist Economies* 2 (1990):3, pp. 347-71.
6. For one recent interpretation of the phenomenon and its correlates, see Vaclav Smil, "Coronary Heart Disease, Diet, and Western Mortality," *Population and Development Review* 15 (1989):3, pp. 399-424.
7. See, for example, Abram Bergson and Hans Heymann, Jr., *Soviet National Income and Product 1940-48* (New York: Columbia University Press, 1954). The fullest exposition of the approach is Bergson's classic study, *The Real National Income of Soviet Russia Since 1928* (Cambridge, MA: Harvard University Press, 1961).
8. For a classic exposition on the distinction between living standards and consumption levels, see Joseph S. Davis, "Standards and Content of Living," *American Economic Review* 35 (1945):1, pp. 1-15.

9. The distinction between health trends and mortality trends is not to be minimized. See, for example, James C. Riley, "The Risk of Being Sick: Morbidity Trends in Four Countries," *Population and Development Review* 16 (1990):3, pp. 403-32, and Christopher J.L. Murray and Lincoln Chen, "Understanding Morbidity Change," *Population and Development Review* 18 (1992):3, pp. 481-503. For better or worse, however, mortality data are generally more available and more reliable today than are morbidity data.

10. The discussion below is premised on the assumption that the economists under consideration operate with production functions in which output is a function of capital and labor inputs—both adjusted for quality of the stocks included—and of technical and allocative efficiency, where these are exogenous parameters. Economies of scale do not figure explicitly in the model outlined above. The discussion assumes that mortality levels do not correlate negatively with other components of "human capital stock," and that there is no correlation between mortality levels and economies of scale.

11. Conventionally, of course, one measures hours of total employment against the economically active population, not the total population. The alternate denominator is used here because we are comparing output per capita for the population as a whole, not per worker.

12. The theoretical grounds for expecting socialist economies to have systemic problems with allocative efficiency were laid out in Ludwig von Mises, *Socialism* (London: Jonathan Cape, 1935), and F. A. von Hayek, ed., *Collectivist Economic Planning* (London: George Routledge and Sons, 1936). Empirical studies of the problem as it actually exists are numerous, but one might point in particular to Josef C. Brada, "Allocative Efficiency and the System of Economic Management in Some Socialist Countries," *Kyklos* 27 (1971):2, pp. 270-85; and Padma Desai and Ricardo Martin, "Efficiency Loss from Resource Misallocation in Soviet Industry," *Quarterly Journal of Economics* 98 (1983):3, pp. 441-56. See also Abram Bergson, "Comparative Productivity: The USSR, Eastern Europe, and the West," *American Economic Review* 77 (1987):3, pp. 342-57, where a measure of the efficiency loss attendant upon Soviet-style socialism is computed (although this loss relates to both technical *and* allocative efficiency).

13. The literature documenting technological lag in Soviet bloc industry is extensive, but noteworthy studies include Ronald Amann, Julian Cooper, and R. W. Davies, eds., *The Technological Level of Soviet Industry* (New Haven, CT: Yale University Press, 1977); Ronald Amann and Julian Cooper, eds., *Industrial Innovation in the Soviet Union* (New Haven, CT: Yale University Press, 1982), and Stanislaw Gomolka, "The Incompatibility of Socialism and Rapid Innovation," *Millenium* 13 (1984):1, pp. 16-26. In the words of Janos Kornai, "To sum up, low efficiency and technological backwardness and conservatism can be attributed to the combined effects of a set of system-specific factors." Janos Kornai, *The Socialist System* (Princeton, NJ: Princeton University Press, 1992), p. 301.

As to general issues relating to Soviet capital stock, see Raymond P. Powell, "The Soviet Capital Stock from Census to Census," *Soviet Studies* 31 (1979):1, pp. 56-75. For 1975, Bergson estimated the USSR's per capita Gross Reproducible Capital Stock (GRCS) to be 73 percent of the U.S. level; by his estimates per capita GRCS in a sample of four socialist countries averaged 71 percent of the level in a sample of seven Western mixed-economy countries, and averaged 77 percent of the Western European level in the socialist economies analyzed. See Bergson, "Comparative Productivity," p. 347.

In East Germany as of 1975, the estimated nominal value of the stock of capital assets was roughly 17 percent of West Germany's—with the former measured in *Marks* and the latter in *Deutschemarks*. On a per capita basis, East Germany's estimated stock of capital assets, on a nominal basis, would have been roughly 63 percent of the West German level; insofar as the price ratio with respect to investment in 1975 was believed to be about 1.16 DM/M, this would have suggested East Germany's capital stock per capita was roughly 73 percent as great as West Germany's in 1975. See Reinhard Pohl, ed., *Handbook of the Economy of the German Democratic Republic* (Guildford, Surrey: Saxon House, 1979), pp. 31-33, and Irwin L. Collier, "The Estimation of Gross Domestic Product and Its Growth Rate for the German Democratic Republic," *World Bank Staff Working Papers*, no. 773 (1985), p. 27.

14. Note that we are comparing two rather different systems for measuring labor force participation; while the results cannot be presumed totally comparable, they are nonetheless illustrative.

15. For one such assessment, see Kenneth Hill and Anne R. Pebley, "Child Mortality in the Developing World," *Population and Development Review* 15 (1989):4, pp. 657-87.

16. This is not to say that German policies pertaining to the economics of unification did not leave room for improvement. A sustained examination and economic critique of those policies may be found, for example, in Gerlinde and Hans Werner Sinn, *Kaltstart: Volkswirtschaftliche Aspekte der deutschen Vereinigung* (Tuebingen: J.C.B. Mohr, 1991), and Horst Siebert, *Das Wagnis der Einheit: Eine Wirtschaftspolitische Therapie* (Stuttgart: Deutsche Verlags-Anstalt, 1992).

References

Amann, Ronald, and Julian Cooper, eds. *Industrial Innovation in the Soviet Union.* New Haven, CT: Yale University Press, 1982.

Amann, Ronald, Julian Cooper, and R. W. Davies, eds. *The Technological Level of Soviet Industry.* New Haven, CT: Yale University Press, 1982.

Anderson, Barbara A., and Brian D. Silver. "Trends in Mortality in the Soviet Population." *Soviet Economy* 6 (1990): 2, pp. 191-252.

Banister, Judith. *China's Changing Population.* Stanford, CA: Stanford University Press, 1987.

Bergson, Abram. *The Real National Income of Soviet Russia Since 1928.* Cambridge, MA: Harvard University Press, 1961.

Bergson, Abram, and Hans Heymann, Jr. *Soviet National Income and Product 1949-48.* New York: Columbia University Press, 1954.

Brada, Joseph C. "Allocative Efficiency and the System of Economic Management in Some Socialist Countries." *Kyklos* 27 (1974): 2, pp. 270-85.

Collier, Irwin L. "The Estimation of Gross Domestic Product and Its Growth Rate for the German Democratic Republic." *World Bank Staff Working Papers*, no. 773 (1985).

Davis, Joseph S. "Standards and Content of Living." *American Economic Review* 35 (1945): 1, pp. 1-15.

Desai, Padma, and Ricardo Martin. "Efficiency Loss from Resources Allocation in Soviet Industry." *Quarterly Journal of Economics* 98 (1983): 3, pp. 441-56.

Dutton, John, Jr. "Changes in Soviet Mortality Patterns, 1959-77." *Population and Development Review* 5 (1979): 2, pp. 267-91.

Eberstadt, Nicholas. "Health and Mortality in Eastern Europe 1965-85." *Communist Economies* 2 (1990): 3, pp. 347-71.

Eberstadt, Nicholas, and Judith Banister. *The Population of North Korea.* Berkeley, CA: University of California, Institute of East Asian Studies, 1992.

Gates, Robert M. "CIA and the Collapse of the Soviet Union: Hit or Miss?" Speech delivered to the Foreign Policy Association, New York, May 20, 1992.

German Federal Statistical Office (Statistiches Bundesamt). *Statistiches Jahrbuch.* Wiesbaden: Metzler Poeschel Verlag, 1991 and 1992 editions.

Gomolka, Stanislaw. "The Incompatibility of Socialism and Rapid Innovation." *Millenium* 13 (1984): 1, pp. 16-26.

von Hayek, Friedrich, ed. *Collectivist Economic Planning.* London: George Routledge and Sons, 1936.

Hill, Kenneth. "An Evaluation of Cuban Demographic Statistics, 1938-80." In Paula E. Hollerbach and Sergio Diaz-Briquets, *Fertility Determinants in Cuba.* Washington, DC: National Academy Press, 1983.

Hill, Kenneth, and Anne R. Pebley. "Child Mortality in the Developing World." *Population and Development Review* 15 (1989): 4, pp. 657-87.

International Labor Office. *Yearbook of Labor Statistics 1989/90.* Geneva: ILO, 1991.

Kornai, Janos. *The Road to Economic Freedom: Shifting from a Socialist System, The Example of Hungary.* New York: W.W. Norton, 1990.

Idem. "Comparative Productivity: The USSR, Eastern Europe, and the West." *American Economic Review* 77 (1987): 3, pp. 342-57.

Idem. *Zur wirtschaftlichen und sozialen Lage in der neuen Bundeslaendern.* Special edition, April 1993.

Idem. *The Socialist System.* Princeton, NJ: Princeton University Press, 1992.

Labedz, Leopold. "Small Change in Big Brother." *Survey* 120 (1984), p. 3.

Lipset, Seymour Martin, and Gyorgy Bence. "Anticipation of the Failure of Communism." *Theory and Society* 23 (1994): 2, pp. 169-210.

von Mises, Ludwig. *Socialism.* London: Jonathan Cape, 1935.

Murray, Christopher J. L., and Lincoln Chen. "Understanding Morbidity Change." *Population and Development Review* 18 (1992): 3, pp. 481-503.

Pohl, Reinhard, ed. *Handbook of the Economy of the German Democratic Republic.* Guildford, Surrey: Saxon House, 1979.

Powell, Raymond P. "The Soviet Capital Stock from Census to Census." *Soviet Studies* 31 (1979): 1, pp. 56-75.

Revelle, Roger. "Introduction to the Issue 'Historical Population Studies.'" *Daedelus* 97 (1968): 2, pp. 352-62.

Riley, James C. "The Risk of Being Sick: Morbidity Trends in Four Countries." *Population and Development Review* 16 (1990): 3, pp. 403-32.

Rosen, Sherwin. "The Value of Changes in Life Expectancy." *Journal of Risk and Uncertainty* 1 (1988): 3, pp. 285-304.

Siebert, Horst. *Das Wagnis der Einheit Eine Wirtschftspolische Therapie.* Stuttgart: Deutsche Verlags-Anstalt, 1992.

Sinn, Gerlinde, and Hans Werner Sinn. *Kaltstart: Volkswirtschaftliche Aspekte der deutschen Vereinigung.* Tuebingen: J. C. B. Mohr, 1991.

Smil, Vaclav. "Coronary Heart Disease, Diet, and Western Mortality." *Population and Development Review* 15 (1989): 3, pp. 399-424.

United Nations. *Demographic Yearbook.* New York: U.N. Department of International Economic and Social Affairs, various issues.

———. *Levels and Trends in Mortality Since 1950.* New York: U.N. Department of International Economic and Social Affairs, 1982.

———. *World Population Prospects 1990.* New York: U.N. Department of International Economic and Social Affairs, 1991.

———. *World Population Prospects: The 1992 Revisions*. New York: U.N. Department of Economic and Social Development, 1993.

United States Central Intelligence Agency. *Handbook of Economic Statistics*. Washington, DC: GPO, 1980, 1988, 1990 editions.

———. *World Factbook 1987*. Washington, DC: GPO, 1987.

Usher, Dan. "An Imputation to the Measure of Economic Growth for Changes in Life Expectancy." In Milton Moss, ed. *The Measurement of Social and Economic Performance*. Cambridge, MA: National Bureau of Economic Research, 1977, pp. 192-226.

USSR State Statistical Committee (Goskomstat). *Tablitsy Smertnosti i Ozhidaemoy Prodalzhitel'nosti Zhizni Naseleniya*. Moscow: Goskomstat, 1989.

Winiecki, Jan. "Are Soviet-type Economies Entering into an Era of Long-Term Decline?" *Soviet Studies* 38 (1986): 3, pp. 325-48.

———. "Transition and the Privatization Problem." *Cato Journal* 11 (1991): 2, pp. 299-309.

World Bank. *World Development Report 1992*. New York: Oxford University Press, 1992.

World Health Organization. *World Health Statistics Annual*. Geneva: WHO, 1988, 1990, 1991 editions.

5

The Soviet Way of Death

I

The statesman and the demographer share a common interest: the untidy world of human affairs. They tend to approach that subject, however, from rather different perspectives. While the former strives to bring some order to daily life for large groupings of people, the latter strains to discern the regularities that may be found there already. No less than for the statesman, orderliness is the preoccupation of the demographer. For a field of inquiry that lies on the cusp of the natural and the social sciences—attending as demography does to the details of birth, family formation, and death within established human communities—the defining challenge is to assure an outside observer that there actually is some measure of generality and even predictability to the tendencies by which human numbers wax or wane, and population structures evolve, in the world's diverse localities.

For better or worse, demographers have suffered enduring frustrations in this quest. Just as in the past, the vital events that transform modern populations have proved to be full of surprises. And in our century, many of the great and terrible surprises that lay in store for demographers—but by no means them alone—are ones that were impressed upon local populations by their own governments.

Through the varied instruments of its growing power, the modern state became increasingly capable of affecting rhythms of birth, life, and death among its citizens. Newly possible interventions with dramatic demographic consequences often conferred widespread and widely desired

107

benefits upon the general populace (public health programs, for example). But in the hands of a less-benign directorate, the state could also use its newfound powers to inflict injury or visit upheaval upon its subjects.

Perhaps no region's population patterns bear the telling and disfiguring scars of state-directed experimentation quite so clearly as the former Soviet Union. Though the Russian Empire was by no means unaccustomed to tragedy by official design, the merciless utopians who seized power in the Bolshevik Revolution elevated these malign acts of state from haphazard practice to studied technique, and in so doing condemned the societies under their command to convulsions, catastrophes, and unnatural distortions.

Thanks to the special therapies administered to it under three generations of Soviet rule, in fact, the populations of Russia and the other newly independent states begin their postcommunist eras as veritable models of demographic irregularity. Already they have experienced trends in death rates, population movement, and contraception that no demographer ever foresaw—or could possibly have foreseen. They enter into independence, moreover, registering new and, once again, completely unexpected population shocks—reverberations, perhaps, from their Soviet past, which may yet have consequential implications for their future.

More directly than for other systems of governance, the progress and prospects of the totalitarian state are illuminated by the population patterns of those who live beneath it. Yet up to now, the Western reader would search in vain for a reliable and accessible presentation of the population history of the Soviet epoch. Happily, with the appearance of Alain Blum's *Naitre, Vivre, et Mourir en URSS, 1917-1991* (*Birth, Life, and Death in the USSR, 1917-1991*) [Paris: Librarie Plon, 1994], this gap has been ably filled. This important little book can be read with profit by a wide audience with varied professional interests. Indeed, it will even reward the reader who is ordinarily indifferent to demographic questions. For in Dr. Blum's retelling, the population history of the USSR is a primal drama set on a massive stage: a conflict framed by the tension between a government that insists upon inflicting "dark blows" (p. 83) and "great disruptions" (p. 108) upon the public, and the manifold "resistance" (p. 127) to these pressures from ordinary men and women, who are quietly intent upon their own "demographic autonomy" (p. 127).

II

Blum comes to his task well trained and well qualified. A graduate of EHESS (École des hautes études en sciences sociales) who is now director of research at INED (Institut national d'études démographiques—France's national demographic research center), he is a scholar of demonstrated accomplishment. His more technical writings—on Soviet population trends and the demographic history of France—have already established his reputation within international circles of specialists. As one might suspect of a man who can claim both Marc Ferro and Herve le Bras as mentors, Blum's inquiries are both solidly grounded and wide-ranging: interdisciplinary in the best sense of the term. And as one might also expect of a writer from this background, he is strongly influenced by the "École d'Annales" approach to history, and makes a point of keeping an eye on long-term social forces even as he depicts the most arresting current events. As Blum puts it: "Population dynamics should not be analyzed in terms of the concerns of the moment or the current political passions. They must be viewed over the longer term" (p.79).

Naitre, Vivre, et Mourir en URSS is composed of three overlapping essays: the first, on the history of Russian and Soviet population statistics; the second, on the violent demographic shocks between the October Revolution and the death of Stalin; and a final one on continuities in local population patterns despite Soviet policies and communist practices. On its face, the schema may appear abstruse, even eccentric, but it actually works quite well. For in telling the story of how the Russian, and later the Soviet, statistical authorities gathered and used population numbers, Blum has also selected a narrative device by which to introduce his readers to the history of the Soviet state apparatus: its founding, construction, and eventual decay. This history, in turn, prepares us for the shocks and challenges awaiting the Soviet peoples in the following chapters of the book.

Like so many other aspects of the Soviet experiment, the USSR's statistical system can be traced back to the French Revolution. This marriage of politics and numbers took on a distinctive character, even in Imperial Russia's initial Napoleonic borrowings, for as Blum points out, "The Minister of the Interior first set in motion the collecting of demographic, agricultural, and industrial information, from the *gubernii* (local administrative organizations) up. This arrangement took form through the creation of a bureau of statistics within the Ministry of Police, in 1811" (p. 33).

As an instrument not just for informing administration, but also for enforcing control under the Czars, this Russian statistical system was quite easily adapted to the purposes of Bolshevik planners, and, in fact, served them well—as long as they could stand to look at the results of their inquiries. From the very start, however, Soviet authorities were ambivalent on precisely this point. With the ascent of Stalin, "the statistics lost their relevance if they did not suit the will of those in power" (p. 40).

It was the particular misfortune of Soviet statisticians to be obliged to conduct a census for Stalin in 1937—in the wake of the devastating terror-famine of 1932-33, and at a time when the Vozhd himself had decreed the country's population to be rising swiftly. The returns from the population count—eight million too low for Stalin's liking—were nullified, and the head of the state's statistical service was shot. Two years later, another count was done: the figures were deliberately padded, and apparently deemed acceptable. Nevertheless, "the results from this census were left practically unpublished, apart from two short articles in *Pravda* and some data broadcast just before, and at the time of, the 1959 census. These were the only published traces of two major population counts that had carried statisticians into the maelstrom of the great purge" (p. 48).

Even under Stalin, deliberate falsification of inconvenient data was the exception, not the rule. "Even as the leadership denied the reality of the famine, and the official ideology affirmed the uninterrupted growth of the Soviet population, statisticians from the Central Board of the National Economy continued, despite everything, to collect and tabulate figures that perfectly expressed the magnitude of the catastrophe" (p. 49). Later, "after the war, the considerable losses suffered by the USSR ought to have required a new census, but there would only be a partial one....Faithful to a logic of concealing, rather than falsifying, the Soviet Regime waited until 1959, six years after the death of Stalin, to conduct its census" (p. 50). Still later, during the Brezhnev years, as health statistics in the USSR began to register broad deteriorations in the public's well being, "the authorities, without falsifying these figures, simply suppressed their publication. The elimination of the numbers was gradual and did not follow a strict logic, as if officials were realizing, as they went along, that one number or another could be used for indirect estimates" (pp. 51-52). With "glasnost," the dying Soviet regime finally disgorged the demographic facts it had taken pains for decades to conceal, making it possible at last for outside researchers to take the full measure of this particular facet of Soviet Union's seventy-year reign.

III

Surveying these newly released numbers, Blum's judgement is un-equivocal: "The history of Imperial Russia, of the Soviet Union, and the fifteen newly independent republics can only be seen as a continuous series of ruptures, indeed catastrophes" (p. 83). In this ongoing process, it was the Soviet government's distinctive innovation to modernize this phenomenon of demographic catastrophe: "Imperial Russian demographic history is that of an *ancien régime*, punctuated by a succession of mortality crises, while Soviet demographic history is interrupted by losses directly tied to conflicts, famines and successive waves of repression" (p. 85). Just what scale of losses were sustained in the construction and maintenance of Soviet socialism? Blum offers a few rough calculations. First, there was the civil war. In terms of battle deaths, that war is said to have cost about 800,000 lives: "but there still, civilian losses were much higher and might have amounted to 8 million people between 1918 and 1920, in terms of mortality above normal levels" (p. 90). There followed the famine of 1921-22, "aggravated by the Great Drought of 1921," but, in fact, provoked by the agricultural "hard line policies" of the new regime (p. 91). "In 1921," notes Blum, life expectancy in Soviet Russia "did not exceed twenty-five years, a level lower than that of France in the middle of the eighteenth century or of Russia at the end of the last century, when expectation of life at birth was around thirty-one years" (p. 94).

Then came the early 1930s, with forced collectivization in the countryside, the pitiless campaign against the *kulak*, and their consequences. "Rarely, in Europe's *entire* demographic history, had a famine resulted in such tremendous losses" (p. 100).

By Blum's reckoning, the USSR's life expectancy at birth in 1933 plunged below neolithic levels (p. 94); for that year alone, "six million deaths were attributable to the famine, in addition to the four million deaths that would be witnessed in normal times" (p. 99). By comparison with this disaster, in Blum's estimation, the terrible purges of the late 1930s—during which the NKVD was shooting hundreds of thousands of innocent people each year—were only a minor perturbation.

The Second World War, we learn, was even more costly to the USSR than is customarily imagined: "For a long time the figure of 20 million deaths in addition to natural deaths, cited by Khrushchev in his speech to the Twenty-First Congress of the CPSU, was regarded as definitive.

But actually, the Secretary General spoke of *more than 20 million deaths....* Reconstructions since then approach 26 to 27 million, out of a population that in 1941 numbered 195 million inhabitants, within the borders at the time" (p. 114). The war was followed, in 1946, by yet another famine, "the last murderous sign of the two decades of Stalinist power... although not of the same magnitude as the famines preceding it" (p. 116).

For all these horrors, we have not yet even mentioned the *gulag:* "In total over 8.2 million persons would pass through the camps between 1943 and 1953, 3.8 million of them between 1934 and 1941.... Thus, nearly one man in seven passed through the camps, not counting all the people passing through the labor colonies" (p. 112). For these unlucky prisoners, the death rate tended to be fearfully high. The deportation of entire suspect nationalities and the involuntary relocation on a massive scale of others were also integral features of the era's "population trends." These, too, exacted a high toll of mortality.

IV

Blum does not offer a total figure for the unnatural losses sustained by the Soviet peoples during these gruesome decades: perhaps because that would require too many assumptions and involve too many contrafactuals. What he permits himself to observe is that "crises of such importance leave indelible traces in the structure of population even if these diminish over time" (p. 117). But diminish with time they do, notwithstanding the harshest blows a modern dictatorship can mete out. And here we come to a central thesis of Blum's book.

Despite brutal, violent, or painfully foolish policies of the modern state, Blum argues, "demography acts, and reacts, over the long run. Continuity has the upper hand" (p. 129). In his view, "Observation of demographic behavior, for the population as a whole, leads to the conclusion that social development has been significantly independent of political evolution. This may seem a heretical proposition, insofar as the USSR's politics so tragically shaped its population.... Soviet propaganda was describing a new world, a utopia achieved, to populations that were searching in every way to save themselves from the effects of a discourse which, in all likelihood, they did not want to hear" (pp. 213-214). As Blum describes it, a sort of popular resistance, expressed through the mundane routines of family formation, not only thwarted the state's grand designs of forced modernization, but contributed to the ultimate failure of the Soviet experiment itself.

In his effort to make this case, Blum concentrates on Soviet demographic trends after the death of Stalin, examining patterns of fertility, mortality, contraception, and nuptiality, in turn. With respect to births, Blum points out that "trends in cohort fertility, which corresponds to the average number of births per woman for each generation, demonstrate without ambiguity that the decline in fertility is scarcely affected by the great catastrophes" (p. 132). At the same time, the fertility trends of the USSR's many separate nationalities seemed to have followed their own particular courses: lowest for the Baltic peoples, highest for the Central Asians of Muslim heritage. "Notably, and in a striking manner, the onset of fertility decline coincided in specific Soviet republics and neighboring countries. Thus, in an epoch when the USSR was virtually shut off from international migration, and the population of the Central Asian republics could not communicate with neighbors of the very same language and culture: Azerbaizhan, the first of the predominantly Muslim Soviet republics to begin this transition, started at the same time as Turkey; Uzbekistan, whose transition was later, began only a few years before Iran" (p. 136). Thus, too, the disposition toward illegitimacy: according to the final Soviet census (1989), the proportion of births outside marriage was high in Estonia and Latvia (paralleling trends in nearby Lutheran Sweden and Finland), low in Central Asia (where "Muslim tradition was unfamiliar with the phenomenon of illegitimate births" [p. 140]). These basic social trends, Blum informs us, "continued to evolve, not according to the rhythm Moscow wanted to impose on them, but rather to that of the cultural area to which they were traditionally linked" (p. 141).

Blum has a similar explanation for Soviet health patterns in the post-Stalin era—in particular, for the anomalous increases in infant mortality that were reported in the 1970s, and the general rise in adult death rates ever since the end of the Khrushchev thaw. "It is not necessary," he writes, "to see in this deterioration a connection between the growth of military expenditures and a decline in the health budget, as has been asserted by some experts. Its origins are more profound and attest to the limits of a determined planning policy strongly stressing a technical conception of medicine." And, he adds, "We could thus understand that such a 'technicalization' could lead, in turn, to a resurgence of mortality, particularly in the adult age groups, that would reach a level more in keeping with the real situation in the country, and would reestablish a more customary rhythm of decrease" (pp. 150, 158). With family planning, "the massive reliance upon abortion effectively distinguishes the USSR from the rest of Europe, to the point of making it a special case. In 1990, for example, more than seven million abortions were performed in the USSR, as against a little over five million live births" (p. 133). Soviet policy attempted to influence the country's fertility by regulating the availability of abortion, but Blum judges this to have been a fruitless project: "The practice of abortion by the ruled—independent of the intentions of the rulers—points to the emergence of a society propelling itself outside of the framework of policies set down by a monolithic party" (p. 177).

Finally, there is the family itself: what Blum calls the "place for preservation" (p. 185). Everywhere he looks, Blum sees "the persistence of traditional family structures. The fractured Estonian family is identical to the Scandinavian family; the extended and patriarchal Uzbek family, which does not allow for living alone, is of Muslim model" (p. 188).

Through marriage choices and household behavior, men and women living under communism resisted the stated Soviet goal of "drawing together" the country's diverse nationalities. In 1988, 90 percent of the Russians in the RSFSR married other Russians; in the Caucasus and Central Asian Republics, the corresponding fractions were even higher (p. 196). According to census results, moreover, the overwhelming majority of the Soviet Union's non-Russian children did not speak Russian as a first or second language, even in the late Brezhnev era: "To the extent that the use of the national language as first language was quasi-universal for all Soviet nationalities, except Ukrainians and Bielorussians, language patterns seemed to indicate, more or less, a grand rejection of assimilation" (p. 200).

This refusal to assimilate, in Blum's assessment, took on a broader political significance in the final days of the Soviet government, as the state headed toward breakup. "Remoteness was not the cause of the breakup. To the contrary: it was proximity, insofar as proximity made for a genuine threat of assimilation, which in turn prompted a resistance across the entire spectrum of civil society that was deviating from the established polity. The first countries to retain their independence were the Baltic nations; as for the political transitions in Uzbekistan or Turkmenistan, these did not lead to an overthrow of the established power structure" (p. 213). Thus "the families of the USSR contributed, in part, to the failure of Soviet integration" (p. 214)—and provided a base for harassing, eroding, and in the final analysis outlasting Soviet power.

V

Naitre, Vivre, et Mourir en URSS is a bold and masterly book. It is likely to be the final word on this important topic for some time to come. Blum presents his interpretation with force and confidence. Even so, for all its considerable merits, it is possible for one to leave this study impressed, but not wholly convinced.

There are smaller and larger reasons for such a reaction. On the one hand, it seems that Blum has not made his own case for demographic continuity and resistance under Soviet rule quite as convincing as it could be. Despite his evident mastery of detail and demographic technique, he neglects some facts that would only make his presentation stronger. There is no mention in his account, for example, of the de-urbanization of the Central Asian republics reported in the censuses of the 1970s and 1980s—a general and deliberate avoidance of the centers of Russian life and Soviet power. Yet this real and quite voluntary phenomenon—unique, to my knowledge, in the contemporary world—dramatically affirms Blum's general thesis. By the same token, there is scarcely a nod in this volume toward the demographic concept of "cohort fertility"—a measure of births to particular women over the course of their lives, in distinction to the "snapshot" view we ordinarily see in any given year of births to women of all different ages. Yet "cohort fertility" patterns in the USSR emphasize continuities in underlying trends, insofar as surviving women of fertile ages timed and spaced their lifetime births around the terrible disruptions of particular dark years.

More fundamental questions, however, concern Blum's very approach to his subject. From an Anglo-American perspective, the *"École d' Annales"* method of analysis appears to be especially prone to two types of errors. The first is in identifying historical or social continuities where these do not, in fact, exist. The second is in underestimating the impact of discrete and particular events—a new idea or outlook; a decisive battle—on the sweep of *"l'histoire longue."* These two vulnerabilities can be seen in Blum's own narrative. For alert as it is to the details of life under Soviet socialism, *Naitre, Vivre, et Mourir en URSS* is also surprisingly insensitive to those aspects of the USSR's demographic experience which might be very new, indeed unprecedented.

Blum's treatment of the long rise in Soviet mortality—a phenomenon reaching from the early 1960s up to the collapse of the system in 1991—betrays precisely such difficulties. In suggesting that the USSR's strange increase in peacetime mortality was simply a return to "more in keeping with the real situation in the country," Blum's argument may maintain its internal consistency, but it suddenly becomes inconsistent with a number of facts. After all, with lower incomes, lower levels of popular education, and only rudimentary medical systems, quite a number of developing countries (Sri Lanka and China among them) achieved higher levels life expectancy at birth than the USSR—and have yet to retrogress to more "historical" levels. Indeed, steady health progress is the rule in the world of modern nations, not the exception; it is long-term stagnation or deterioration that requires explanation.

The broad setbacks in health status that afflicted the USSR's population (and in particular, the populations of the USSR's "European" republics) during the last generation of Soviet power can be explained in terms of specific proximate factors: heavy drinking, heavy smoking, bad diet, inappropriate health and hygiene policies, and so on. But the USSR's health crisis—let us call it by its proper name—may also have been strongly influenced by factors no less important for being hard to quantify: the attitudes, outlook, and hopes of the general public. Blum insists that "Soviet man never existed, except in the imagination of some political figures" (p. 211). An alternative hypothesis could be that the new Soviet man was indeed created—but that he turned pessimist, and that his change of mood helped to undermine not only his own health but the power of the state above him.

Indeed, if *homo Sovieticus* were truly an imaginary creature, if the social continuities beneath the vicissitudes of politics were truly the *leitmotive* of the USSR's population history, we would be led to expect a fairly smooth demographic transition from the old order to the new one now evolving in the territories of the fifteen independent republics. Yet the end of communism, despite having occurred with an almost astonishing absence of violence and bloodshed, has ushered in a period of brutal demographic shocks, evocative in their magnitude of total war or crippling famine.

Consider: after two decades of relative stability, the total fertility rate in Russia proper began to plummet in 1991, and had dropped by fully a third by early 1994. Death rates, for their part, have skyrocketed: indeed, Russia's crude death rate in early 1994 was over 40 percent higher than it had been in 1989. Death rates for virtually all Russian age groups, male and female, have jumped since the collapse of the Soviet state, and at the moment more than three Russians are dying for every two born.

The same troubling pattern, incidentally, is replicated in all the Baltic Republics, in Ukraine, in Belarus, in Moldova—and in varying degree, throughout the Eastern European regions of the former Warsaw Pact. The area currently experiencing these peacetime demographic convulsions, one need hardly emphasize, comprises an amalgam of peoples—populations with distinct (if not strikingly different) cultures, traditions, levels of material attainment, degrees of political stability, and immediate economic prospects.

Demographers may be no worse than other social scientists at forecasting the future, but they find themselves called to do so more often and in greater detail: typically, to humbling consequence. Population developments in Russia and the other newly independent states in the years ahead may prove to be a matter of international interest. What sorts of trends may we expect?

Dr. Blum's analysis would seem to suggest that more traditional trends will resume, or redouble, once the hand of state repression is lifted. He may well prove to be correct, and I hope that he is. My own concern, however, is that living populations that have until now known only Soviet communism may still, in some sense, be imprisoned, even though the jail door is open for them—and that this dissonance may have repercussions that are demographic, but not demographic alone.

6

Health and Mortality in Eastern Europe: Retrospect and Prospect

Over the past generation, demographic data from the Soviet Union and Warsaw Pact Europe have detailed an anomalous and disturbing trend: stagnation, even retrogression, in overall health conditions and general mortality levels. For industrialized countries during peacetime, such an interruption of health progress is historically unprecedented. It is also unique, being limited—at least to date—to those populations living under governments established with the direct assistance of the Soviet Red Army. The pervasive nature of this health crisis within the states of the former Warsaw Pact is all the more striking when one considers the historical and cultural differences that otherwise divide the peoples commonly afflicted.

The epicenter of the Warsaw Pact's health crisis was within the Soviet Union, the first Warsaw Pact state to experience secular increases for men and women of various ages. It is also on the territory of the former Soviet Union that, by a variety of measures, the deterioration of overall health conditions, seems, to date, to have been most pervasive and severe. But for the more than 100 million people of what was Warsaw Pact Europe, the reverberations of this long-term health crisis have been far from negligible. Rising death rates have been characteristic of broad segments of the public in all of these countries over the past generation. For the region as a whole, moreover, overall mortality levels, when appropriately standardized, appear to have been higher at the end of the 1980s than they had been in the mid- to late 1960s.

This chapter explores this grim aspect of communism's social legacy in Eastern Europe.[1] We will begin by examining the dimensions of the health crisis that beset Warsaw Pact Europe between the mid-1960s and the "revolutions of 1989," tracing its trajectory over that generation. It then examines some of the proximate factors accounting for these perverse health patterns. Deteriorating health conditions have a direct bearing upon individual welfare; they also have implications for the states under which these syndromes emerged. Some of those implications will be discussed. Finally, this chapter touches briefly upon the health prospects for the populations of Eastern Europe now that Warsaw Pact communism has collapsed.

Dimensions of the Eastern European Health Crisis from about 1965 to about 1989

Specialists in public health and social affairs are by now familiar with the story of health crisis in the Soviet Union.[2] From the end of World War II until the early 1960s, health progress in the USSR appears to have been steady, rapid, and general. According to recent estimates by the United Nations (U.N.) Population Division, for example, the USSR's infant mortality rate fell by over half in the decade 1950/55-1960/65, and its overall life expectancy at birth rose by more than five years during that same decade.[3] By the mid-1960s, however, all-union death rates were registering a rise for certain cohorts of men in late middle age. The situation subsequently worsened. By the early 1970s, rising death rates were reported for adult males of almost every age group, for women beyond the childbearing years, and even for newborn infants. Sensitive to the political interpretations of such figures, Soviet authorities imposed a virtual blackout on mortality statistics for a decade, from the mid-1970s through the mid-1980s. By the final years of the Soviet era, data on mortality in the Soviet Union were once again widely available. These data were not without their defects and shortcomings.[4] Nevertheless, they pointed to a syndrome of broad, severe, and long-term deterioration in the country's public health conditions. According to official data, death rates in the Soviet Union were higher in 1989 than they had been thirty years earlier for a large portion of the country's population: men thirty-five years of age or older, and women fifty-five or older.[5] By the U.N. Populations Division's assessment, overall life expectancy at birth was actually slightly lower in the Soviet Union in the late 1980s than it had been in the early 1960s.[6]

Although the health record of Central and Eastern Europe has not occasioned as much commentary as the former Soviet Union, there are, nonetheless, striking parallels between the two. Like the Soviet Union, Warsaw Pact Europe began the cold war with a burst of health progress that encompassed virtually all groups and areas within the region. As in the Soviet Union, rapid and uninterrupted improvements in public health continued only up to the early 1960s. Thereafter, health progress came to a halt for a growing portion of the populations of the Central and Eastern European countries, as it did in the Soviet Union. Long-term stagnation, even decline, in health status came to typify the trends for major segments of each society within the Warsaw Pact alliance.

Health status is a subtle and complex quantity; it cannot be captured in a single, summary statistic. But perhaps the best way to chart the shifting health fortunes of Central and Eastern Europe's various populations is by means of local mortality trends. As an indicator of health conditions, mortality has obvious limitations: death rates cannot speak to the physical state of persons who actually manage to survive from one year to the next.[7] Nevertheless, mortality trends are meaningful in and of themselves, broadly suggestive of attendant changes in health circumstances, and by their nature more reliable and intrinsically comparable than many other data pertaining to health status. In short, there is probably no better first approximation of public health conditions for a population as a whole than those afforded by its mortality trends.

The most comprehensive, and intuitively clear, measure of overall mortality is probably life expectancy at birth. Official "life tables"[8] from the six countries of Warsaw Pact Europe provide an initial glimpse at the region's emerging health troubles. Results from these official calculations are presented in table 6.1. Between the mid-1960s and the late 1980s, according to these estimates, overall life expectancy in Warsaw Pact Europe did, in fact, rise, but just barely: taken together, the unweighted average for males and females is an increase of about one year. In aggregate, these six countries experienced no improvement in male life expectancy at birth whatever in the decades under consideration; two of the six states—Bulgaria and Hungary—actually estimated their male life expectancies to have declined. The situation was better for females, who were estimated to have enjoyed an increase in life expectancy at birth averaging a little more than two years. Yet even these improvements look far from favorable when set in international perspective. By the U.N. Population Division's assessment, Warsaw Pact Europe's female gains, in terms of years of life expectancy at birth, were less than half as great as those for the rest of Europe over the

TABLE 6.1

Expectation of Life at Birth in Eastern Europe
c. 1965-1989 (years)

Country	Male	Female
Bulgaria		
1965/67	68.81	72.67
1987/89	68.33	74.70
- increment	-0.47	+2.03
Czechoslovakia		
1964	67.76	73.56
1988	67.76	75.29
- increment	0.00	+1.73
GDR		
1967	68.35	73.43
1987/88	69.81	75.91
- increment	+1.46	+2.48
Hungary		
1964	67.00	71.83
1989	65.44	73.79
- increment	-1.54	+1.96
Poland		
1965/66	66.85	72.83
1988	67.15	75.67
- increment	+0.30	+2.84
Romania		
1964/67	66.45	70.51
1987/89	66.51	72.41
- increment	+0.06	+1.90

Sources: For GDR 1967: *Statistiches Jahrbuch Der Deutschen Demokratischen Republik 1970* (Berlin: Staatsverlag der Deutschen Demkratischen Republik, 1970), p. 470. For all others: United Nations, *Demographic Yearbook* (New York: U.N. Department of International Economic and Social Affairs), various issues.

period 1960/65 to 1985/90.[9] Apart from the Soviet Union, no other region of the world, by this indicator, is believed to have experienced such a marginal improvement in overall female health status over those decades. Despite its well-publicized economic and social travails, for example, the Latin American and Caribbean region is estimated to have significantly outpaced Eastern Europe in life expectancy improvements for men and women alike over that generation.

What accounts for the region's poor performance over these recent decades? In an arithmetic sense, the answer can be exposed by separating the populations in question into component parts. All Central and Eastern European countries reported steady, if undramatic, declines in their infant mortality rates between the mid-1960s and the late 1980s. The situation for their non-infant population was rather different (see table 6.2). In four of these six countries, overall life expectancy at age one was somewhat lower in the late 1980s than it had been several decades earlier; it was lower for males in all countries. For the region as a whole, it appears that such health progress as was achieved between the mid-1960s and the late 1980s can be attributed entirely to improvements in infant mortality; life expectancy at age one for the region as a whole looks to have been slightly lower at the end of that period than it had been at its beginning.

If general health conditions for Central and Eastern Europe's non-infant populations were characterized by stagnation, the plight of adult groups in particular was marked by pervasive deterioration. As table 6.2 illustrates, life expectancy at age thirty for males is estimated to have fallen in all six countries of Warsaw Pact Europe. Some of these declines were little short of catastrophic. Hungary, for example, registered a drop of nearly four years. In five of the six Eastern European states, overall life expectancy was lower in the late 1980s than it had been a generation earlier, and in the GDR—the sole exception to the regional trend—it was only very slightly higher.

Changes in age-specific mortality rates highlight the adverse health trends that befell Eastern European adults (see table 6.3). During the quarter century between 1965 and the revolutions of 1989, death rates in all of these countries were up for at least some adult male cohorts; for many of these groups, the increases recorded were dramatic and alarming. In Hungary, for example, death rates for men in their forties fully doubled between 1966 and 1989. The patterns for Central and Eastern European women were less unfavorable. Even so, Hungary re-

TABLE 6.2

**Expectation of Life at Age One and Age 30:
Warsaw Pact Region, c. 1965-c.1989**

Country	Life Expectation at One Year of Age (years)		Life Expectation at Age 30 (years)	
	Male	Female	Male	Female
Bulgaria				
1965/67	70.28	73.81	43.06	45.99
1987/89	68.42	74.64	40.87	46.53
- increment	-1.86	+0.83	-2.19	+0.54
Czechoslovakia				
1964	68.44	73.96	41.15	45.84
1988	67.70	75.07	39.73	46.62
- increment	-0.74	+1.11	-1.42	+0.78
East Germany				
1967-68	69.77	74.70	42.46	46.70
1987-88	69.53	75.46	41.67	47.08
- increment	-0.24	+0.76	-0.79	+0.38
Hungary				
1964	69.08	73.45	41.74	45.45
1989	65.58	73.86	37.84	45.55
- increment	-3.50	+0.41	-3.90	+0.10
Poland				
1965/66	68.98	74.43	41.68	46.46
1988	67.37	75.70	39.60	47.29
- increment	-1.61	+1.27	-2.08	+0.83
Romania				
1964/67	68.93	72.53	42.04	45.09
1987/89	67.53	73.13	40.45	45.56
- increment	-1.40	+0.60	-1.59	+0.47

Sources: United Nations, *Demographic Yearbook* (New York: U.N. Department of International Economic and Social Affairs), various issues.

TABLE 6.3

Changes in Age-Specific Death Rates for Cohorts Aged 30-69: Warsaw Pact Region, c. 1965-c. 1989 (percent)

Country and Sex	Cohort Age							
	30/34	35/39	40/44	45/49	50/54	55/59	60/64	65/69
Males								
Bulgaria (1966-89)	+ 19	+ 32	+ 62	+ 70	+ 56	+ 47	- 16	+ 14
Czechoslovakia (1965-89)	- 5	+ 8	+ 19	+ 40	+ 33	+ 29	+ 15	+ 6
East Germany (1965-88)	- 5	- 8	- 5	+ 7	+ 3	+ 1	- 15	- 17
Hungary (1966-89)	+ 67	+ 96	+ 100	+ 131	+ 93	+ 69	+ 46	+ 25
Poland (1966-88)	+ 9	+ 17	+ 36	+ 51	+ 47	+ 38	+ 23	+ 6
Romania (1966-89)	+ 32	+ 36	+ 43	+ 61	+ 44	+ 32	+ 35	+ 15
Unweighted average	+ 20	+ 30	+ 43	+ 60	+ 46	+ 36	+ 15	+ 8
Soviet Union (1965/66-89)	- 5	0	+ 21	+ 25	+ 24	+ 25	+ 20	+ 25
Females								
Bulgaria (1966-89)	- 11	- 15	- 10	+ 4	- 4	- 4	- 7	- 6
Czechoslovakia (1965-89)	- 13	- 23	- 14	- 9	- 10	0	- 3	- 9
East Germany (1965-88)	- 12	- 15	- 14	- 12	- 12	- 10	- 16	- 17
Hungary (1966-89)	+ 33	+ 26	+ 26	+ 33	+ 23	+ 22	+ 7	- 2
Poland (1965-88)	- 27	- 25	- 9	- 9	- 2	- 1	- 3	- 14
Romania (1966-89)	- 8	+ 13	+ 4	- 3	0	- 2	- 3	- 3
Unweighted average	- 6	- 7	- 3	+ 1	- 1	+ 1	- 4	- 9
Soviet Union (1965/66-89)	- 21	- 17	- 4	- 3	+ 2	+ 11	+ 4	+ 19

Note: All changes rounded to the nearest percentage point. Percentages derived from sources.

Sources: For Soviet Union 1965/66: John Dutton, Jr., "Changes in Soviet MortalityPatterns, 1959-77," *Population and Development Review*, vol. 5, no. 2 (1979), pp. 276-77. All other data: United Nations, *Demographic Yearbook* (New York: U.N. Department of International Economic and Social Affairs), various issues.

ported broad rises in adult female mortality, and both Bulgaria and Romania registered at least some long-term increases in mortality for specific female age groups. On the whole, deterioration of health appears to have been most serious for Eastern European men and women in their forties and fifties. Poor as the Soviet performance with respect to public health may have been over the past generation, it is worth noting that there appear to be numerous instances in Eastern Europe in which specific adult cohorts suffered even sharper reversals than those experienced by contemporaries in the former Soviet Union.

Those reversals are all the more dramatic when viewed against the backdrop of the decades immediately following World War II. Between 1945 and 1965, mortality declines were more rapid in Eastern than Western Europe. To many observers East and West, that differential pace of progress seemed to open the possibility that the countries of Soviet Bloc Europe might match, and ultimately surpass, the health performance of "capitalist" Europe. By the mid-1960s, "convergence" did, in fact, suggest itself. "Age-standardized mortality rates"[10] emphasize this point (see table 6.4). In 1965/69, according to calculations of the World Health Organization (WHO), mortality rates for WHO's four contemporary members from Warsaw Pact Europe, when standardized against the WHO's "European Model" population, looked to be only slightly higher than those of eighteen countries in Western Europe: for females, the differential was about 8 percent; for males, less than 3 percent.

Yet by the eve of the revolutions of 1989, a great gap had opened between Eastern and Western Europe. For both males and females, age-standardized death rates were, on an unweighted average, over 40 percent higher in Warsaw Pact Europe. Between the mid-1960s and the late 1980s, Western European age-standardized mortality rates had been falling steadily; overall rates dropped by about 25 percent between 1965/69 and 1989. In Eastern Europe, by contrast, the overall impact of mortality change was to raise combined rates of age-standardized mortality somewhat, as secular increases in male death rates more than made up for the slight improvements that were registered by females.

A generation of stagnation, and even deterioration, in general health conditions took its toll on Central and Eastern Europe's standing in relation to other areas of the world. By 1989, there was no longer any meaningful comparability in general health conditions between the two portions of divided Europe. Age-standardized mortality rates underscore the contrast. As of 1989, these death rates were higher, for males and females alike, in Eastern Europe's "healthiest" state (the GDR), than in Ireland—the state then registering the highest levels of overall mortal-

TABLE 6.4

Age-Standardized Mortality Rates in Selected Eastern European Countries and in Western Europe: 1965/69-c. 1989 (deaths per 100,000)

Country or group	1965/69	c.1989	change (%)
Bulgaria			
males	1228.4	1396.6	+13.7
females	956.8	917.8	-4.1
Czechoslovakia			
males	1496.0	1522.8	+1.8
females	978.7	888.4	-9.2
Hungary			
males	1444.2	1624.9	+12.5
females	1044.5	933.4	-10.6
Poland			
males	1388.5	1498.0	+7.9
females	922.6	838.5	-9.1
Unweighted average,			
4 Eastern European countries			
males	1389.3	1510.6	+8.7
females	975.7	894.5	-8.3
Unweighted average,			
18 Western European countries			
males	1344.9	1041.2	-22.6
females	903.2	626.9	-30.6
Ratio, Selected Eastern			
to Western European countries			
(Western Europe = 100)			
males	103	145	
females	108	143	

Notes: Mortality rates are standardized against the WHO "European Model" population. Western Europe: Austria, Belgium, Denmark, Finland, France, Federal Republic of Germany, Greece, Iceland, Ireland, Italy, Luxembourg, Netherlands, Norway, Portugal, Spain, Sweden, Switzerland, United Kingdom (England and Wales). Western European figures for 1965-69 do not include Italy. Western European figures for c. 1989 are 1989, except Belgium (1986), Italy (1988), Spain (1987), and Sweden (1988).
Sources: World Health Organization, *World Health Statistics Annual* (Geneva: WHO), 1988 edition (1989), table 12; 1990 edition (1991), table 10; 1991 edition (1992), table 11.

TABLE 6.5

Age-Standardized Mortality Rates for Eastern Europe and Selected Other Populations, c. 1989 (deaths per 100,00)

Country or group	male	female	total
Bulgaria 1989	1396.6	917.8	1141.0
Czechoslovakia 1989	1522.8	888.4	1158.0
GDR 1989	1313.7	828.4	1014.7
Hungary 1989	1624.9	933.4	1229.6
Poland 1989	1498.0	838.5	1118.7
Romania 1988	1462.0	1051.1	1240.5
Unweighted average, 6 Eastern European countries	1469.7	909.6	1150.4
Unweighted average, 18 Western European countries c. 1989	1041.2	626.9	803.1
Unweighted average, 6 Selected Latin American countries, late 1980s	1210.7	819.7	997.2
USSR 1988	1565.2	915.8	1159.9
Ratios			
USSR:Eastern Europe	106	101	101
Eastern Europe:Western Europe	141	145	143
Eastern Europe:Latin America	121	111	115

Notes: Mortality rates are standardized against the WHO "European Model" population. For Western European countries, see table 4.
The six selected Latin American countries are Argentina (1987), Chile (1987), Costa Rica (1988), Mexico (1986), Venezuela and Uruguay (1987).
Sources: World Health Organization, *World Health Statistics Annual* (Geneva: WHO), 1990 edition (1991), table 10; 1991 edition (1992), table 11.

ity in Western Europe. By the criterion of age-standardized mortality, in fact, health conditions appeared to be better in any industrialized democracy on any continent than in any Warsaw Pact state.

Health conditions in the communist countries of Central and Eastern Europe also fared poorly by comparison with a growing number of developing countries. Table 6.5 contrasts age-standardized mortality rates for Warsaw Pact Europe around 1989 with an unweighted average for six Latin American countries in the late 1980s: Argentina, Chile, Costa Rica, Mexico, Uruguay, and Venezuela. As may be seen, mortality levels were by then significantly higher in Eastern Europe. On an unweighted average, female death rates were over 10 percent higher; for males, the differential was over 20 percent. By the end of its communist era, in fact, not even the GDR could claim to have an age-standardized death rate as low as the average for these six Latin American populations. Nor were these the only Latin American countries with health conditions superior to those of Warsaw Pact Europe. WHO judges fifteen territories in Latin America and the Caribbean to have sufficiently complete data to permit computation of their age-standardized mortality rates; by WHO's reckoning, overall mortality by this measure was lower than the Eastern European average in eleven of them, and lower than the GDR's in nine.

Even against the unexacting standard of Soviet performance, age-standardized mortality rates in Eastern Europe in the late 1980s do not look especially favorable. One must remember that the WHO "European model" population, against which all death rates in table 6.5 were standardized, is weighted toward adult working-age groups—and thus towards cohorts registering Eastern Europe's most severe health reversals. Nevertheless, by this particular criterion, overall health levels for certain groups—including females from Bulgaria and Romania, and Hungarians of both sexes—actually appear to have been worse than the USSR's own on the eve of the revolutions of 1989.

The health situation in the European communist countries considered here, then, was characterized by both absolute and relative decline over the past generation. But while Soviet bloc Europe suffered setbacks in health conditions between the mid-1960s and the late 1980s, this outcome was not the result of a single, unremitting trend. On the contrary: two quite different trends are in evidence during those years. From the mid-1960s through the mid-1980s—roughly from 1965 until 1985—overall rates of age-standardized mortality in these countries were generally rising, with modest declines in female rates being more than offset by the increases for males. Between 1985 and 1989, however, there appears to have been something of a turnaround. After decades of worsening health conditions for men, age-standardized mortality for males suddenly started to improve. Progress in reducing female mortality, for its part, appears to have accelerated in much of the region (see figures 6.1 and 6.2).

This resumption of broad mortality declines, however, was not enough to draw communist Europe's levels closer to those of non-communist

FIGURE 6.1

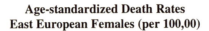

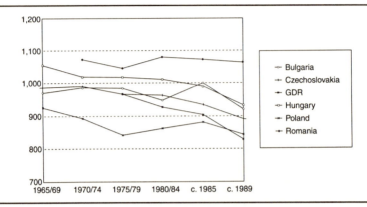

Notes: Morality rates are standardized against WHO "European Model" population; "c. 1985"=1986 (Poland) and 1984 (Romania); "c. 1989"=1988 (Romania)
Sources: *World Health Statistics Annual* (Geneva: WHO), various editions

FIGURE 6.2

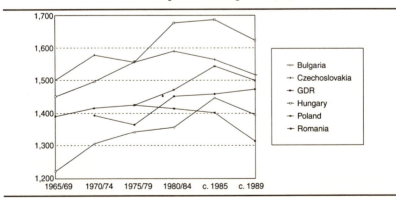

Notes: Morality rates are standardized against WHO "European Model" population; "c. 1985"=1986 (Poland) and 1984 (Romania); "c. 1989"=1988 (Romania)
Sources: *World Health Statistics Annual* (Geneva: WHO), various editions

Europe. During those same years, the latter countries were experiencing rapid improvements in mortality. Between 1985 and 1989, for example, overall age-standardized mortality fell by more than 11 percent in Austria; in Portugal it dropped by fully 12 percent. Though the region's rate of mortality decline was less rapid overall, it was nonetheless well ahead of that in the European communist states. Thus, even though European communist countries managed to stabilize and reduce death rates during the final years under communism, the gap between their health circumstances and those on the other side of the Iron Curtain apparently continued to widen up to the very collapse of the communism itself.

Proximate Causes and Underlying Influences

How are the peculiar health patterns witnessed in Eastern Europe over the past generation to be explained? We may begin by examining a few hypotheses that *do not* adequately explain the phenomenon.

The first of these suggests that the region's rising death rates were, in large measure, a statistical artifact: a function of improvements in the region's vital registration systems. This hypothesis can be rejected out of hand. Death registration remains spotty for infants in several Eastern European countries—and egregiously incomplete in Romania[11]—but this is not the cohort whose death rates were reported to be on the rise. Throughout Eastern Europe, by contrast, the mortality data for non-infants, and in particular for adults, seem to have been characterized by near-universal coverage since at least the mid-1960s.

A second hypothesis argues that mortality rates in Central and Eastern Europe are indeed genuine, but that they may be due to factors preceding the communist interlude. By this theory, today's health problems are in large measure a delayed consequence of shocks and stresses suffered during World War II.[12] On its face, such a "cohort effect" is certainly plausible; excess mortality appears to have been characteristic of certain cohorts of combatant populations that survived the two World Wars.[13] But the hypothesis is of little use in explaining the most anomalous and disturbing features of Eastern Europe's postwar health performance. As we saw in table 6.3, death rates for Central and Eastern European men in their early forties were, on the whole, much higher around 1989 than around 1965. This is to say that mortality was higher for persons born *after* World War II than for earlier cohorts who lived through it. "Cohort effects," moreover, cannot explain why age-standardized mortality has risen over the past generation in most Eastern European countries even as it was rapidly declining in (for example) Japan—a society that suffered severe wartime losses and endured great postwar privation. Nor can this hypothesis cast light on the divergent mortality trends in the GDR and Federal Republic of Germany (FRG), territories that experienced the Second World War as a single nation (see table 6.6). Note that, as of 1989, GDR-FRG mortality differentials for younger men and women (ages 15-44) were quite similar to those of their older counterparts who had survived World War II (45 and older).

Hypotheses to the contrary notwithstanding, the health problems of the formerly communist countries of Central and Eastern Europe today are all too real; moreover, they appear to reflect the consequence of events and developments since the advent of Socialist rule, not just the aftershocks from World War II. But rejecting these hypotheses only begs the question of explanation. If these particular theories are inadequate to account for Eastern Europe's prolonged health crisis, what factors are responsible for it?

TABLE 6.6

Age-Specific Death Rates: East and West Germany, 1989
(deaths per 100,000)

Age	Males			Females		
	GDR	FRG	Ratio (FRG=100)	GDR	FRG	Ratio (FRG=100)
0	889.6	845.1	105	618.6	638.8	97
1-4	42.5	43.3	98	38.5	34.3	112
5-14	28.2	21.5	131	15.1	14.6	103
15-24	100.7	87.7	115	42.2	34.6	122
25-34	142.4	113.4	126	63.3	50.2	126
35-44	288.5	214.2	135	129.6	118.7	109
45-54	744.0	571.5	130	353.2	286.0	123
55-64	1845.2	1495.3	123	917.2	696.5	132
65-74	4396.4	3601.1	122	2561.7	1828.5	140
75+	13578.0	11340.8	120	10471.1	8297.3	126

Source: World Health Organization, *World Health Statistics Annual 1990* (Geneva: WHO, 1991), pp. 226, 228.

One initial approach to the puzzle is offered by reported cause-of-death patterns for the region's various populations. Such data must be handled with appropriate care;[14] they are, after all, conditioned by an unavoidable element of subjectivity. Specialists have noted variations in diagnosis and coding practices for death certificates among countries in the European Community.[15] Similarly, in a recent experiment in the United States, roughly half of the certificates queried were upon further investigation amended with respect to cause of death.[16] We should not expect cause-of-death data from Eastern Europe to attain a higher standard of reliability than that evidenced in OECD countries—all the more because of the indications that these figures were shaped by political considerations under at least some Eastern European regimes.[17] For all these qualifications, cause-of-death data may nevertheless afford a view of the proximate causes of the region's health troubles, and by doing so, may be broadly suggestive of the underlying factors propelling large population groups toward reduced life expectation.

Intriguing indications and trends emerge from these data for a variety of reported causes of death: among them, cirrhosis and chronic liver disease (often associated with heavy drinking); lung cancer (heavy smoking); and accidents or injuries (a category defined to include both suicide and homicide).

Evocative of broader conditions though such reported causes of death might be, they account for only a relatively minor share of total deaths. On an age-standardized basis, in fact, deaths ascribed to lung cancer, cirrhosis, and suicide accounted for about a tenth of overall male mortality and for less than a twenty-fifth of overall female mortality in Eastern Europe in the mid-1980s.[18] The region's recent mortality patterns and trends, rather, are dominated and indeed shaped by deaths attributed to cardiovascular disease (CVD): afflictions of the heart and the circulatory system, including ischemic heart disease (heart attacks) and cerebrovascular disease (strokes).

The importance of CVD-attributed deaths in Central and Eastern Europe's health crisis can be seen in table 6.7. In the late 1960s, according to WHO data, age-standardized mortality rates for deaths ascribed to CVD were quite similar in Eastern and Western Europe. By around 1989, however, Eastern European countries had CVD-ascribed mortality rates vastly higher than Western Europe's: in this particular comparison, over 75 percent higher for men, and over 85 percent higher for women. Between 1965/69 and 1989, age-standardized CVD-ascribed mortality had fallen substantially in non-communist Europe: on average, by about a fourth for men, and by about a third for women. In contrast, Eastern European countries were subject to an explosion of CVD-ascribed mortality. The region's men suffered an ostensible epidemic of these noncommunicable diseases; in Bulgaria, the increase over the period in question was placed at over 50 percent. Nor were women spared: most of these countries reported long-term rises in female CVD as well. So severe was the apparent upsurge in cardiovascular mortality that by around 1989, age-standardized   CVD-ascribed death rates were on average higher for women in the states of communist Europe than for men in noncommunist European countries.

Table 6.8 illustrates that the level of mortality attributed to cardiovascular disease by the Soviet bloc countries around 1989 was vastly higher than the rates ostensibly prevalent in contemporary Western Europe, or among economically advanced regions of Latin America. Indeed, the absolute level of CVD-ascribed mortality (appropriately standardized) within the Soviet bloc in the 1980s was historically unprecedented. These deaths were by 1989 the principal proximate determinant of overall differences in mortality between Eastern and Western Europe. Over three-fourths of the mortality differential for males, and over nine-tenths of that for females, in the two regions by that time were accounted for by differences in death rates attributed to CVD. The same pattern holds for more specific comparisons of countries from the two regions (see table 6.9). On the eve of German reunification, about seven-eighths of the total difference in death rates for males and females alike between the GDR and FRG could be accounted for by their reported differences in CVD mortality.[19]

In proximate terms, it would appear that the factor mainly responsible for today's gap in mortality levels between Eastern and Western Europe is deaths attributed to cardiovascular disease. CVD-ascribed mortality also appears to be the proximate factor most clearly associated with the region's increases in overall mortality levels over the past generation. (Conversely, the slight declines in overall mortality rates reported for the 1985-89 period are born of reported declines in CVD mortality.) It would seem, then, that the key to explaining postcommunist European countries lies in the distinctive and worrisome movements of the region's CVD-ascribed death rates.

There is much about cardiovascular disease that is poorly, or incompletely, understood at present.[20] Even the relationship between preva-

TABLE 6.7

Age-Standardized Mortality Attributed to Cardiovascular Disease (CVD):
Selected Eastern and Western European Countries, 1965/69-c. 1989
(deaths per 100,000)

Country or group	1965/69	c.1989	change (%)
Bulgaria			
males	531.3	808.8	+52.2
females	512.7	595.2	+16.1
Czechoslovakia			
males	682.4	787.6	+15.4
females	505.8	507.9	+ 0.4
Hungary			
males	747.0	785.7	+ 5.2
females	603.0	506.3	-16.1
Poland			
males	523.6	758.8	+44.9
females	381.2	465.3	+22.1
Unweighted average			
males	621.1	785.2	+26.4
females	500.7	518.7	+ 3.6
Unweighted average, 18 Western European countries			
males	601.9	447.0	-25.7
females	425.7	279.2	-34.4
Ratio, Selected Eastern to Western European countries (Western Europe = 100)			
males	101	176	
females	118	186	

Notes: Mortality rates are standardized against the WHO "European Model" population.
For Western Europe, see table 4.

Sources: World Health Organization, *World Health Statistics Annual* (Geneva: WHO),
1988 edition (1989), table 12; 1990 edition (1991), table 10; 1991 edition (1992), table 11.

TABLE 6.8

**Age-Standardized Mortality Attributed to Cardiovascular Disease (CVD):
Eastern Europe and Selected Other Populations
c. 1989 (deaths per 100,000)**

Population group or ratio	male	female	total
Unweighted average Eastern Europe c.1989	774.1	540.9	636.9
USSR 1988	830.9	583.7	672.5
Unweighted average, 18 Western Countries c.1989	447.0	279.2	351.3
Unweighted average, 6 Selected Latin American Countries, late 1980s	424.5	314.8	364.8
Ratio			
USSR:Eastern Europe	107	108	106
Eastern:Western Europe	173	194	181
Eastern Europe:Latin America	182	172	175
Proportion of overall Difference in age-standardized mortality accounted for by reported differences in CVD mortality; Eastern Europe vs.:			
Western Europe	76	93	82
Selected Latin America	135	251	178

Notes: Mortality rates are standardized against the WHO "European Model" population. For Western Europe, see table 6.4. For Latin America, see table 6.5.

Sources: World Health Organization, *World Health Statistics Annual* (Geneva: WHO), 1990 edition (1991), table 10; 1991 edition (1992), table 11.

TABLE 6.9

Differences in Age-Standardized Cause-of-Death Structures:
East vs. West Germany, 1989
(deaths per 100,000)

Ratio Selected Cause of Death	GDR 1989	FRG 1989	Absolute (FRG=100)	as % of over-all difference
All Causes				
male	1313.7	1075.5	122	100
female	828.4	634.0	131	100
Infectious and Parasitic				
Diseases				
male	5.4	7.8	69	1
female	3.3	4.9	67	1
Malignant Neoplasms				
male	245.5	279.5	88	14
female	150.0	166.1	90	8
Diseases of the Circulatory				
System				
male	689.1	483.6	142	86
female	473.8	300.2	158	89
Diseases of the Respiratory				
System				
male	92.3	77.7	119	6
female	34.4	28.9	119	3
Chronic Liver Diseases and				
Cirrhosis				
male	28.6	29.9	96	1
female	10.5	12.4	85	1
Injury and Poisoning				
male	94.6	61.4	154	14
female	41.7	27.3	153	7
— of which, suicide and				
self-inflicted injury				
male	37.7	22.0	171	7
female	13.3	8.2	162	3

Notes: Mortality rates are standardized against the WHO "European Model" population.
Source: Derived from World Health Organization, *World Health Statistics Annual 1990* (Geneva: WHO, 1991), pp. 380-81.

lence or severity of CVD and resultant mortality in industrialized countries is a matter of considerable uncertainty. Yet CVD does seem to be associated with a variety of identifiable and specific factors. Heavy smoking is one of them. Poor diet, lack of exercise, and obesity are others. Insofar as hypertension bears upon CVD, heavy drinking appears to play a role. And researchers now suspect that psychological stress or emotional strain may have an impact on CVD.[21]

Observers of the scene in the postcommunist countries of Central and Eastern Europe have commented widely on the extent to which these populations are today exposed to these diverse risk factors. Statistical sources strongly suggest that per capita consumption of cigarettes and hard spirits rose dramatically in Eastern Europe between the mid-1960s and the 1980s.[22] No parallel quantitative measure is available for gauging psychological stress or emotional strain, although contemporary literature from Eastern Europe may perhaps offer a view of the changing "mood of the times." It is, at the very least, quite plausible that Central and Eastern Europe ran an increasing risk of CVD during their last generation under communism because of a variety of characteristic changes in personal behavior and lifestyle.

Yet in and of themselves, behavioral factors can only offer an incomplete explanation for changing patterns of health, disease, and death. After all, government health policies are framed and pursued on the premise that public interventions can stabilize and reduce overall mortality levels—and even insulate the individual from the consequences of his own adverse actions. More generally, health and welfare policies undertaken by governments in the modern era are expected to protect vulnerable segments of society, even during times of economic dislocation or crisis.

In retrospect, it is clear that the last generation of "health strategies" and social welfare policies implemented by Central and Eastern European governments failed badly. In the view of its exponents and admirers, the Soviet-style health system—with its universal coverage, extensive regimen of contacts between medical personnel and the population at large, and its provision that medical treatment costs be borne directly by the state—was a model for the enhancement of public health. Secular increases in national death rates throughout the Warsaw Pact countries speak to the contrary.

Yet they also speak more broadly to the performance of the regimes in question. Mortality conditions are affected by a constellation of social, economic, and environmental factors. Education, housing conditions, and pollution are but a few of the areas bearing upon health in which modern governments routinely intervene. For centrally planned economies, where the state arrogates a more far-reaching authority over the social and economic rhythms of life, the correspondence between mortality trends and government performance is presumably all the more comprehensive and direct.

Despite the claims made on their behalf, the fact remains that the Warsaw Pact governments, during their last generation of power, presided over an extraordinary and unique decline in the well being of their subjects. Mortality patterns provide incontrovertible proof of this. Yet those same patterns raise questions not only about the health of the citizenry, but of the states that governed them. In the final analysis, the health crisis of the Eastern European peoples in their last generation of communism may be diagnosed as a crisis of the system under which they were living.

Some Implications of the Health Crisis in Communist Europe

That long-term increases in death rates are unwelcome should hardly require emphasis—by definition they signify a diminution of public health. They speak to real reductions in individual and social well being. Moreover, their economic consequences are predictably adverse and far-reaching. For the consumer, reductions in life expectancy will occasion unanticipated alteration of consumption patterns;[23] for producers it means a smaller and quite possibly more debilitated labor force. Because of the complementary nature of the various quantities together known as "human capital," moreover, rising death rates might be expected to have considerable indirect economic repercussions as well.

Not all the implications of Central and Eastern Europe's health crisis, however, concern the populations afflicted by it. These unpredicted, and still largely unexplained patterns of health reversal speak directly to the state of Western knowledge about, and understanding of, this collectivity of countries during its final generation under communist rule.

The notion that an industrialized society under a stable administrative system, and at a time of peace, should experience prolonged deteriorations in public health is, to put it mildly, inconsistent with contemporary Western expectations. Yet an entire grouping of such societies, bound together by a tight and far-reaching alliance, was characterized by exactly these sorts of health setbacks. The perverse health trends witnessed throughout the region, indeed, were not only distinctive, but by almost any reading fundamental in their significance. Taken together, these simple but basic facts would seem to frame a compelling case: namely, that conventional Western assessments of Soviet bloc states seriously missed the mark in important respects for at least a generation before their collapse.

What sorts of judgements do the region's health trends suggest? One general tendency surely concerns economic performance. In and of themselves, for example, Eastern European mortality trends would seem consistent with the proposition that contemporary Western studies (with very few exceptions) seriously overestimated levels of per capita output, per capita consumption, and rates of per capita growth of the countries in question during their last generation under communism.

Take the case of the GDR. In 1988, the Central Intelligence Agency's Handbook of Economic Statistics placed the GDR's 1987 per capita GNP (in current U.S. dollars) at $12,330—a level almost identical with its estimate for per capita GNP within the European Community ($12,340).[24] Yet around 1989, age-standardized mortality for males was about 26 percent higher in the GDR than the FRG; for females the difference was about 32 percent. The relationship between mortality levels and productivity levels is admittedly neither tight nor mechanistic. Yet the discrepancy between estimated levels of productivity and actual levels of mortality is glaring, and would seem to require explanation. In the absence of a plausible explanation, one would be drawn to the conclusion that the GDR's per capita output had been dramatically overstated.

Similar questions arise with respect to consumption levels. As we saw in table 6.5, mortality levels in the communist countries of Central and Eastern Europe around 1989 were typically higher than those recorded in Latin America's more materially advanced societies in the late 1980s. Yet conventional Western estimates at the time indicated that per capita consumption was far higher in Eastern Europe than in those Latin American societies. Is it possible that levels of per capita consumption could have been far higher in the group of countries whose mortality levels were substantially the worse? In theory, yes; but the juxtaposition is peculiar, and would require explanation. In the absence of a convincing explanation, one would be drawn to the conclusion that the levels of per capita consumption in communist Europe in the late 1980s were not so different from those in various Latin American societies at the time.

Outside estimates of economic growth in Warsaw Pact Europe are subject to parallel questions. As table 6.10 indicates, official U.S. estimates of per capita growth between 1966 and 1989 were roughly similar for a number of Eastern and Western European countries. Yet whereas all the Western countries could point to declines in male mortality over those years, the Central and Eastern European countries reported increases. In Eastern Europe, as in noncommunist Europe, men made up the bulk of the workforce during this period, and men accounted for the great majority of hours worked in any given year. Could such radically different trends in male mortality be consistent with similar tempos of long-term economic growth? If so, the explanation that would reconcile these contrasting patterns is not immediately evident.

If health trends in Central and Eastern Europe during the period of communist rule appear to argue implicitly for a reassessment of the region's economic performance, they would also seem to merit examination from a political perspective. For a striking political coincidence is now evident in communist and formerly communist states. As of 1992, the world's only remaining Marxist-Leninist governments—China, Cuba, North Korea, North Vietnam—could all claim to have presided over long-term mortality improvements for the populations under their supervision. By contrast, the governments of the Warsaw Pact, all of which collapsed between 1989 and 1991, had each witnessed secular deteriorations in public health conditions over the previous generation.

Is this cleavage an entirely random outcome? Probably not. It may be unwise to overemphasize the role of demographic trends in political developments. Yet demographic trends may at times serve as political indicators. The Warsaw Pact countries' long-standing inability to effect mortality decline was arguably a fact of considerable political significance. It bespoke many things: one of them was regime fragility. With the benefit of hindsight, it may be easier now to appreciate just how fragile those regimes were in the years preceding their demise.

Health Prospects and the Transition toward a Market Order

With the collapse of Warsaw Pact communism, the populations of Eastern Europe are free to experiment with new political and economic arrangements, to embrace new policies, and to identify new social objectives. While individuals and organized groups will surely differ on the particulars of many postcommunist programs and proposals, the

TABLE 6.10

CIA Estimates of Changes in Per Capita GNP vs. WHO Estimates
of Changes in Age-Standardized Male Mortality:
Selected Warsaw Pact and Western European Countries
c. 1965-c. 1989

Country	Estimated Changes in Per Capita GNP 1966-89 (percent)	Estimated Changes in Age-Standardized Male Mortality, 1965/69-89 (percent)
Bulgaria	+ 61.2	+ 13.4
Czechoslovakia	+ 62.7	+ 1.8
Hungary	+ 57.3	+ 12.5
Poland	+ 62.3	+ 7.9
unweighted average	+ 60.9	+ 8.9
Netherlands	+ 63.4	- 11.5
Sweden[1]	+ 61.1	- 13.3
Switzerland	+ 51.6	- 27.1
United Kingdom	+ 63.0	- 25.1
unweighted average	+ 59.8	- 19.4

Notes: Mortality rates are standardized against the WHO "European Model" population.
    [1] = 1988
Sources: Derived from U.S. Central Intelligence Agency, *Handbook of Economic Statistics*: 1980 edition, p. 29; 1990 edition, p. 44; World Health Organization, *World Health Statistics Annual*: 1988 edition, table 12; 1990 edition, table 10; 1991 edition, table 11.

need to improve national health conditions is an objective that is likely to be universally endorsed.

As citizens and officials contemplate health prospects in the new Central and Eastern Europe, they are confronted by two basic questions. First: How heavily are the perverse health patterns from the old communist era impressed upon the region's contemporary populations? Second: Will the economic and social transformations now underway jeopardize the quest for health progress?

That the postcommunist governments of the region must overcome health problems bequeathed to them by the regimes they have replaced is clear enough. Unfortunately, this social legacy of communism looks more troubling as it is examined more closely. Not only are mortality levels throughout the area strangely high, but the pattern of illness and disease they reflect is one that may prove unexpectedly resistant to public health policy interventions.

The formidable challenges posed by the region's health problems are outlined by a simple comparison with materially advanced areas of Latin America. Poland (1989) and Argentina (1987) are used in tables 6.11 and 6.12 to frame the contrast, although other combinations could do so just as well. On the whole, mortality in Poland is slightly higher for females than in Argentina, and is significantly higher for males. Differentials are greatest for the population conventionally considered to be of working ages. Economically inauspicious as higher general levels of mortality may appear, the incidence of Poland's "excess mortality" in relation to Argentina would seem all the more disadvantageous.

Despite Poland's generally higher levels of mortality, Poland does not register higher death rates than Argentina for all reported categories of deaths. If cause-of-death statistics can be trusted, for example, Poland compares quite favorably with Argentina in its fatalities from certain types of disease, especially those classified as "infectious and parasitic" in nature. On the other hand, mortality levels ascribed to cancer and cardiovascular diseases are vastly higher in Poland than Argentina.

Taken as a category, infectious and parasitic diseases tend to be amendable to immediate control through discrete, and often relatively inexpensive, public health interventions. Cancer and CVDs, on the other hand, are noncommunicable conditions that tend to be chronic in nature, and to reflect physical insults and abuses that have accumulated over the course of a lifetime. Under the best of circumstances, a new regimen of medical and public health policies might be expected to

TABLE 6.11

Ratio of Age-Specific Death Rates:
Poland 1989 vs. Argentina 1987
(Argentina = 100)

Age group (years)	Male	Female
0	61	59
1-4	67	66
5-14	83	83
15-24	112	63
25-34	147	68
35-44	135	81
45-54	138	103
55-64	127	118
65-74	118	119
75+	110	103
Age-Standardized Mortality Rate, WHO "European Model"	116	100

Source: Derived from World Health Organization, *World Health Statistics Annual* (Geneva: WHO); 1990 edition (1991), p. 282; 1991 edition (1992), p. 92.

make fewer immediate inroads against cancer and CVD than against infectious and parasitic diseases.

The best of circumstances, moreover, do not obtain in contemporary Poland. In a country at Poland's level of economic attainment, health care costs must be a consideration in policy, and chronic diseases are especially expensive to treat. (Health benefits may be expected from less expensive preventative measures, but their impact tends to be greatest in the longer run.) The intrinsic financial problems presented to these postcommunist societies by their disease profiles are exacerbated further by the population structure now characteristic in Eastern Europe. A generation of fertility near or below the net replacement level has made for populations composed disproportionately of elderly and middle-aged adults—groups most likely to be at risk from cancer and CVD.

The constraints on public health policies for Central and Eastern Europe are formidable, but hardly insuperable. To the contrary: properly framed and implemented policies, pursued on realistic budgets, should be capable of eliciting steady improvements in general health conditions throughout the region. Indeed, even under the highly questionable public health policies of the region's *anciens régimes*, some general if belated improvements in public health conditions were registered during the second half of the 1980s.

Initial readings from the postcommunist Central and Eastern Europe, however, suggest that the region's health policies have not been adequate to the task of controlling and reducing mortality during the first steps toward a market order. As table 6.13 details, male mortality rose between 1989 and 1990 in Bulgaria, Czechoslovakia, Hungary, and Poland; in Hungary female mortality rose as well. One may appreciate

TABLE 6.12

**Difference in Age-Standardized Cause-of-Death Structures:
Poland (1989) vs. Argentina (1987) (deaths per 100,000)**

Causes	Poland 1989	Argentina 1987	Ratio (Argentina=100)
All Causes			
Male	1498.0	1291.7	116
Female	838.5	834.6	100
Infectious and Parasitic Diseases			
Male	14.2	38.6	37
Female	5.3	26.7	20
Malignant Neoplasms			
Male	291.2	232.7	125
Female	154.1	144.7	106
Diseases/Circulatory System			
Male	758.8	603.5	126
Female	465.3	419.7	111
Diseases/Respiratory System			
Male	81.1	95.3	85
Female	28.2	50.7	57
Diseases/Digestive System			
Male	46.9	67.7	69
Female	26.0	36.7	71
Chronic Liver Disease and Cirrhosis			
Male	17.4	22.7	72
Female	6.9	6.4	108
Injury and Poisoning			
Male	122.4	86.6	138
Female	34.9	32.5	107
Suicide and Self-inflicted Injury			
Male	20.9	13.4	156
Female	3.8	4.1	93

Note: Mortality rates are standardized against the WHO "European Model" population.
Source: Derived from World Health Organization, *World Health Statistics Annual 1990* (Geneva: WHO, 1991), table 11.

the potential health stresses attendant upon the "revolutions of 1989" without presuming that great economic and social dislocations necessarily result in rising mortality rates. In Latin America and the Caribbean, for example, there is to date no evidence that widely cited shocks of the debt crisis and "adjustment policies" of the 1980s brought about pervasive increases in mortality—even in the most severely affected countries.[25]

More ominous than the upticks in mortality evidenced in the four aforementioned countries are the initial changes registered in the GDR. The East German situation, after all, may be seen as constituting some-

TABLE 6.13

Age-Standardized Mortality
in Eastern Europe, 1989-1990
(deaths per 100,000 population)

Country and Sex	Year 1989	1990	% change
Bulgaria			
Males	1396.6	1397.3	+ 0.1
Females	917.8	913.5	- 0.5
Czechoslovakia			
Males	1522.8	1552.1	+ 1.9
Females	888.4	874.1	- 1.6
Hungary			
Males	1624.9	1670.6	+ 2.9
Females	933.4	955.0	+ 2.3
Poland			
Males	1498.0	1670.6	+ 1.2
Females	838.5	833.0	- 0.7

Note: Mortality rates are standardized against the WHO "European model" population.
Sources: World Health Organization, *World Health Statistics Annual* (Geneva: WHO), 1990 edition (1991), table 10; 1991 edition (1992), table 11.

TABLE 6.14

Reported Changes in Age-Specific Death Rates
Eastern Germany, 1989-1990 (percent)

	0	1/4	5/9	10/14	15/19	20/24	25/29	30/34	35/39	40/44
Male	- 2	+ 48	+ 11	+ 68	+ 44	+ 37	+ 26	+ 24	+ 24	+ 4
Female	+ 6	+ 23	+ 63	+118	+ 18	+ 12	+ 23	-3	+ 17	- 2

	45/49	50/54	55/59	60/64	65/69	70/74	75/79	80/84	85/89	90+
Male	+ 36	+ 8	+ 3	0	+ 4	- 15	+ 16	+ 6	+ 2	+ 7
Female	+18	0	+ 1	+ 5	+ 2	- 18	+ 10	- 2	- 2	+ 2

Sources: Statistiches Bundesamt, *Statistiches Jahrbuch 1991 Fuer Das Vereinte Deutschland* (Wiesbaden: Metzler Poeschel Verlag, 1991). p. 87; unpublished data, Statistiches Bundesamt.

thing like the best of all possible postcommunist transitions. With unification, East Germany was subsumed into a stable political order and a highly developed "social market economy." Moreover, the German government has been underwriting the unification process with subsidies on a scale unlikely to be repeated in any other postcommunist region. Despite these promising forensics, pervasive increases in death rates for male and female cohorts alike were reported between 1989 and 1990 (see table 6.14).

The general deterioration of health conditions in formerly communist Europe in the immediate aftermath of the revolutions of 1989 has widened still further the mortality gap that separates these countries from other European countries. Even if one were to posit an immediate resumption, and acceleration, of mortality declines, it would be many years before these countries could hope to achieve levels characteristic of contemporary Europe. On the extremely optimistic assumption of a continuing 2 percent per annum decline in age-standardized mortality—a pace to date maintained over time in only a few countries—it would take more than twelve years for mortality levels in Eastern Germany to reach those registered today in Western Germany, and well over twenty years for Hungary's to reach the current average for Western Europe as a whole.

That proposed trajectory, it should be emphasized, is optimistic; it may actually take considerably longer for Eastern European countries to attain the levels of public health evident in the rest of Europe. Thus, like the communist interlude itself, the postcommunist recovery from this aspect of the region's legacy promises to be an historic process.

Notes

1. Only Warsaw Pact Europe will be surveyed in this chapter; developments in Yugoslavia and Albania (where trends differed somewhat from the patterns described above) will not be analyzed here.
2. See, for example, John Dutton, Jr., "Changes in Soviet Mortality Patterns, 1959-77," *Population and Development Review* 5 (1979):2, pp. 276-91; Christopher Davis and Murray Feshbach, *Rising Infant Mortality in the USSR in the 1970s* (Washington, DC: U.S. Bureau of the Census, International Population Reports, series P-95, no. 74, 1980); Murray Feshbach, "Soviet Health Problems," *Proceedings of the Academy of Political Science* 35 (1984):3, pp. 81-97; Barbara A. Anderson and Brian D. Silver, "The Changing Shape of Soviet Mortality, 1958-1985: An Evaluation of Old and New Evidence," *Population Studies* 43 (1989):2, pp. 243-65; and Murray Feshbach and Alfred Friendly, Jr., *Ecocide in the USSR: Health and Nature under Siege* (New York: Harper Collins Books, 1992).
3. United Nations, *World Population Prospects: The 1992 Revision* (New York:

U.N. Department of Economic and Social Development, 1993), p. 202.

4. For one assessment of some of these problems, see Barbara A. Anderson and Brian D. Silver, "Trends in Mortality of the Soviet Population," *Soviet Economy* 6 (1990):3, pp. 191-252.

5. Comparisons based upon data presented in United Nations, *Demographic Yearbook* (New York: United Nations), various issues.

6. *World Population Prospects: The 1992 Revision*, p. 202.

7. For an extended examination of the distinction between morbidity and mortality trends, see James C. Riley, "The Risk of Being Sick: Morbidity Trends in Four Countries," *Population and Development Review* 16 (1990):3, pp. 403-32.

8. "Life tables" are standard demographic constructs that trace survival chances across all ages for males and females in a given population.

9. Derived from *World Population Prospects: The 1992 Revision*, p. 192.

10. "Age-standardized mortality rates" provide a summary measure of overall mortality by applying age-specific death rates for a given population against a specifically selected age-sex structure; such adjustments afford a greater comparability across countries and over time.

11. See Nicholas Eberstadt, "Health and Mortality in Eastern Europe, 1965-85," *Communist Economies* 2 (1990):3, esp. pp. 349-50.

12. For one exposition of this hypothesis, see R.H. Dinkel, "The Seeming Paradox of Increasing Infant Mortality in a Highly Industrialized Nation: The Example of the Soviet Union," *Population Studies* 39 (1985):1, pp. 87-97.

13. Shiro Horiuchi, "The Long Term Impact of War on Mortality: Old Age Mortality of the First World War Survivors in the Federal Republic of Germany," *Population Bulletin of the United Nations* 15 (1983), pp. 80-92.

14. As is explained in Lado T. Ruzicka and Alan D. Lopez, "The Use of Cause-of-Death Statistics for Health Situation Assessment: National and International Experiences," *World Health Statistics Quarterly* 43 (1990):2, pp. 249-58.

15. Zbigniew J. Brzezinski, "Mortality Indicators and Health-for-All Strategies in the WHO European Region," *World Health Statistics Quarterly* 39 (1986):4, p. 365.

16. Harry M. Rosenberg, "Improving Cause-of-Death Statistics," *American Journal of Public Health* 79 (1989):5, pp. 563-64.

17. "Health and Mortality in Eastern Europe, 1965-85," p. 354.

18. Derived from ibid., p. 356.

19. For a more detailed examination, see Charlotte Hoehn and John Pollard, "Mortality in the Two Germanies in 1986 and Trends 1976-1986," *European Journal of Population* 7 (1991):1, pp.1-28.

20. Some of these uncertainties are outlined in G. Lamm, *The Cardiovascular Disease Programme of WHO in Europe: A Critical Review of the First 12 Years* (Copenhagen: WHO Regional Office in Europe, 1981).

21. See, for example, U.S. Department of Health and Human Services, Public Health Service, *Health Consequences of Smoking: Cardiovascular Disease: A Report of the Surgeon General* (Washington, DC: Government Printing Office, 1983); Vaclav Smil, "Coronary Heart Disease, Diet, and Western Mortality," *Population and Development Review* 15 (1989):3, pp. 399-424; Erkki Vartianinen, Du Dianjun, and James S. Marks, "Mortality, Cardiovascular Risk Factors, and Diet in China, Finland, and the United States," *Public Health Reports* 105 (1991):5, pp. 41-46; U.S. Department of Health and Human Services, Public Health Service, *Seventh Report to the Congress on Alcohol and Health from the Secretary of Health and Human Services, January 1990* (Washington, DC: Government Printing Office, 1990); Richard J. Contrada, "Type A Behavior, Personality Hardiness, and Car-

diovascular Responses to Stress," *Journal of Personality and Social Psychology* 59 (1989):5, pp. 895-903.

22. "Health and Mortality in Eastern Europe, 1965-85," pp. 362-65.

23. Dan Usher, "An Imputation of the Value of Improved Life Expectancy," in Milton Moss, ed., *The Measurement of Social Life and Economic Performance* (Cambridge, MA: NBR, 1977), pp. 192-226.

24. U.S. Central Intelligence Agency, *Handbook of Economic Statistics 1988* (Washington, DC: CIA, 1988), pp. 24-25.

25. See, for instance, Kenneth Hill and Anne R. Pebley, "Child Mortality in the Developing World," *Population and Development Review* 15 (1990):4, pp. 657-87.

References

Anderson, Barbara A., and Brian D. Silver. "The Changing Shape of Soviet Mortality, 1958-1985: An Evaluation of Old and New Evidence." *Population Studies* 43 (1989):2, pp. 243-65.

——. "Trends in Mortality of the Soviet Population," *Soviet Economy* 6 (1990):3, pp. 191-252.

Brzezinski, Zbigniew J. "Mortality Indicators and Health-for-All Strategies in the WHO European Region." *World Health Statistics Quarterly* 39 (1986):4.

Contrada, Richard J. "Type-A Behavior, Personality Hardiness, and Cardiovascular Responses to Stress." *Journal of Personality and Social Psychology* 59 (1989):5, pp. 895-903.

Davis, Christopher, and Murray Feshbach. *Rising Infant Mortality in the USSR in the 1970s.* Washington, DC: U.S. Bureau of the Census, International Population Reports, series P-95, no. 74, 1980.

Dinkel, R. H. "The Seeming Paradox of Increasing Infant Mortality in a Highly Industrialized Nation: The Example of the Soviet Union." *Population Studies* 39 (1985):1, pp. 87-97.

Dutton, John, Jr. "Changes in Soviet Mortality Patterns, 1959-77." *Population and Development Review* 5 (1979):2, pp. 276-91.

Eberstadt, Nicholas. "Health and Mortality in Eastern Europe, 1965-85." *Communist Economies* 2 (1990):3, pp. 347-71.

Feshbach, Murray. "Soviet Health Problems." *Proceedings of the Academy of Political Science* 35 (1984):3, pp. 81-97.

Feshbach, Murray, and Alfred Friendly, Jr. *Ecocide in the USSR: Health and Nature under Siege.* New York: Harper Collins Books, 1992.

FRG Federal Statistical Office. *Statistiches Jahrbuch 1991 Fuer Das Vereinte Deutschland.* Wiesbaden: Metzler Poeschel Verlag, 1991.

——. unpublished data.

GDR State Statistical Committee. *Statistiches Jahrbuch Der Deutschen Demokratischen Republik 1970.* Berlin: Staatsverlag der DDR, 1970.

Hill, Kenneth, and Anne R. Pebley. "Child Mortality in the Developing World." *Population and Development Review* 15 (1990):4, pp. 657-87.

Hoehn, Charlotte, and John Pollard. "Mortality in the Two Germanies in 1986 and Trends 1876-1986." *European Journal of Population* 7 (1991):1, pp. 1-28.

Horiuchi, Shiro. "The Long Term Impact of War on Mortality: Old Age Mortality of the First World War Survivors in the Federal Republic of Germany." *Population Bulletin of the United Nations* 15 (1983), pp. 80-92.

Lamm, G. *The Cardiovascular Disease Programme of WHO in Europe: A Critical*

Review of the First 12 Years. Copenhagen: WHO Regional Office in Europe, 1981.

Riley, James C. "The Risk of Being Sick: Morbidity Trends in Four Countries." *Population and Development Review* 16 (1990):3, pp. 403-32.

Rosenberg, Harry M. "Improving Cause-of-Death Statistics," *American Journal of Public Health* 79 (1989):5, pp. 563-64.

Ruzicka, Lado T., and Alan D. Lopez. "The Use of Cause-of-Death Statistics for Health Situation Assessment: National and International Experiences." *World Health Statistics Quarterly* 43 (1990):2, pp. 249-58.

United Nations. *Demographic Yearbook.* New York: U.N. Department of International Economic and Social Affairs, various issues.

——. *World Population Prospects: The 1992 Revision.* New York: U.N. Department of Economic and Social Development, 1993.

U.S. Central Intelligence Agency. *Handbook of Economic Statistics.* Washington, DC: CIA, various editions.

U.S. Department of Health and Human Services, Public Health Service. *Health Consequences of Smoking: Cardiovascular Disease: A Report of the Surgeon General.* Washington, DC: Government Printing Office, 1983.

——. *Seventh Report to the Congress on Alcohol and Health from the Secretary of Health and Human Services, January 1990.* Washington, DC: Government Printing Office, 1990.

Vartianinen, Erkki, Du Dianjun, and James S. Marks. "Mortality, Cardiovascular Risk Factors, and Diet in China, Finland, and the United States." *Public Health Reports* 105 (1991):5, pp. 41-46.

World Health Organization, *World Health Statistics Annual.* Geneva: WHO, various editions.

7

Demographic Shocks in Eastern Germany, 1989-1993

One recent population movement in Eastern Germany has already occasioned considerable commentary. This was the mass exodus of Eastern Germans to Western Germany—a tumultuous out-migration between 1989 and 1992 of over one million persons from a territory whose population now stands at less than 16 million.[1] Dramatic though that shift may appear, an even more fundamental series of changes has been quietly registered in Eastern Germany's vital trends since unification: its patterns of births, marriages, and deaths. In this chapter, I examine each of these in turn.

Fertility

During the decade before the end of East German communism, aggregate fertility levels were relatively stable. Between 1980 and 1988, for example, the annual number of live births in the German Democratic Republic ranged between 216,000 and 245,000; crude birth rates per thousand residents fluctuated, gradually declining from 14.6 at the beginning of the decade to 12.9 in 1998 (see table 7.1). Patterns changed drastically after 1989. In the two years between 1989 and 1991, the number of live births reported in Eastern Germany fell by over 91,000, or about 46 percent. The downslide continued thereafter. By 1992, births amounted to a mere 44 percent of the 1989 total, and birth rates were 53 percent lower than they had been three years earlier. Data through early 1993 suggest that fertility levels in Eastern Germany had not yet stabilized. In the first five months of 1993, Eastern Germany's total number of live births was down by more than 60 percent from the same period in 1989; whereas the region's crude birth rate had been 13.3 per thousand for January-May 1989, it was under 5.1 per thousand in January-May 1993.

TABLE 7.1

	Natality in Eastern Germany, 1980-1993	
	Number of live births (thousands)	**Crude birth rate (per 1000 population)**
1980	245.1	14.6
1981	237.5	14.2
1982	240.1	14.4
1983	233.8	14.0
1984	228.1	13.7
1985	227.6	13.7
1986	222.3	13.4
1987	226.0	13.6
1988	215.7	12.9
1989	198.9	12.0
1990	178.5	11.1
1991	107.8	6.8
1992	88.3	5.6
1993 (Jan-May)	NA[1]	5.1

Notes: NA = not available; [1] = annualized total extrapolated from January-May 1993 births would be 79.6 thousand.
Sources: DDR Statistisches Amt, *Statistisches Jahrbuch Der Deutschen Demokratischen Republik 1990* (Berlin: Rudolf Haufe Verlag, 1990), pp. 403-404; BRD Statistisches Bundesamt, *Zur wirtschaftlichen und sozialen Lage in den neuen Bundeslaendern* (Stuttgart: Metzler-Poeschel Verlag), April 1993, pp. 5, 7; *Wirtschaft und Statistik*, 1993(5), p. 304; 1993(6), p. 368.

Such an abrupt and precipitous drop in fertility is unprecedented for an industrialized society during peacetime. In the past, human populations have on occasion experienced sudden and dramatic reductions of childbearing of comparable proportion, but only during times of catastrophe, desperate privation, and widespread loss of life. Among the low-income agrarian societies, for example, China is estimated to have cut its birth rate roughly in half between 1957 and 1961[2]—in the wake of the disastrous "Great Leap Forward" campaign, which shattered the country's agricultural system and set the stage for mass starvation in the countryside. Industrialized societies, for their part, have scarcely ever registered such radical declines in fertility—not even during the chaos and destruction attendant upon defeat in total war. Nazi Germany and Imperial Japan both saw their national birth rates sink as they headed toward unconditional surrender, but neither drop was proportionately as severe as the drop in crude birth rates in Eastern Germany between 1989 and early 1993.[3] To locate a drop in crude birth rates for an industrialized population in the recent past that is comparable in relative magnitude with the one registered in Eastern Germany since the collapse of the Honecker regime, one must demarcate small areas, such as Berlin during World War II, where cataclysmic events reduced the crude birth rate by 52 percent between 1942 and 1946.[4]

While the relative decline in fertility in Eastern Germany since the end of communism can be fitted to historical parallels, albeit not without difficulty, the absolute level of fertility now being recorded in that territory appears to be a completely new phenomenon—at least for sizable naturally constituted populations. Eastern Germany's adults appear to have come as close to a temporary suspension of childbearing as any such population in the human experience. The contrast with Western Germany puts the matter in perspective. Western Germany's contemporary birth rate, of course, is famously low; nevertheless, it was over twice as high—11.3 per thousand—as Eastern Germany's in 1992.

What accounts for this extraordinary change? As is always true with fertility trends, it is much easier to outline the proximate factors in the shift than to identify underlying causes. The timing of Eastern Germany's birth collapse, for example, can be detailed by monthly numbers of reported live births (see figure 7.1). Some downward drift is evident over the course of 1989 (a tendency partly reflecting the sudden outmigration of Eastern Germans in large numbers in the second half of that year). Monthly birth totals, however, do not begin to drop sharply

FIGURE 7.1

Births in Eastern Germany, January 1989-April 1993

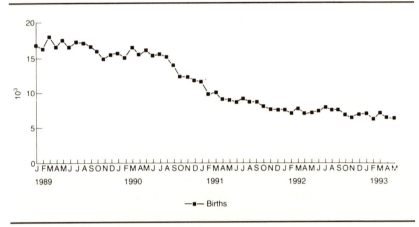

Sources: DDR Statistisches Amt, *Statistisches Jahrbuch 1990*; Statistisches Bundesamt, *Wirtschaft und Statistik*, various issues.

FIGURE 7.2

Number and Ratio of Abortions: Eastern Germany, 1980–92

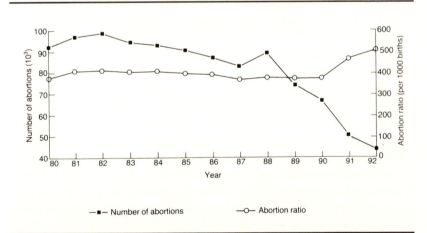

Sources: Statistisches Bundesamt, unpublished data; *Zur wirtschaflichen und sozialen Lage*, special edition, April 1993.

until August 1990—in other words, until nine months after the fall of the Berlin Wall.[5] Birth totals appear to have stabilized somewhat between April and July 1991. Then, in July 1991—nine months after the October 1990 reunification—birth totals resume their descent. *Die Wende* of 1989, it would seem, was just as precise (and unexpected) a "turning point" for Eastern German fertility as it was for Eastern German politics.

The timing of Eastern Germany's falloff of births—or more precisely, the sudden and precipitous nature of this decline—also raises questions about the techniques by which such a dramatic reduction was effectuated. Since Eastern Germany was (and through May 1993 remained) a region recognizing the right to abortion on demand, one might suspect abortion played a major role in this birth collapse. Perhaps surprisingly, official data on induced abortions suggest otherwise (see figure 7.2). Between 1989 and 1992, according to these figures, the number of induced abortions in Eastern Germany fell steadily: from about 74 thousand to about 44 thousand, or by 40 percent. (Because the drop in births during this same period was even sharper, however, the abortion ratio— the number of abortions to live births—did rise after 1990.)[6]

While Eastern Germany's abortion ratio was and is distinctly lower than those in most of the rest of the erstwhile Soviet bloc, it was and continues to be higher than the abortion ratio in Western Germany.[7] In newly unified Germany, opinion in Eastern Germany appears to be more supportive of liberalized abortion laws than the public opinion of the Western German region.[8] Disposition toward the abortion issue notwithstanding, abortion per se appears to have been a peripheral factor in Eastern Germany's postcommunist fertility decline. Pregnancy avoidance, not pregnancy termination, appears to explain most of the change in the region's fertility level.

Demographic figures can provide information on the components of this "birth shock," as well as its timing. Arithmetically, the total number of live births in any population is a function of (1) the population's absolute size; (2) its age and sex structure; and (3) the age-specific fertility rates for its women of childbearing ages. We can break down Eastern Germany's birth drop between 1989 and 1991 in relation to changes in these three elements. (Not all the data needed in this exercise are as yet available for 1992). As I noted above, reported live births in Eastern Germany fell by about 91 thousand (or about 46 percent) between 1989 and 1991. Of this overall drop, roughly one-ninth can be attributed to sheer decline of Eastern Germany's population during those two years.

About one-twelfth of the decline in birth numbers can be attributed purely to changes in Eastern Germany's age-sex structure between 1989 and 1991. (Most of these shifts involved women eighteen to twenty-five years of age; women from this cohort bore the majority of Eastern Germany's infants in 1989, and were more likely than the population as a whole to migrate westward.)[9] But over four-fifths of the total falloff in births was due directly to reductions in age-specific fertility rates for Eastern German women. Although population decline and changes in the region's age-sex structure did contribute to Eastern Germany's birth falloff, the drop itself was essentially driven by a radical change in childbearing behavior.

Eastern Germany's dramatic drop in age-specific fertility between 1989 and 1991 is depicted in figure 7.3. The dimensions of the decline are highlighted by the total fertility rate (TFR), a summary measure that indicates the consequences of adhering to current age-specific fertility patterns for the full course of a woman's life. To attain generational replacement, Eastern Germany's women of childbearing age today would have to give birth to an average of about 2.07 infants over the course of their lives.[10] In 1989, Eastern Germany's age-specific fertility rates summed to a TFR of 1.57—a level considerably lower, if continued over time, than would be required for population replacement. By 1991, Eastern Germany's TFR had dropped to 0.98—less than one birth per woman per lifetime, by this synthetic measure. This is, perhaps, the lowest TFR ever calculated for a large population; even so, we can be fairly confident that the TFRs for Eastern Germany for 1992 and 1993 will be lower still.

Although Eastern Germany's TFR fell by 38 percent between 1989 and 1991, not all age groups were equally affected. Fertility rates for teenagers and women in their forties exhibited little change—but the contributions of these two groups to the overall rate was negligible to begin with in 1989. On the other hand, declines in age-specific fertility rates for women throughout what had been the prime years of childbearing in the GDR were especially pronounced. Eastern German women aged twenty-five to thirty-four—the prime childbearing ages for Western German women, their new peers—reported a drop in fertility of over 45 percent during these two years.

That the "birth shock" would be unevenly distributed with respect to maternal age may not surprise. More surprising, perhaps, has been its distribution with respect to marital status. Between 1989 and 1992 live births in Eastern Germany dropped by a reported 56 percent—but out-of-wedlock births fell by 45 percent, whereas births within a marital

FIGURE 7.3

Fertility Rates by Age of Women: Eastern Germany, 1989 vs. 1991

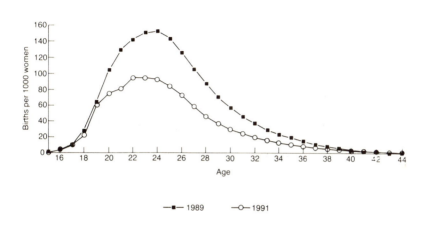

—■— 1989   —○— 1991

Sources: BRD Statistisches Bundesamt, *Statistisches Jahrbuch 1992* and unpublished data.

union fell by 62 percent. As a result, Eastern Germany's illegitimacy ratio rose sharply (see figure 7.4). By 1991 and 1992 nearly 42 percent of the infants born in Eastern Germany were delivered to single mothers (as against 12 percent in Western Germany in the latter year.) As figure 7.5 illustrates, the proportion of babies born to unwed parents rose for mothers of nearly every age between 1989 and 1991.

Eastern Germany's illegitimacy ratio in the 1980s, it is true, was singularly high among Soviet bloc countries, and had been rising—partly in response, it has been argued, to pronatalist GDR policies that offered special benefits to single parents.[11] Yet Eastern Germany's illegitimacy ratio veered upward after these incentives (and the state that provided them) had vanished. Insofar as abortion on demand remained readily available in Eastern Germany in the early 1990s, this rise in illegitimacy ratios cannot be ascribed to a sudden deterioration in access to previously utilized family planning techniques. In many respects, the systemic economic changes in Eastern Germany between 1989 and 1992 might have been presumed to favor childbearing by two-parent unions; to judge by events, however, married couples in Eastern Germany have apparently signaled that they do not concur with such an assessment.

FIGURE 7.4

Out-of-Wedlock Births: Eastern Germany, 1980-92

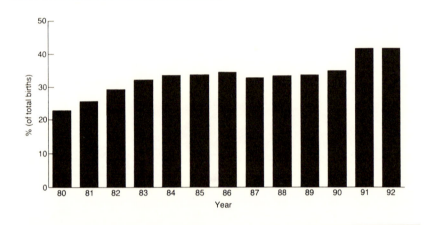

Sources: DDR Statistisches Amt, *Statistisches Jahrbuch 1990*; BRD Statistisches Bundesamt
unpublished data.

FIGURE 7.5

**Out-of-Wedlock Births: Percentage of Total Eastern
German Births, 1989 vs. 1991**

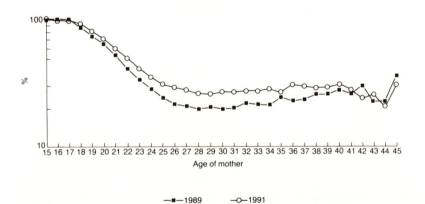

Sources: Statistisches Bundesamt, *Statistisches Jahrbuch*, 1992 ed., p. 78; 1993 ed., p. 79.

Marriage

If the collapse of East German communism and the subsequent rapid transition to the market system has had an especially profound effect upon natality within marriage, they have had a similarly dramatic impact on the formation of such unions themselves. Like birth trends, aggregate figures on new marriages in the GDR evidenced a certain stability between 1980 and 1988 (see table 7.2).[12] Just as with births, registered marriages in Eastern Germany commenced a precipitous slide after 1989. By 1992 the number of marriages celebrated was a mere 37 percent of the 1989 total. Marriage rates per thousand persons in Eastern Germany fell nearly equally sharply. Whereas Eastern Germany's marriage rate had been consistently higher than Western Germany's during the 1980s, by 1992 it was less than half as high.

It is hard to identify a historical parallel for such a "marriage shock." Between 1935 and 1938—amidst the conflagration of its devastating civil war—Spain's marriage rate fell by but 26 percent; that of the city

TABLE 7.2

Nuptiality in Eastern Germany, 1980-1992

	Annual number of marriages (thousands)	Marriage Rate (per 1000 population)
1980	134.2	8.0
1981	128.2	7.7
1982	124.9	7.5
1983	125.4	7.5
1984	133.9	8.0
1985	131.5	7.9
1986	137.2	8.3
1987	141.3	8.5
1988	137.2	8.2
1989	131.0	7.9
1990	101.9	6.3
1991	50.5	3.2
1992	48.2	3.1

Sources: DDR Statistisches Amt, *Statistisches Jahrbuch Der Deutschen Demokratischen Republik 1990* (Berlin: Rudolf Haufe Verlag, 1990), pp. 403-404; BRD Statistisches Bundesamt, *Zur wirtschaftlichen und sozialen Lage in den neuen Bundeslaendern*, April 1993, pp. 4, 7.

of Berlin between 1942 and 1946, by only 30 percent.[13] As for its absolute level, Eastern Germany's marriage rate is today lower than that of
any other society in which such legally formalized adult unions prevail.
Indeed, crude marriage rates in Eastern Germany are currently lower
than in such countries as Jamaica and Panama, where consensual unions
are the typical living arrangement.

Figure 7.6 illustrates monthly marriage figures reported in Eastern
Germany between January 1989 and May 1993. These offer insight into
the timing of the recent wedding slump. In Eastern Germany, as in most
of the rest of the world, marriage rates tend to follow the seasons: wed-
dings are much more likely to be set for summertime than winter. Between November 1989 and June 1990, the tally of marriages appears to
have been largely unaffected by the radical political events that were
unfolding. For the period January-June 1990, for example, Eastern Germany recorded 97 percent as many marriages as it had during the same
six months in the previous year. Wedding totals collapsed in July 1990.
For that month registered marriages were down 41 percent from July
1989; despite seasonal fluctuations, the trend has continued downwards
since. The onset of this falloff in marriages is significant, for it coin-
cides precisely with currency union—Eastern Germany's changeover
to the Deutschemark, and thereby to the "social market economy."

Mortality

Repercussions from Eastern Germany's sudden political and economic transition reverberate not only through current fertility and marriage trends, but through mortality trends as well. Data for 1991 point
to a broad upsurge in death rates among most segments of the Eastern
German population.

Figure 7.7 outlines the changes in Eastern Germany's age-specific
mortality patterns between 1989 and 1991. The steep falloff in births
following unification seems to have coincided with a significant improvement in survival chances for those infants born. Men and women
over sixty-five years of age also enjoyed some improvements in survival chances in the immediate aftermath of the GDR's collapse. Nearly
every other group in the Eastern German population, however, suffered
reversals. Children, teenagers, young adults, and middle-aged people
all experienced increases in their mortality rates. Many of these increases
were very sharp. For women between the ages of thirty-five and forty-

FIGURE 7.6

Marriages in Eastern Germany, January 1989-April 1993

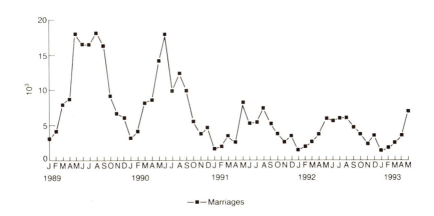

— ■ — Marriages

Sources: BRD Statistisches Bundesamt, *Wirtschaft und Statistik*, various issues.

four, reported death rates rose by nearly 20 percent; among men of the same ages, death rates jumped by nearly 30 percent. Some younger age groups registered even more alarming increases: death rates for girls aged ten to fourteen, for example, were up by nearly 70 percent.

In reviewing the data that depict such startling and unexpected mortality trends, two questions immediately come to mind. First: Are the numbers themselves reliable, or are the patterns in figure 7.7 simply some sort of statistical artifact? Second: Even if these trends are genuine, might they not reflect the strong influence of selective migration, that is to say, of the disproportionate exit of healthy Eastern Germans in search of westward opportunities after 1989?

The first question can be answered the more confidently of the two. The rises in age-specific mortality indicated by Eastern Germany's demographic data do not appear to be statistical artifacts. Vital registration statistics for Eastern Germany appear to be quite complete and accurate, both for the period since unification and for the last years of the Honecker era. It is possible that migration to Western Germany was

FIGURE 7.7

Changes in Age-Specific Mortality Rates: Eastern Germany, 1989-91

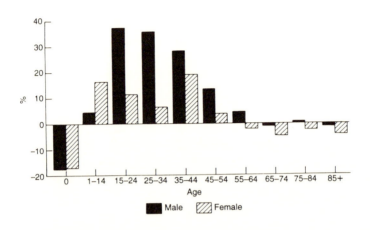

Source: Derived from BRD Statistisches Bundesamt, unpublished data.

somewhat underreported for Eastern Germany for the base year of 1989. Such a circumstance could result in marginal underestimates of age-specific mortality for that year, slightly biasing 1989-91 mortality trends for certain cohorts in the process. At the same time, however, one must recognize that no plausible scale of unreported out-migration could possible produce the marked shifts that are indicated for many different male and female age groups. While some of the increases in age-specific mortality rates between 1989 and 1991 may have been exaggerated by Eastern German data, the increases themselves, unfortunately, look all too real.

With regard to the second question, one could indeed imagine how a massive and selective out-migration might affect the denominator from which Eastern German age-specific mortality rates for 1991 were computed. Such selective migration, however, would not be expected to influence the numerator in these calculations, that is, the absolute number of deaths reported. Yet for many different male and female age groups these totals did increase between 1989 and 1991, even as the size of those age groups shrank. Selective migration, in short, could have contributed to recent perverse increases in mortality rates in Eastern Germany, but was clearly not the driving force behind them. Other explanations for these troubling trends are also required.

Anomalous as it may be for industrialized societies during peacetime, rising age-specific mortality was hardly unknown to Soviet bloc countries in the generation before the downfall of their communist regimes. To the contrary: between the mid-1960s and the late 1980s, secular increases in mortality were characteristic among the male population of these countries, and, in some of them, characteristic of adult females as well.[14] Such perverse trends, however, were less heavily imprinted on the GDR than any other Soviet bloc country. While health progress in the GDR under Ulbricht and Honecker may have been lackluster, females of all ages and males of nearly every age group registered some decline in mortality rates between 1965 and 1989. Thus, far from constituting a continuation of trends already extant under communist rule, the worsening of Eastern Germany's mortality patterns since 1989 represent a sharp departure from the past.

While the magnitude of the sudden upsurge in mortality registered by certain Eastern German cohorts is in itself extraordinary, it is the broad span of the age groups registering rising death rates that might most concern the epidemiologist or the specialist in public health. After all, health risks differ for men and women, and they change over the course of the life cycle. For death rates to worsen for both girls on the verge of grade school and men on the verge of retirement, a variety of illnesses and causes of death must presumably be exacting a greater toll than was the case only a few years earlier.

If reliable cause-of-death data were available from Eastern Germany's communist era, we could follow the impact of particular diseases and conditions on the region's overall mortality. Unfortunately, the GDR's cause-of-death statistics were not nearly as accurate as its vital statistics at large. Political considerations prompted the Honecker regime to misrepresent certain causes of death (such as suicides, which were included in the mortality totals but routinely reclassified under other causes).[15] Inadvertent technical mistakes also marred these compilations. An examination by the German Federal Statistical Office of 2,500 randomly selected GDR death certificates identified inconsistencies between the examiner's report and the coded cause of death in nearly 40 percent of the cases sampled; in 15 percent of the cases sampled, major errors were evident. Without reliable base-period data, it is impossible to chart overall cause-of-death trends accurately.[16]

TABLE 7.3

Age-Standardized Mortality Rates (per 100,000 population) by Selected Causes of Death: Eastern Germany (EG) and Western Germany (WG), 1990/91

Total Population	Eastern Germany	Western Germany	Index for EG (WG = 100)	Percentage of total difference between EG and WG
Males, all causes	1314.2	1023.3	128	100
-cardiovascular disease	647.1	450.1	144	68
-injuries (including suicide)	68.9	36.5	189	11
-cirrhosis of the liver	50.4	28.7	181	8
Females, all causes	1378.2	1066.8	129	100
-cardiovascular disease	824.6	550.1	150	88
-injuries (including suicide)	43.3	27.0	160	5
-cirrhosis of the liver	21.2	15.1	140	2
Population Ages 30-44				
Males, all causes	317.7	191.9	165	100
-cardiovascular disease	55.1	32.4	170	18
-injuries (including suicide)	65.0	25.4	256	32
-cirrhosis of the liver	41.4	13.8	300	22
Females, all causes	128.1	96.9	132	100
-cardiovascular disease	21.0	13.1	160	25
-injuries (including suicide)	16.2	6.6	245	31
-cirrhosis of the liver	13.4	6.8	197	21

Note: Mortality data in this table are standardized against Germany's 1987 age-sex structure by the Statistisches Bundesamt.
Source: Gunter Brueckner, "Todesursachen 1990/1991 Im Vereinten Deutschland," *Wirtschaft und Statistik*, 1993:4, pp. 248-253.

Nevertheless, some inferences can be drawn on the basis of the Statistisches Bundesamt's new data on causes of death in Eastern Germany (see table 7.3). In 1990-91, age-standardized mortality by these calculations was 28 percent higher for males and 29 percent higher for females in Eastern Germany than in Western Germany. Differences in mortality rates were even more pronounced for deaths attributed to three major causes: cardiovascular diseases, injuries (including suicide), and cirrhosis of the liver. These three factors appear to be responsible for most of the gap between Eastern and Western German death rates.

Mortality differences for Eastern and Western Germany's men and women between the ages of thirty and forty-four are of particular interest. This group suffered especially severe increases in mortality in Eastern Germany after 1989; for this reason, differences currently registered between Eastern and Western German patterns should strongly reflect recent changes. For these young adults, differences in mortality rates ascribed to cardiovascular disease, injuries, and cirrhosis are even more extreme than for the population as a whole. One may also note that deaths attributed to injuries (including suicide) and cirrhosis account for most of the current difference in mortality levels among young adults in unified Germany's two principal regions. Limited though these indications may be, it would seem reasonable to guess that heart disease, injuries (including suicide), and cirrhosis played a major role in driving up Eastern German death rates after 1989.

A rise in mortality due to cirrhosis, injuries, and cardiovascular disease would be suggestive of a number of general pathologies: among these, a serious turn toward heavy drinking. But owing to the lack of appropriate data, etiological speculations for the moment are mainly conjectural. On the other hand, we can be quite sure that death rates from all causes together rose in Eastern Germany between 1989 and 1991 for male and female age groups comprising nearly four-fifths of the region's total population. No matter what was propelling Eastern Germany's age-specific death rates upward, these sudden and broadly based mortality increases signified declines in health status for large portions of the general public—and by this most important of measures, real reductions in material well being.[17]

Concluding Observations

If there are any lingering doubts as to whether Eastern Germany's unexpected and rapid transition from communism to "social market economy" has been a time of shock and crisis for the general public of the former GDR, they should be dispelled by the region's demographic trends. This conjuncture of extreme and anomalous tendencies—the upswing in mortality and the collapse of births and new marriages—portrays a society convulsed by its stresses. Such demographic shocks, moreover, would ordinarily be consistent with severe reductions in material well being in a population experiencing them.

The paradox, of course, is that economic data can be read to suggest that transition and unification have ushered in a time of marked economic improvement and unparalleled plenty for the residents of Eastern Germany. The restructuring of the Eastern German economy is being underwritten by extraordinary subsidies and transfers from Western Germany; in 1991 and 1992, the region's net import of goods and services nearly equaled its own gross domestic product. Though still considerably lower than in Western Germany, Eastern Germany's average monthly wage virtually doubled between late 1990 and late 1992. Moreover, Eastern German disposable household income by late 1992 was nearly twice the nominal level of 1989—and in 1992 purchasing power was articulated in Deutschemarks, not Ostmarks.[18]

Despite these blandishments and improvements, Eastern Germans are not *behaving* like a population whose living standards have been significantly increased. Mortality increase is not usually the handmaiden of prosperity; such setbacks, to the contrary, constitute in themselves a self-evident reduction in levels of general welfare. (Evidently, the Federal Republic's highly regarded medical system and its vaunted network of targeted social benefits were not adequate to forestall these health reversals.) Moreover, to the extent that decisions about childbearing or marriage are affected by financial calculations or expectations, Eastern Germany's recent fertility and marriage patterns would appear to register a profound and broadly felt lack of confidence in the economic future.

Pervasive uncertainty about the economic future would be easy to understand. Eastern Germany's almost overnight transition from central planning to the market has entailed enormous dislocations in its economy. Although comparisons of economic activity in communist and market systems are plagued by methodological problems, German researchers have estimated that gross domestic output in Eastern Germany fell by over two-fifths between 1989 and 1991, and that output was still nearly two-fifths lower in 1992 than during the last full year of

GDR communism.[19] Labor market data indicate that 15 percent of the Eastern German workforce was unemployed in early 1993, with another 12 percent engaged in "short work," retraining, or job-creation programs.[20] These are circumstances that could only engender insecurity and stress. Yet it is important to remember that such profound macroeconomic changes would not appear to be historically unique—or even unprecedented in Germany. To the contrary: by such quantitative measures as total output, unemployment rates, or changes in price levels, Germany between the two world wars experienced periods of comparable, or even more intense, economic instability.[21] Yet interwar Germany never suffered the sorts of demographic shocks that Eastern Germany is now witnessing.

This stark difference in demographic responses to economic disruptions of ostensibly similar magnitude may simply underscore what we already know: namely, that the path back from communism is *terra incognita*, and that historical analogies are of only limited utility in describing that terrain. For populations who have known only the planned economy and the closed society, transition to the liberal market order might be expected to entail far-reaching, often traumatic adjustments. Eastern Germany's demographic data document dramatic, unexpected, and in many ways unprecedented adjustments by the local populace to their new socioeconomic environment. Until the transition in postcommunist societies is completed, such demographic data may provide a useful supplement, or even corrective, to available economic data for assessing changes in local levels of material welfare.

Notes

1. Between January 1989 and June 1992, a total of 1.127 million persons reportedly emigrated from Eastern Germany; net out-migration over this period—the excess of emigrants over immigrants—is put at about 955,000. Statistisches Bundesamt, *Zur wirtschaftlichen und sozialen Lage in den neuen Bundeslaendern*, special edition, April 1993, p. *8.
2. Judith Banister, *China's Changing Population* (Stanford, CA: Stanford University Press, 1987), p. 354.
3. United Nations, *Demographic Yearbook 1948* (New York: U.N., 1949), pp. 255, 257, 263. Japan's birth rate fell by a reported 25 percent between 1941 and 1945. For Germany, birth rates reportedly fell between 1941 and 1945 by 24 percent in what became the American zone of occupation, and by 34 percent in the French zone.
4. Ibid., p. 263; rates pertain only to West Berlin. Earlier in the twentieth century, it appears that some of the combatant powers during World War I may have registered comparable "birth shocks" between 1914 and 1918. See Robert R. Kuczynski,

The Balance of Birth and Deaths (New York: Macmillan, 1928).

5. One of the first studies to recognize the significance of these timing effects was Juergen Dorbritz, et. al., "Wandel des generativen Verhaltens und der Familienbildung in den neuen Bundeslaendern infolge des Austausches der Wirtschaftsund Sozialordnung und der sozialstrukturellen Transformation," *KSPW*, Berlin, November 1992.

6. Closer examination of these data indicate that the rise in Eastern Germany's abortion ratio after 1989 was mainly due to a rise in ratios for women between the ages of fifteen and twenty-four—the group, one may note, with the very *lowest* abortion ratios under the old regime.

7. Henry P. David, "Abortion in Europe, 1920-91: A Public Health Perspective," *Studies in Family Planning* 23 (1992):1, p. 2.

8. *Politbarometer*, January 1993.

9. Helmut Schultze and Hans-Joachim von der Muelbe, "Bevoelkerungsentwicklung 1989 bis 1991," in Statistisches Bundesamt, *Zur wirtschaftlichen und sozialen Lage in den neuen Bundeslaendern*, special edition, December 1992, pp. 26-27.

10. Slightly more than two births are necessary for net population replacement because some infants do not survive to childbearing age.

11. Alain Monnier, "Bilan de la Politique Familiale en Republique Democratique Allemande: Un Reexamen," *Population*, vol. 44, no. 2 (March-April, 1989).

12. Over the postwar period as a whole, both total average rates and age-specific marriage probabilities had been declining in Eastern Germany. See Juregen Dorbritz, "Nuptialitaet, Fertilitaet, und familiale Lebensformen in der sozialen Transformation—Uebergang zu einer neuen Bevoelkerungsweise in Ostdeutschland?" *Zeitschrift fuer Bevoelkerungswissenschaft*, vol. 18, no. 3 (1992). The same was true in most of the rest of Eastern Europe. See Jean-Paul Sardon, "Marriage et Divorce en Europe de l'Est," *Population*, vol. 46, no. 3 (May-June 1991). Broadly similar trends were evident in Western Europe as well. See *idem.*, "La Primo-nuptialite Feminine en Europe: Elements pour une Typologie," *Population*, vol. 47, no. 4 (July-August 1992).

13. U.N., *Demographic Yearbook 1948*, p. 465.

14. See, among other studies on this phenomenon, Nicholas Eberstadt, "Mortality in Eastern Europe: Retrospect and Prospect," in James R. Millar and Blair Ruble, eds., *The Social Legacy of Communism* (New York: Cambridge University Press, 1994 [Chapter 6 in this volume]).

15. Eberstadt, "Health and Mortality in Eastern Europe," p. 354.

16. Gunter Brueckner, "Todesursachen 1990/91 Im Vereinten Deutschland," *Wirtschaft und Statistik*, 1993, no. 4, p. 257.

17. For elaboration on the economic significance of rising mortality rates in Eastern Germany and elsewhere, see Nicholas Eberstadt, "Mortality and the Fate of Communist States," *Communist Economies and Economic Transition* 5 (1993):4.

18. These assessments are all derived from Statistisches Bundesamt, *Zur wirtschaftlichen und sozialen Lage in den neuen Bundeslaendern*, special edition, April 1993.

19. Deutsches Institut fuer Wirtschaftsforschung, *Sozialprodukt und Einkommenskreislauf, I/1989 Bis IV/92* (Berlin: DIW, 1993), table A-11; estimates are for constant 1991 prices.

20. *Zur wirtschaftlichen und sozialen Lage in den neuen Bundeslaendern*, April 1993, pp. 12-17.

21. For example, German industrial production fell by 47 percent between 1929 and 1932; unemployment was over 26 percent among salary and wage earners in

1933; and in September 1930 over 36 percent of Germany's union members were either unemployed or on "short work." In 1923, moreover, price levels in Germany rose by a factor of more than one million. See Gustav Stolper, *The German Economy 1870 to the Present* (New York: Harcourt, Brace and World, 1967), chap. 4; Burton H. Klein, *Germany's Preparations for War* (Cambridge, MA: Harvard University Press, 1959), p. 67; and Harold James, *The German Slump* (Oxford: Clarendon Press, 1986), p. 113.

References

Anderson, Barbara A., and Brian D. Silver. "The Effects of the Registration System on the Seasonality of Births: The Case of the Soviet Union." *Population Studies* 42 (1988):2.

————. "Trends in Mortality of the Soviet Population." *Soviet Economy* 6 (1990):3.

Banister, Judith. *China's Changing Population.* Stanford: Stanford University Press, 1987.

Blades, Derek, ed. *Statistics for a Market Economy.* Paris: Organization for Economic Cooperation and Development, 1991.

Bratkowski, Andrzej S. "The Shock of the Transformation or the Transformation of the Shock?" *Communist Economies and Economic Transformation* 5 (1993):1.

Brueckner, Gunter. "Todesursachen 1990/91 Im Vereinten Deutschland." *Wirtschaft und Statistik*, 1993, no. 4.

DDR Statistisches Amt. *Statistisches Jahrbuch der Deutschen Demokratischen Republik 1990.* Berlin: Rudolf Haufe Verlag, 1990.

Deutsches Institut fuer Wirtschaftsforschung. *Sozialprodukt und Einkommenskreislauf, I/1989 Bis IV/92.* Berlin: DIW, 1993.

Dorbritz, Juergen. "Nuptialitaet, Fertilitaet, und familiale Lebensformen in der sozialen Transformation—Uebergang zu einer neuen Bevoelkerungsweise in Ostdeutschland?" *Zeitschrift fuer Bevoelkerungswissenschaft*, 18 (1992):3.

Dorbritz, Juergen, et al. "Wandel des generativen Verhaltens und der Familienbildung in den neuen Bundeslaendern infolge des Austausches der Wirtschaftsund Sozialordnung und der sozialstrukturellen Transformation," *KSPW*, Berlin, November 1992.

Eberstadt, Nicholas. "Health and Mortality in Eastern Europe, 1965-1985." *Communist Economies* 2 (1990):3.

————. "Mortality in Eastern Europe: Retrospect and Prospect." In James R. Millar and Blair Ruble, eds., *The Social Legacy of Communism.* New York: Cambridge University Press, 1994 [Chapter 6 in this volume].

German Federal Statistical Office (BRD Statistisches Bundesamt). *Statistik Im Uebergang Zur Marktwirtschaft: Probleme und Loesungsansaetze.* Stuttgart: Metzler-Poeschel Verlag, 1991.

————. *Statistisches Jahrbuch*, various issues.

————. unpublished data.

————. *Wirtschaft und Statistik*, various issues.

————. *Zur wirtschaftlichen und sozialen Lage in den neuen Bundeslaendern.* Stuttgart: Metzler-Poeschel Verlag, April 1993.

James, Harold. *The German Slump.* Oxford: Clarendon Press, 1986.

Klein, Burton H. *Germany's Preparations for War.* Cambridge, MA: Harvard University Press, 1959.

Kuczynski, Robert R. *The Balance of Birth and Deaths*. New York: Macmillan, 1928.

Lipton, David, and Jeffrey Sachs. "Creating a Market Economy in Eastern Europe: The Case of Poland." *Brookings Papers on Economic Activity*, 1990, no. 1.

Monnier, Alain. "Bilan de la Politique Familiale en Republique Democratique Allemande: Un Reexamen." *Population*, vol. 44, no. 2 (March-April, 1989).

Nazarov, M. "The Market and Statistics." *Problems of Economics*, vol. 34, no. 7 (November 1991).

Polish Statistical Association. *Poverty Measurement for Economies in Transition in Eastern European Countries*. Warsaw: Central Statistical Office, 1992.

Politbarometer, January 1993.

Powers, Susan. "Statistical Needs in Eastern Europe." *Monthly Labor Review*, 115 (1992):3.

Sardon, Jean-Paul. "Marriage et Divorce en Europe de l'Est." *Population* 46 (1991):3.

————. "La Primo-nuptialite Feminine en Europe: Elements pour une Typologie." *Population* 47 (1992):4.

Schultze, Helmut, and Hans-Joachim von der Muelbe. "Bevoelkerungsentwicklung 1989 bis 1991." In BRD Statistisches Bundesamt, *Zur wirtschaftlichen und sozialen Lage in den neuen Bundeslaendern*, December 1992.

Stolper, Gustav. *The German Economy 1870 to the Present*. New York: Harcourt, Brace and World, 1967.

United Nations. *Demographic Yearbook 1948*. New York: U.N., 1949.

Wolf, Charles. *Economic Transformation and the Changing International Economic Environment*. Santa Monica: RAND Corporation, 1993.

Part III

Global Population Problems

8

Justifying Population Control:
The Latest Arguments

For convinced proponents of international policies to promote what was once known as "population control" and is currently called "stabilizing world population," the 1980s was a grim decade: a time not only of frustration, but of bitter and often unexpected reversals. The most public and publicized of the many setbacks for population activists during those years took place in Mexico City in 1984, when the Reagan administration's delegation to the International Conference on Population upstaged the assembled anti-natalist contingents and altered the rhetoric of the population debate with their assertion that "population growth is, by itself, a neutral phenomenon."

The bad news for the population control movement, however, was not always carried live on CNN, or splashed over the front page of the *New York Times*. For, as sophisticated observers immediately recognized and rank-and-file population activists gradually came to understand, the movement suffered one of its severest blows in the 1980s from a slender summary report with a modest circulation: the 1986 National Academy of Sciences (NAS) reassessment of the population question. *Population Growth and Economic Development: Policy Questions* offered a cautious and highly qualified assessment of the potential risks posed by rapid population growth, substantially revising and toning down the warnings issued in the NAS's previous report on the topic fifteen years earlier. The change in scholarly thought about the population-development relationship prompted by the NAS study struck at the intellectual underpinnings of the global policy apparatus that had been

175

constructed to elicit fertility reduction in less developed regions, for it suggested that the rationale for these interventions was by no means as clear-cut as supporters claimed. (Adding insult to this injury, the 1986 NAS study had been requested and sponsored by institutions themselves enthusiastically embracing anti-natalist population policy, including the U.S. Agency for International Development and the Rockefeller Foundation.)

The 1980s, however, are behind us, and so is the dark mood of defeat and disarray within the international population community. Population activists have entered the 1990s vigorously pressing their agenda on the political and intellectual fronts, by all indications confident that they can recapture lost ground. The two publications here under review* may be seen as emblems in this greater campaign and, indeed, were so intended by their sponsoring institutions.

As Overseas Development Council (ODC) President John Sewell writes in the foreword common to the two publications,

> It was against this backdrop [Mexico City and the 1986 NAS report], and in anticipation of the third international population conference in Cairo in 1994, that ODC was asked by the World Bank and The Rockefeller Foundation to undertake an analysis of current research on[1] the relationship between population and development. (pp. ix and vii, respectively)

Project director Robert Cassen affirms the study's purpose in the Policy Essay accompanying the larger report. "Recent policy announcements by the Clinton administration," he writes, "have signaled a welcome return of the United States to the international population community after a significant retreat during the Reagan and Bush years" (p. 5); and population experts can now offer policymakers "broader and more balanced understandings of the relationship between population and development" than could be found in the "1986 National Academy of Sciences study," which he terms "quietist" (p. 1).

Population and Development: Old Debates, New Conclusions contains contributions by sixteen authors. In addition to Robert Cassen, the authors represented included Dennis Ahlburg, Nancy Birdsall, Allen Kelley, Cynthia Lloyd, William McGreevy, Thomas Merrick, Sharon

---

*Robert Cassen et. al., *Population And Development: Old Debates, New Conclusions* (New Brunswick, NJ: Transaction Publishers, 1994) [referred to hereafter as "Book"]

Robert Cassen with Lisa M. Bates, *Population Policy: A New Consensus* (Washington, DC: Overseas Development Council, 1994, [referred to hereafter as "Policy Essay"]

Russell, and Michael Teitelbaum. Among the assembled authors, more-over, are two who had participated in the preparation of the "quietist" 1986 NAS study: Ahlburg and Birdsall.

Cassen, in his capacity as spokesman for the group, summarized its findings as follows:

> [T]here is a new international consensus among and between industrial and developing countries that individuals, countries, and the world at large would be better off if population were to grow more slowly.... [A] number of widely accepted and well-supported research studies now provide the grounds for active population policies. (Policy Essay, p. 12)

The case for action, as Cassen describes it, is buttressed by a new consensus on the implications of rapid population growth:

> [I]n the near term, rapid population growth under conditions of high fertility has clear and negative effects at the individual and household levels, particularly for the health and opportunities of women and children. Rapid population growth also constrains governments' abilities to provide adequate education and health services and to ensure employment opportunities for a growing labor force. The impact of population growth on national and global concerns such as the environment and migration is more long term and is mediated by a number of other factors.... However, to alleviate pressures that will exacerbate the problems in the long run, it is necessary to take action on population issues now. (Policy Essay, pp. 1-2)

Cassen identifies three overlapping but conceptually distinct population issues as the locus for policy action and, he warns, "it matters greatly that action be taken sooner rather than later." (Policy Essay, p. 13)

The first issue is the reduction of unwanted fertility in high-fertility regions, which is depicted as a major problem:

> [L]arge numbers of couples who want to limit their fertility do not have access to modern family planning methods; it is estimated that the demand for contraception of some 125 million married and single women in developing countries goes unmet. (Policy Essay, p. 12)

The second is "socioeconomic change to reduce high desired fertility." (Policy Essay, p. 44) Among the changes required are improved infant and child survival, greater educational opportunities, "empowerment of women," and,

> since most of these require an increase in the income of the poor as increased public action, other measures to improve the productivity and income-earning opportunities of poor people. (Policy Essay, p. 45)

The third issue is braking the demographic momentum in high-fertility countries. Cassen identifies "population momentum" as a significant problem for developing countries in the years ahead:

> On average, half of all future population growth will be due to population momentum, the growth that will occur even after replacement fertility is reached.... Momentum is a neglected topic, in part because it is often regarded as somewhat inevitable. But it can be addressed. (Policy Essay, p. 45)

The means for addressing the problems of demographic momentum and unwanted fertility, in Cassen's view, are straightforward: active, far-reaching, and well-designed family planning programs for low-income populations. Such programs, Cassen stresses, should be seen as effective instruments for altering demographic patterns in low-income societies, and should be expected to achieve substantial demographic impacts over long periods. In and of themselves, he states, family planning programs "have an independent influence on fertility behavior" (Policy Essay, p. 26); and "considerable evidence suggests that family planning efforts *can* be a significant factor in fertility decline if designed properly." (Policy Essay, p. 3; italics in original)

To this end, Cassen endorses a draft proposal giving a new estimate of resource requirements for population programs ("better reasoned than those of the past") (Policy Essay, p. 48) and submitted in advance to the Cairo conference. That draft called for $3.8 billion in developed-country giving for "population assistance" for 1995, nearly four times the volume of such donations actually transferred by OECD governments in 1991 and, while earmarking money for reproductive health, STD prevention, and data and policy analysis, reserved nearly four-fifths of its proposed budget for family planning programs. "All donors," writes Cassen, "should be willing ... to spur donor coordination along the lines discussed above." (Policy Essay, p. 64)

Cassen's support for this agenda, though, extends beyond issues of program funding. Without mentioning the lengthy document by name, he implicitly affirms the soundness of the detailed "Programme of Action" prepared for Cairo (lauding its "simultaneous" concern for "family planning and related health measures, and the promotion of human development") (Policy Essay, p. 65). Looking toward the then-upcoming International Conference on Population and Development (ICPD), Cassen explains that "The research findings reported here" not only "justify" the Conference's "goals," but "also by and large form the basic motivation for support of these activities." (Policy Essay, pp. 65-66)

Designed as they are to appeal to potential constituents at an impending convention, Cassen's two essays do not dwell on the finer points of the research studies commissioned for the project. Individual chapters in this collection, nonetheless, will make worthwhile reading for students of population and development. The contribution on reproductive health issues by Deborah Main et al., for example, makes the important but often overlooked point that "family planning can decrease maternal deaths, but it cannot help women give birth safely. Only access to emergency obstetric care can do that." (Book, p. 219) The essay by Allen Kelley and William McGreevey is a brief but useful survey of the economics profession's postwar "population debate" and of the state of economic research on population and development before the Industrial Revolution. Michael Teitelbaum and Sharon Stanton Russell provide a concise and informative summary of current issues and questions in international migration policy.

Yet whether one reads Cassen's essays by themselves or together with the studies they are meant to draw upon, what is perhaps most surprising about these volumes is their essential modesty. For while this project concludes with a ringing endorsement of current international population policies and calls for major increases in domestic spending and foreign aid monies for population activities, both the collected studies and the parallel policy essay shy away from the economic arguments traditionally employed to justify such interventions, conceding that the empirical record can buttress only a much more limited intellectual case for action. And even within the more narrowly defined, and seemingly sheltered, intellectual terrain in which its defense of population programs and aid is newly cast, there is almost no meaningful attempt to deal with research findings or to address policy questions that might challenge the project's own proclaimed "new conclusions."

Cassen abandons the macroeconomic rationale for population policy virtually at the outset, with a declaration that "the available evidence from empirical studies does not clearly show that population growth exerts a negative influence on development." (Book, p. 2) Elaborating on the theme, he writes that

> [T]he issue of whether per capita economic growth is reduced by population growth remains unsettled. Attempts to demonstrate such an effect empirically have produced no significant and reliable results, although most of these studies have

examined developing countries in the aggregate rather than individually. (Policy Essay, p. 15)

Cassen also dismisses the Malthusian, and neo-Malthusian, argument that population growth might outstrip food production:

Today, the issue of adequate food supplies is not usually seen as a problem of capacity so much as an environmental and economic problem: the food can be produced, at least in the short run. (Policy Essay, p. 17)

Not even the long-stipulated connection between rapid population growth and poverty is adduced by this project: as Dennis Ahlburg concludes in his study, "the importance of population growth's contribution to poverty is far from clear....[I]t is not clear whether population growth causes poverty in the long run or not." (Book, pp. 142- 43)

Cassen gamely suggests that the failure, after over three decades of research, to establish persuasively the widely presumed negative influence of rapid population growth on economic development may simply be due to a lack of adequate econometric investigation (Policy Essay, pp. 16-17; Book, pp. 9-11, 13). But Allen Kelley, no mean econometrician himself, offers a different view in his essay coauthored with William McGreevey:

The contradictions in the mind of Malthus still confront many analysts and policymakers in the population field, those whose feelings, impressions, and personal certainties about the negative effects of population growth are not supported by a careful sifting of the facts. (Book, p. 124)

Heretofore, population activists have customarily invoked the notion of economic externality purported discrepancies, for example, between the private and social costs of childbearing, to support their calls for government action to reduce fertility. But as these volumes counsel that "macroeconomic arguments now take a back seat in the debate about development and population" (Policy Essay, p. 16), so they also steer proponents of international population policy away from the familiar claim that "externalities" necessitate the programs they prefer.

In his lengthy and spirited defense of international population programs, Cassen discreetly omits the externality argument altogether. It is a judicious decision, considering the relevant background papers in the collection. For in his chapter on population, environment, and development of a traditional venue for broad claims of environmental externality, Theodore Panayotou, in perhaps the collection's strongest essay, declines the invitation to issue a sweeping anti-natalist license:

[E]vidence from all regions of the developing world supports the eclectic view that population growth can be an agent either of sustainable development or of environmental degradation depending on how free households, communities, and societies are to respond.

Where markets are not functioning, mobility is restricted, land and wealth are skewedly distributed, and government policies counter or block the avenues of individual and social response, a low-level trap is artificially created where diminishing returns to land lead to resource depletion and degradation, rather than to investment and innovation. (Book, pp. 150, 176)

By contrast, Nancy Birdsall's essay on the scope for government interventions in population affairs reads as a quest to enumerate any and all externalities that might conceivably justify policy action. This far-ranging hunt eventually transports the reader into the realm of epistemology by implicitly redefining "externality" to mean forces external to the individual that affect his or her welfare. To her credit, Birdsall cites the one major study in recent years that attempted to calculate rather than simply speculate about externalities to childbearing in some less developed countries; this inconvenient reference (Lee and Miller 1991), however, in fact, concluded that the discrepancies between private and social costs in such high-fertility societies as Bangladesh and Kenya appear to be minimal.

Displeased though Cassen may be by the "very low-keyed and non-urgent tone" (Book, p. 4) of the 1986 NAS report, neither he nor his contributors challenge any of the substantive conclusions from that study. Thus, these volumes signal a major shift: a decision by advocates of international population policy to retreat from argumentation in the economic arena, and to rest the case for population action on seemingly safer pillars: the problem of "population momentum"; the problem of "unmet need" for modern contraceptives; and the related assertion that family planning programs "work" to lower birth rates. Unfortunately, even these fallback positions are more problematic than Cassen and contributors seem to appreciate.

Consider the issue of demographic momentum. Both Cassen and Thomas Merrick, in his chapter on population prospects for developing countries, identify this as a significant problem, one appropriately addressed through population policies. That proposition, admittedly, is taken as an article of faith by many within the population community, a fact that may help explain why neither Cassen nor Merrick spells out the specific reasons that "population momentum" should require corrective policy interventions. Yet it is far from obvious how they would attempt to convince an uncommitted listener to endorse the course of action they recommend.

Demographic momentum, after all, exerts its influence during that period in which a society's pace of natural increase is decelerating, and, in fact, is approaching zero; arguments about the ills of rapid population growth, even if any such arguments were offered, consequently should not obtain. Moreover, since Cassen et al. do not insist that the "carrying capacity" of the globe and its regions should be a salient concern for policymakers, then neither should the increased demand for food and other renewable or nonrenewable resources that will come with demographic momentum. As demographic momentum spends itself, a society will become more densely populated; but as most population economists now acknowledge, the available evidence hardly suggests that increased population density adversely affects a country's development. A society being transformed by demographic momentum, other things equal, can expect a decreasing share of children in its total population and a rising share of adults in the economically active age groups; ordinarily, such trends are not viewed as a cause for alarm. Between the onset of net replacement fertility and the advent of zero natural increase, a typical population will tend to become grayer: its median age will rise, and the elderly will comprise a sharply larger proportion of its citizens. But surely a looming future surfeit of pensioners is not what agitates population activists when they contemplate demographic momentum—if it were, they presumably would not be pressing for policies to lower fertility here and now.

The magnitude of the "unmet need" for modern contraception and the demographic efficacy of family planning programs are important issues, but these studies do not seriously contend with any of the evidence on these topics that conflicts with the project's preferred policy options. Yet such contrary evidence is considerable and in some respects compelling. Lant Pritchett's recent article (1994) for example, presents a powerful brief for the case that "excess fertility" in developing countries is being overestimated by demographic research and, along with it, the scope for fertility reduction through voluntary "supply side" approaches. Cassen notes this objection, then brushes it aside by simply repeating his claim that "The extent of unwanted fertility as measured by demographic surveys in developing countries is considerable, as much as one birth in four by some estimates." (Policy Essay, p. 26) It is precisely the *reliability* of those same estimates, however, that Pritchett's study calls into question.

Pritchett's essay has caused a commotion in the population community because it seems to have caught so many specialists and scholars by surprise. But formidable as Pritchett's critique may be, it is hardly novel: Kingsley Davis (1967), after all, raised many of the same points three decades earlier, and others have raised them since. After more than a generation of gradual introduction to the approach, many population experts still seem to have trouble dealing with what are sometimes termed the "demand side" issues in population policy. An inability to appreciate the motivations and desires of individuals who may wish to have children is often evident—and often clearest in discussions of the consequences of childbearing at the household or individual level. The Policy Essay, for example, offers this evaluation of the implications of high-fertility regimes for individual welfare:

> Mothers are more likely to die in childbirth if they have large numbers of children; they will also spend a high proportion of their adult lives pregnant, breast-feeding, and providing childcare. (Policy Essay, p. 18)

All of this, of course, is perfectly true. It is equally true that those Americans who live to a ripe old age are more likely to die of chronic degenerative diseases and that they risk spending a high proportion of their adult lives out of the work force, relegated to nursing homes, or afflicted by Alzheimer's disease. Yet most researchers and policymakers concerned with such matters do not view those arguably unpleasant attributes of old age as arguments for curtailing the number of America's elderly, insofar as they appreciate that the desire to enjoy a long life is a *preference* of the persons in question and typically, of their families as well.

In both his Policy Essay and his overview for this collection of studies, Cassen ends his defense of anti-natalist population policies for developing countries with the proposition that "virtually everything that needs doing from a population point of view needs doing anyway." (Policy Essay, p. 67; Book, p. 23) By such reasoning, however, population programs are all but stripped of an independent rationale and are submitted to the public instead as simply one more worthy cause, yet another claimant upon a relatively fixed pool of social spending funds.

Some readers will rightly sense that we have been over this ground before. Indeed, at the World Population Conference, not Cairo but Bucharest, Paul Demeny, editor of *Population and Development Review*, had these apposite and tart words for the population specialists of 1974:

> To argue that people who want contraceptives for their own good reasons do benefit if somebody else namely, the general taxpayer pays the bill is, of course, self-evident. But so would be the argument that people would benefit from free breakfast, lunch, or dinner, or free shoes, free toothpaste, or free haircuts paid for from public funds. Those who seek to establish population programs as simply a social service program—one among the potential many that provide people with what they want—have no convincing argument that places pills over porridge. No wonder that family planning programs are poorly supported by national budgets. (Demeny 1984, p. 355)

The wonder today, ironically, is how very much budgetary support proponents of international population policies propose to claim. As envisioned by Cairo's schedule, donor governments will soon be devoting as much to international population activities as they have been spending on all other health-related programs in developing countries *combined* (for estimates of the latter, see World Bank 1993, pp. 165-67; Michaud and Murray 1993). This prospective reallocation of aid resources is ultimately justified not by the relative merits of competing projects, but by raw political facts: most important among them, the success of the anti-natal lobby in the 1992 American presidential elections. In the arena of politics, power may serve as its own justification.

But politics has its vicissitudes. Alignments tend to re-align; and tides turn, sometimes unexpectedly. Proponents of international population programs will need more than a few well-placed patrons at the top to assure the continued success of their venture. They will need convincing arguments. If the "rationale for population assistance programs" elucidated in these volumes does, indeed, represent "the best current assessment of what is known about the consequences for development of rapid population growth," as their two forewords assert, the intellectual structure undergirding this great venture would seem almost as exposed as a sand castle at low tide.

Note

1. The phrase "current research on" appears only in the foreword to the book.

References

Davis, Kingsley. 1967. "Population Policy: Will current programs succeed?" *Science*, 10 (November): 730:39.

Demeny, Paul. 1984. "Population on the world agenda, 1984: A view from Bucharest." *Population and Development Review* 10, no. 2: 353-59.

Lee, Ronald D. and Timothy Miller. 1991. "Population growth, externalities to child-bearing, and fertility policy in developing countries," *Proceedings of the World*

Bank Annual Conference on Development Economics 1990. Washington, DC: World Bank, pp. 275-304.

Michaud, Catherine, and Christopher Murray. 1993. "Aid flows to the health sector in developing countries: A detailed analysis 1972-1990," Health Transition Working Paper No. 93-08. Harvard Center for Population and Development Studies.

Pritchett, Lant H. 1994. "Desired fertility and the impact of population policies." *Population and Development Review* 20, no. 1: 1-55.

World Bank. 1993. *World Development Report 1993.* New York: Oxford University Press.

9

Starved for Ideas: Misconceptions that Hinder the Battle Against World Hunger

Why do we live in a world in which millions upon millions of children and adults suffer from the scourges of extreme hunger and malnutrition? Why does famine—that age-old terror—still stalk the earth today?

These are profound and terrible questions. We gather here at the World Food Summit to confront these questions at the end of a great—but also a terrible—era. Our century has been a time of extraordinary wonder—and of extraordinary horror. It is the paradox of our time that we can marvel at the tempo of technical advance, even as the global gap between what can be done and what is being done grows ever wider—indeed, that in the century when the formula for attaining mass affluence was finally perfected, more people should perish from famine than ever before in human history.

This paradox invests your deliberations here in the days ahead with a special and grave responsibility. As we are all too aware from events well within living memory, the power of modern government and the potentialities of collective international action can alter the human prospect for the better—but they can also alter it very much for the worse.

Esteemed parliamentarians. I hope you will indulge me if I speak frankly today, and take my frankness as a sign of my respect. As delegates to the World Food Summit, and as legislators in your own countries, you occupy positions of considerable influence on the global food situation. Through your efforts and activities you can accelerate the pace of progress against global hunger, and bring us closer to the day when famine is permanently conquered. But your official decisions, here and in your home countries, can equally hinder the international struggle for worldwide food security, and exacerbate the risk of mass starvation for vulnerable populations in the years ahead.

Of course we are all gathered here in good will, possessed of noble purpose. It is apparent that we share the same concerns and cherish the same ultimate objective. The success of our venture, however, is not predetermined by the intensity of our intentions. Success will instead depend on just how we choose to pursue our common objective. Effective policies and initiatives must be based on a realistic understanding of the problems we are striving to solve.

Why should I begin with so obvious a point? Because it is often forgotten when people of good will talk about world hunger. For some perhaps primordial reason, it seems that contemplating the problems of starvation and famine can cause the vision of ordinarily brilliant intellectuals, learned academicians, and clearheaded statesmen suddenly to blur. This peculiar phenomenon, moreover, is not confined to any particular country or group of countries. All around the world today, specialists and policymakers continue to entertain beliefs and accept premises about the world food situation that are demonstrably invalid—sometimes even glaringly invalid.

To a strange and disturbing degree, modern international man is, quite literally, starved for ideas. Widely accepted misconceptions, stubborn *idées fixes* and crude ideological notions about the nature of hunger and famine in the modern world are impeding the quest to achieve food security for all. Guided—or more exactly, misguided—by fundamentally flawed assessments of the prevalence and causes of global hunger, we cannot hope to attain satisfactory results. At best, our well-meaning efforts will be merely ineffective; at worst, we risk making bad conditions worse, and injuring those we seek to help.

Modern-day myths about the world food problem are legion. Today I wish to discuss three that seem to me particularly fashionable—and particularly pernicious. The first concerns the current dimensions of the hunger problem. The second might be described as the "Malthusian specter." The third bears on the relationship between hunger and political morality.

I

According to what is by now a large body of major studies by reputable and authoritative organizations, the magnitude of the global malnutrition problem in the modern era is vast—so vast, in fact, as to be almost incomprehensible. According to some of these studies, moreover, the problem has, at least in some respects, been worsening over time.

A few citations may be illustrative. In 1950, Lord Boyd-Orr, the first director general of the U.N. Food and Agriculture Organization (FAO), warned that "a lifetime of malnutrition and actual hunger is the lot of at least two-thirds of mankind."[1] Thirty years later, a United States Presidential Commission on World Hunger concluded that "[t]his world hunger problem is getting worse rather than better. There are more hungry people than ever before."[2] In 1991, the World Food Council declared that "the number of chronically hungry people in the world continues to grow."[3] And at the World Food Summit today, a principal FAO document puts the undernourished population of the world at well over 800 million—indicating that one out of five persons from developing countries was suffering from chronic undernutrition in the early 1990s.[4]

That most recent FAO estimate seems to suggest both absolute and relative improvement in the world food situation over the long period since Lord Boyd-Orr issued his grim assessment. On the other hand, the FAO's third World Food Survey—back in 1963—concluded that a fifth of the developing world was undernourished at that time. By that benchmark, we would seem to have made no relative progress whatever against Third World hunger over the intervening decades; given the growth of population in the less developed regions (a topic to which I will return), the absolute number of hungry people in the world would have increased tremendously over the past generation.

On the whole, these expert findings paint a disheartening picture. There is just one small thing wrong with this picture: the methodologies of the studies from which it is drawn. Astonishing as it may sound to the non-specialist, the approach underpinning every one of the major international studies over the past two generations that has attempted to quantify global hunger is demonstrably and deeply flawed—although the specific methodological defects vary from one study to the next.

Using the methods employed in any one of these oft-quoted studies, it would be impossible even under ideal circumstances to derive an accurate impression of the global hunger situation—and the conditions under which some of those studies were prepared were far from ideal. For citizens and policymakers committed to charting a course against world hunger, these studies offer a distorted and misleading map.

The troubles with the studies are sometimes technical, but they are never difficult to describe. In every instance, their calculations pivot upon questionable and, indeed, unsupported assumptions about individual nutritional needs in large populations, and upon equally questionable assumptions about the correspondence between national food supplies and individual food intake. Remember: malnutrition is a condition that affects *individuals*. Short of clinical or biomedical examination, there is really no reliable means for determining a person's health or nutritional status. Lacking such information, these studies draw necessarily crude inferences about individual well being from highly aggregated economic and agricultural data. They cannot cope with such exacting, but important, issues as whether individuals with lower caloric intake have lower than average caloric requirements; whether individual metabolic efficiency adjusts in response to changes in the nutritional supply; or whether individuals predicted by their models to be undernourished actually suffer from identifiable nutritional afflictions. To pose these questions is not to presuppose an answer to them; rather it is simply to discharge a basic duty of careful inquiry.

Sometimes the results of these hunger studies could be dismissed after the most casual inspection. In 1980, for example, the World Bank published a paper purporting to show that three-fourths of the population of the less developed regions suffered from "caloric deficits."[5] This ominous conclusion, however, was reached by a chain of dubious suppositions, the final and most spectacular of which was that anyone receiving less than the average "recommended dietary allowance" was underfed. In reality, of course, about half of any population will need less than the average *allowance*—that is the meaning of the word "average." Consequently, this model could only generate nonsense numbers. Its computations, for example, showed that nearly half the people in prosperous Hong Kong were getting too little food!

To their credit, the World Bank researchers on this particular project recognized that their work failed the "reality test," and went back to the drawing board to improve their product. Unfortunately, others working on the problem have not always met the same standards of intellectual accountability. Lord Boyd-Orr, for example, never explained the method underlying his now-famous estimate of the prevalence of world hunger. After reviewing contemporary FAO data, one of the leading agricultural experts of the day, Professor Merrill K. Bennett, surmised that the estimate might have been an elementary computational mistake—a misreading of the figures in two particular columns of an FAO table. The FAO, however, never replied to Professor Bennett's inquiry, and has never offered substantiating evidence for Lord Boyd-Orr's original assertion.

Other FAO estimates about world hunger have remained similarly protected against outside inspection: most of the data and calculations in the first three FAO World Food Surveys, for example, are still unavailable to the public. In more recent FAO studies, where somewhat greater intellectual openness is in display, we can see that the FAO's definition of the caloric threshold level for undernutrition has been steadily climbing over time. But why? These upward revisions do not seem to reflect any obvious changes in the scientific consensus concerning nutritional norms—but they do produce higher totals for any given estimate of the number of hungry people in the world.

If we could only for a moment extricate ourselves from this numerical house of mirrors, we would see that there are, indeed, meaningful data that bear upon the actual nutritional status of humanity—and that they tell a rather different story from the tales you may be hearing here in Rome.

Household spending patterns in less developed regions, for example, can reveal how the poor assess *their own* nutritional status. If a family treats food as a "superior good"—that is to say, if an increase in income raises the overall share of the household budget going to food—it renders a telling judgment that its members have too little to eat. By this criterion, the incidence of serious hunger in the world would be far lower than the FAO currently suggests: about two thirds lower, for ex ample, in some years for India (a country which happens to have reasonably good household expenditure data).[6]

Mortality rates, for their part, offer a direct and unambiguous measure of the material condition of any population. Despite the limitations of demographic data in some regions today, it is nonetheless clear that the so-called Third World has experienced a revolution in health conditions over the past generation. According to estimates and projections by the Population Division of the U.N. Secretariat, life expectancy at birth in the less developed regions rose by an average of almost a decade and a half between the early 1960s and the early 1990s; over that same period, infant mortality in the less developed regions is estimated to have dropped by nearly half.[7] Can one really imagine that such dramatic gains were entirely unaccompanied by nutritional progress?

A precise and reliable method for estimating the incidence and severity of worldwide malnutrition has yet to be devised. We can be all too sure that scores of millions in our world suffer from heart-rending, life-impairing hunger. But exaggerating the current scope of the problem, and minimizing the strides we have already made against it, will serve no worthy purpose. Hungry populations certainly do not benefit from such misapprehensions. In an age of "compassion fatigue," these misrepresentations of reality tend instead to discourage action by depicting the problem as almost insurmountably large. To make matters worse, they may misdirect available humanitarian resources away from the places where they might have made the most difference. And by obscuring true patterns of nutritional change, these misrepresentations obstruct our efforts to learn from experience. Denying the existence of progress against global hunger denies us as well the hope of studying, and attempting to replicate elsewhere, local strategies that have actually resulted in progress.

II

Let us turn now to the Malthusian specter. As you know, the postwar variant of the Malthusian worldview holds that the globe cannot support the enormous increase in human numbers that we are witnessing—and holds further that we will be faced by rising poverty, mass hunger, and perhaps even worldwide catastrophe unless we somehow check this uncontrolled demographic growth. Overpopulation, increasing scarcity of food and natural resources, and famine, Malthusians argue, are clear and present dangers—the existence of which, they say, demonstrably validates their explication of how the world works.

In intellectual and political circles, the influence of Malthusian ideology today ranges wide and often runs deep; not surprisingly, it is especially evident in deliberations about the world food outlook. For its proponents, Malthusianism has some of the trappings of a secular faith. Matters of faith, as we know, do not readily lend themselves to testability—or to disproof. If we try to treat the Malthusian specter as an empirical rather than a theological proposition, though, we will find little evidence that its advent is nigh.

Consider the problem of "overpopulation." So much has been said about this problem over the years that it may surprise you to hear that there is no fixed and consistent demographic definition for the term. I repeat: none exists. How would we define it? In terms of population density? If so, Bermuda would be more "overpopulated" than Bangladesh. In terms of rates of natural increase? In that case, pre-

Revolutionary America would have been more "overpopulated" than contemporary Haiti. In terms of the "dependency ratio" of children and the elderly to working-age populations? That would mean Canada was more "overpopulated" in 1965 than India is today!

We could go on, but I trust you see my point. If "overpopulation" is a problem, it is a problem that has been misidentified and misdefined. The images evoked by the term—hungry children; squalid housing; early death—speak to problems all too real in the modern world. But these are properly described as problems of *poverty*. The risk of poverty, however, is obviously influenced—indeed, principally determined—by a panoply of non-demographic forces, not the least of these being the impact of a government's policies upon its subjects or citizens. As for the particulars of the relationship between population growth and poverty, these are more complex and far less categorical than one is often led to suppose.

At the very least, we know for a fact that rapid and sustained population growth does not preclude rapid and sustained economic and social advance. If it did, the vast material transformation we have already witnessed in the twentieth century could not have occurred.

Since the beginning of this century, according to the best available estimates, the world's population has more than tripled. Nothing like this had ever taken place before—and although the tempo of global population growth appears to have peaked and to be declining, it is still proceeding with extraordinary speed by historical perspective. This unprecedented demographic explosion, however, did not consign humanity to penury and destitution. Just the opposite: it was accompanied by a worldwide explosion of prosperity. According to the eminent economist Angus Maddison, the world's per capita GDP quadrupled between the turn of the century and the early 1990s.[8] In Latin America and the Caribbean, per capita GDP, by his estimates, has *more* than quadrupled this century; in Asia and the Pacific, it has more than quintupled; and even in troubled Africa it may have more than doubled. While such calculations cannot be exact, there should not be the slightest doubt about the consequence of the trends they represent.

Why has the most rapid period of population growth in the history of our species been the occasion for the most extraordinary economic expansion in human experience? Part of the answer may lie in the "population explosion" itself—or more precisely, in its proximate causes. The modern "population explosion" was sparked not because people suddenly started breeding like rabbits, but rather because they finally stopped dying like flies. That is to say, it wasn't that fertility rates soared; rather, mortality rates plummeted. Since the start of our century, the average life expectancy at birth for a human being has probably doubled—it may have more than doubled. Every corner of the earth has joined in this health revolution—and on the whole, incidentally, health progress in our century has been more dramatic in the less developed regions than the more affluent ones.

Improvements in health are conducive to improvements in productivity. It is not just that healthier populations are able to work harder: improvements in health and reductions in mortality enhance the potentialities of what economists now call "human capital": education, training, skills, and the like. By so doing, they significantly relieve constraints against attaining higher levels of per capita output.

And what about fertility, which so many influential voices today posit as "excessive" in one or another region of the world? Unlike better health and longer life, which are universally regarded as desirable, there is no "universal" view on optimal family size. The number of children that parents wish to have, like other big decisions in a person's life, is an inescapably subjective choice—while it may surely be shaped by economic, cultural, or religious factors, in the final analysis, it is a personal choice. Before we speak of "excess fertility," we should ponder what we imply by questioning other peoples' choices about family size. Let me be blunt. Human beings are not heedless beasts. They do not procreate with utter disregard for their own well being, much less the welfare of their own children.

With the tremendous growth of human numbers, and of per capita output, the world's GDP has grown phenomenally in our century: Maddison's aforementioned research, for example, suggests a fourteen-fold rise.[9] Despite this awesome surge in demand, however, the prices for foodstuffs and natural resources have not rocketed skywards over the course of the twentieth century. In fact, the long-term trend for primary commodity prices has been heading in exactly the opposite direction. According to one careful study, for example, inflation-adjusted prices for primary commodities—including energy products—had dropped by over a third between the turn of the century and the 1980s.[10] And as you may already have heard in the past few days from our friends from UNCTAD and the "Group of 77," the real price of primary commodities has fallen still further since then.

I regale you with these details about price trends because prices are meant to measure scarcity. Other things being equal, scarce items are supposed to cost more; plentiful items, less. Yet by the very information that prices are intended to convey, it would appear that foodstuffs and natural resources have been growing *less* scarce—not more—despite mankind's steadily increasing demand for them!

For convinced Malthusians, this seeming contradiction constitutes an unsolved mystery—and indeed an unsolvable one, if they are to maintain faith in their doctrine. We may note, however, that there are perfectly good explanations for the divergent directions of these long-term trends—not the least of these involving an appeal to economic reasoning and an attention to the actual workings of the modern economic process.

And what of famine? Malthusians expect famines to strike what they call "overpopulated" region—what we might call very poor regions. It is surely true that the margin for error for the very poor is perilously thin. But it does not follow that the very poor in the modern world are inexorably consigned to mass starvation—or that they are pushed there by their own fertility trends. If we examine the actual record, we will see that modern famines are a quintessentially political phenomenon. In the modern world, people starve *en masse* not because famine is unavoidable. They starve instead because their own rulers happen to be indifferent to their plight—or because the state under which they live has actively contrived to bring about their death.

Recall the most fearsome famines that have gripped nations in our century. Over six million people perished in the Ukraine in 1933. That was Stalin's terror-famine: it was provoked by a deliberately punitive collectivization of agriculture, designed to subjugate an unwilling people. As many as three million people died in Bengal, India, in 1943. That was when the British vice-regency, with available stocks of grain at hand, refused to enact the empire's stipulated relief procedures, lest those somehow compromise the overall war effort. Between 1959 and 1961, China lost as many as 30 million people through abnormally high death rates. That was Mao's cruel utopian experiment: first his forcible communization of the countryside shattered the nation's agriculture, then his government closed the country to outside view, denied there was a hunger problem, refused foreign help, and made a point of exporting food. Perhaps a million Biafrans perished from famine in the late 1960s. That was the Nigerian civil war, when food blockades were consciously employed literally to starve the rebels into submission. In the late 1970s, perhaps a million—maybe more—died from abnormal mortality in Cambodia. That was the Khmer Rouge's methodical and barbaric program of auto-genocide. If the details of the more recent tragedies differ in some specifics from the earlier famines I have mentioned, rest assured that the patterns are entirely the same.

Amartya Sen, the distinguished economist and philosopher, and perhaps the pre-eminent student of contemporary famine, has stated it starkly: "Famines are, in fact, extremely easy to prevent. It is amazing that they actually take place, because they require a severe indifference on the part of the government."[11]

Esteemed parliamentarians: in our epoch, famine has been caused not by an ominous excess of people, but instead by a frightening surfeit of callous rulers and killer states. Malthusian delusions would distract us from this central and gruesome fact, just as they divert us from probing too deeply into the reasons that some countries have, anomalously, experienced persistently poor economic performance, or even economic retrogression, in our age of progressive global economic advance.

III

Finally, let me turn directly to the relationship between hunger and political morality—a topic upon which we have already touched, if indirectly. At international gatherings, it is sometimes regarded as *déclassé* to observe that one form of national political or legal arrangements might be preferable to others manifest elsewhere in the world. To the urbane, the latter view sometimes sounds embarrassingly provincial. In any case, many intellectuals and not a few political figures would contend that such considerations have no bearing on the pragmatic quest to conquer hunger. They would agree with the renowned playwright Bertolt Brecht: *"Erst kommt das Fressen, dann kommt die Moral"*[12]: food first, morality after.

Brecht's famous and seemingly worldly dictum is at once cynical and appallingly naive. How can we reflect upon the history of our century without being struck by the singular role certain political principles have played in abetting mankind's escape from hunger—and the dark role of other political philosophies in perpetuating the threat of hunger and starvation? At the end of the day, this much is crystal clear: economic liberty is the enemy of hunger, and political freedom is the nemesis to famine.

Permit me to quote Amartya Sen once more: "In the gruesome history of famines there is hardly any case in which a famine has occurred in a country that is independent and democratic, regardless of whether it is rich or poor."[13] We can take this point further. There are practically no instances of famine in any setting where local newspapers were free to criticize their own government, or where citizens enjoyed the substantive right to participate in an opposition party. In open and accountable political systems where governments serve at the sufferance of the voter, there is tremendous pressure and incentive for policies that forestall famine. Impoverished as it is often said to be, India has not suffered famine since its independence. Far from being a luxury that only the rich can afford, as some would have it, political freedom is thus actually an indispensable necessity for the very poor.

Marxist-Leninists have sneered at the liberal conception of political freedom; they still dismiss it as a dangerous illusion. But as the nightmare of totalitarianism at last begins to pass, and its legacy of worldwide wreckage is finally laid bare, there can be no more dispute about just who was entranced by perilous political fantasies. For all their proclamations about enshrining "people's rights," Marxist-Leninist regimes never did divide those vaunted rights into individual portions. And while terrible atrocities were committed in our time by regimes of many political hues, only the totalitarians committed atrocities out of cold-blooded principle.

Just as political liberties place a systemic check on the threat of famine, so economic liberties can dynamically reduce the risk of severe malnutrition. This is so, quite simply, because the institutional framework for securing economic liberties happens also to be conducive to material advance, productivity improvement, and, ultimately, the escape from poverty. Rule of law; protection of individual rights, including property rights; enforceability of contracts; sound money; the sanction of mutually beneficial economic exchange: from the standpoint of protecting liberty, all these things are virtues in their own right. But insofar as they decrease the uncertainty, lower the costs of obtaining information, and reduce what are called the "transaction costs" that confront individual economic agents, the underpinnings of economic liberty stimulate economic activity and enhance economic welfare.

One may also make the case, as some of us have elsewhere, that economic liberty is *especially* important to the poor, the vulnerable, and the marginalized—the groups, in other words, least capable of fending for themselves in an economic and political system that is neither regular nor just.

In much of the world—including areas where basic political freedoms are secure—the ordinary workings of domestic and international markets are today regarded with suspicion, even hostility, in many elite circles. Such circles speak gravely of the perils of "market failure," and claim these perils justify far-reaching interventions into economic life. Truth to tell, markets, like all human inventions, *are* imperfect. Some specific instances of modern "market failure," moreover, have been conspicuous. But before learning all the fascinating exceptions to the rules, it is best to get the rules themselves straight. For it is the opportunities that lie in market development, and under a regimen of economic liberty, that offer the greatest inherent scope for improving the purchasing power of the world's poor, for stabilizing their access to food supplies, and thus for promoting nutritional security for vulnerable populations.

What development specialist Deepak Lal termed "the *dirigiste* dogma" is still deeply entrenched in many of the world's poorest, and hungriest, spots. As many here will recognize, this dogma commands faithful followers within FAO and other multilateral institutions as well. Alas: adherents of the *dirigiste* dogma have an unsettling tendency to discover "market failures" where none, in fact, exist—and to misdiagnose the adverse consequences of their own preferred therapies as "market failures" that will only be remedied through further *dirigiste* treatments. To belabor the obvious once more, such a state of affairs does not relieve the plight of the world's poor, or expedite progress against global hunger.

IV

As we look toward the coming century, we have more than a presentiment of some of the challenges that will face us. With the enormous increases in world population anticipated in the coming generations, we will need to arrange for commensurately enormous increases in agricultural production capabilities—or disproportionately enormous increases, if we hope to improve the world's dietary quality. Moreover, insofar as agricultural production is just one facet of the complex modern economy, we must be prepared to let agriculture make its fullest contribution to *overall* development; man's needs and desires, after all, extend far beyond a sufficient dinner. And in the world's hungriest regions, establishing effective, responsive, and limited governance is a task barely begun—much as it was when Lord Peter Bauer warned us so over a generation ago.[14]

That will be the hard work. What I have discussed today—the need to redress some obvious misconceptions—is the easy part. But you will not be able to get around to the hard work unless you do the easy work first. Esteemed parliamentarians and distinguished guests: As you begin the work ahead, which will affect millions of lives, I leave you with a reminder, and a plea. Never forget that harm can come from even the best of intentions. And as you consider the tasks before you, set your course by an injunction as old as the desire to do good itself: first, do no harm. First, do no harm. Ladies and gentlemen, please: *first, do no harm.*

Notes

This chapter was originally presented as a keynote address at Parliamentarians' Day on the occasion of the World Food Summit, Rome, November 1996.

1. Lord John Boyd-Orr, "The Food Problem," *Scientific American*, vol. 183, no. 2 (1950), p. 11-15; citation at p. 11.
2. Presidential Commission on World Hunger, *Overcoming World Hunger: The Challenge Ahead* (Washington, DC: Government Printing Office, 1980), p. 182.
3. World Food Council, "Hunger and Malnutrition in the World: Situation and Outlook," Seventeenth Ministerial Session, Agenda item 2(A), Helsingor, Denmark, June 1991, p. 5; quoted in Thomas T. Poleman, "Global Hunger: The Methodologies Underlying the Official Estimates," *ARME Working Paper no. 95-07*, Cornell University, June 1995, p. 1.
4. Food and Agriculture Organization, "Food, Agriculture and Food Security: Developments Since the World Food Conference and Prospects," Technical background document no. 1, World Food Summit, Rome, November 1996; Executive Summary, p. 8.
5. Shlomo Reultinger and Harold Alderman, "The Prevalences of Calorie Deficient Diets in Developing Countries," *World Bank Staff Working Paper*, no. 374 (1980).
6. This comparison contrasts the most recent FAO estimate for the incidence of undernutrition in Southeast Asia 1969/71 (33 percent) with the proportion of the rural Indian population July 1968/June 1969 in households at income levels where food is a superior good (9.5 percent). "Food, Agriculture, and Food Security," p. 8, and V. V. Bhanoji Rao, "The Measurement of Deprivation and Poverty Based on the Proportion Spent on Food: An Explanatory Exercise," *World Development*, vol. 9, no. 4 (1981), pp. 33-353, citation at p. 351.
7. United Nations, *World Population Prospects: The 1994 Revision* (New York: Department for Economic and Social Information and Policy, 1995), p. 462.
8. Angus Maddison, *Monitoring the World Economy* (Paris: Organization for Economic Co-operation and Development, 1995), p. 212.
9. Ibid., p. 227.
10. Enzo R. Grilli and Maw Cheng Yang, "Primary Commodity Prices, Manufactured Good Prices, and the Terms of Trade of Developing Countries: What the Long Run Shows," *World Bank Economic Review*, vol. 2, no. 1 (1988), pp. 1-47.

11. Amartya Sen, "Nobody Needs Starve," *Granta*, no. 52 (1995), pp. 215-20; citation on p. 220.
12. Bertolt Brecht, *Die Dreigroschenoper*, Act 2, scene iii; finale; cf. Bertolt Brecht, *Stuecke*, vol. 3 (Berlin: Suhrkamp Verlag, 1958), p. 99.
13. Sen, "Nobody Needs Starve," p. 217.
14. P.T. Bauer, *Dissent on Development: Studies and Debates in Development Economics* (Cambridge, MA: Harvard University Press, 1972), pp. 90-92.

References

Bauer, P.T. *Dissent on Development: Studies and Debates in Development Economics.* (Cambridge, MA: Harvard University Press, 1972).

Bord-Orr, Lord John. "The Food Problem." *Scientific American*, vol. 183, no. 2 (1950), p. 11-15.

Brecht, Bertolt. *Die Dreigroschenoper.*cf. idem., *Stuecke*, vol. 3 (Berlin: Suhrkamp Verlag, 1958).

Food and Agriculture Organization. "Food, Agriculture and Food Security: Developments since the World Food Conference and Prospects." Technical background document no. 1, World Food Summit, Rome, November 1996; Executive Summary.

Grilli, Enzo R. and Maw Cheng Yang. "Primary Commodity Prices, Manufactured Good Prices, and the Terms of Trade of Developing Countries: What the Long Run Shows." *World Bank Economic Review*, vol. 2, no. 1 (1988), pp. 1-47.

Maddison, Angus. *Monitoring the World Economy.* (Paris: Organization for Economic Co-operation and Development, 1995).

Presidential Commission on World Hunger. *Overcoming World Hunger: The Challenge Ahead.* (Washington, DC: Government Printing Office, 1980).

Rao, V. V. Bhanoji. "The Measurement of Deprivation and Poverty Based on the Proportion Spent on Food: An Explanatory Exercise." *World Development*, vol. 9, no. 4 (1981), pp. 333-353.

Reultinger, Shlomo and Harold Alderman. "The Prevalences of Calorie Deficient Diets in Developing Countries." *World Bank Staff Working Paper*, no. 374 (1980).

Sen, Amartya. "Nobody Needs Starve." *Granta*, no. 52 (1995), pp. 215-20.

United Nations. *World Population Prospects: The 1994 Revision.* (New York: Department for Economic and Social Information and Policy, 1995).

World Food Council. "Hunger and Malnutrition in the World: Situation and Outlook." Seventeenth Ministerial Session, Agenda item 2(A); Helsingor, Denmark, June 1991, p. 5; quoted in Thomas T. Poleman. "Global Hunger: The Methodologies Underlying the Official Estimates." *ARME Working Paper No. 95-07*, Cornell University, June 1995.

10

Population Prospects for Eastern Asia to 2015: Trends and Implications

As the Eastern Asian[1] financial panic of 1997/98 has vividly demonstrated, certain kinds of important regional developments, rife with profound long-term consequence for economics, politics, and strategy, are intrinsically difficult to anticipate in advance. Some kinds of important regional developments, though, are much easier to foresee. Population change qualifies as one of these. For the Eastern Asian region as a whole, and for most of the countries within it, we can today speak with reasonable confidence and often in quite surprising detail about what lies in store over the next fifteen to twenty years (barring, of course, the contingency of utter catastrophe).

Two factors make possible such demographic foresight for Eastern Asia. The first is that the techniques of demography happen to be rather good, under normal circumstances, for predicting many characteristics of any given modern population a decade or two hence. "Population science," to be sure, provides no reliable insight into future trends in national fertility; this glaring disciplinary shortcoming is not about to be surmounted any time soon. Nevertheless, demographers are quite good at estimating the number of survivors that can be expected in coming decades from any specific population today. (That actuarial capability underlies and informs the modern life insurance industry, among other things.) So long as a country is not visited by cataclysmic upheaval or completely transformed by an influx or exodus of migrants, a reasonably accurate future profile of its population for cohorts currently alive is in theory a manageable proposition. Second, Eastern Asian particulars at this juncture contribute to the accuracy of population projections with a fifteen-to twenty-year time horizon.

Given its current, and generally low, levels of mortality and fertility, the overwhelming majority of people who will be inhabiting Eastern Asia in, say, the year 2015 are already there, alive today. In fact, at this writing (mid-1998), it would be reasonable to suppose that individuals now living in the region will account for nearly three-fourths of the Southeast Asian populace of the year 2015; for East Asia, the corresponding figure is closer to four-fifths.[2]

At the moment, furthermore, demographic information for most of Eastern Asia is fairly good. Unlike the 1970s, when so much of Eastern Asia was still shrouded in demographic mystery, every country in that region has now conducted at least one official census;[3] most of those countries are not only holding regular counts of national population, but are gathering many additional kinds of information on population trends as well. Because we have a reasonably clear picture of Eastern Asia's population situation today, attempting to peer into the region's population conditions for the year 2015 is that much less of a strain.

Eastern Asia's Population: Today and Tomorrow

At mid-year 1995, by the estimate of the United Nations' Population Division, about 1.9 billion people lived in Eastern Asia (see table 10.1). At this writing, Eastern Asia's population totals roughly 2 billion people (give or take a few tens of millions), and accounts for roughly one-third of the world's entire population. Approximately 1.5 billion of those two billion reside in East Asia, with the other half-billion in Southeast Asia. Of all the large regions of the earth, only "South-Central Asia,"[4] with its current estimated population of slightly over 1.4 billion, can even approach the absolute magnitude of human numbers found in Eastern Asia.

Perhaps not surprisingly, the Eastern Asian region contains three of the eight most populous states in the world today—China, number 1 with about 1.25 billion inhabitants; Indonesia, number 4 with about 200 million; and Japan, number 8 with about 125 million. In addition, five other Eastern Asian states today have populations estimated at over 40 million people: Vietnam (about 77 million); the Philippines (about 71 million); Thailand (almost 60 million); Burma/Myanmar (about 47 million); and the Republic of Korea (about 45 million).[5]

TABLE 10.1

Estimated Population of Eastern Asia, 1995 (millions)

Country/ Region	Population	Country/ Region	Population
East Asia	**1,421.3**	**Southeast Asia**	**481.9**
China	1,198.0	Indonesia	197.5
Japan	125.1	Vietnam	73.5
Republic of Korea	44.9	Thailand	58.2
Mongolia	24.6	Philippines	67.8
DPRK	22.1	Myanmar	45.1
Taiwan	21.3	Singapore	33.3
Hong Kong	61.2	Malaysia	20.1
Macau	.4	Cambodia	10.0
		Laos	4.9
		East Timor	.8
		Eastern Asia	**1,903.2**

Notes: U.N. sources include Taiwan within China. This table does not.
Sources: *World Population Prospects: The 1996 Revision* (New York: U.N., 1998) and ROC *Statistical Yearbook of the Republic of China*, 1997.

To a considerable degree, Eastern Asia's population trends between now and the year 2015 have been set already by mortality and fertility trends from the relatively recent past.

Despite a succession of gruesome local paroxysms that claimed many millions of lives,[6] Eastern Asia has enjoyed a veritable explosion of health over the post-World War II era (see table 10.2). Between the early 1950s and the late 1990s, average life expectancy at birth for East Asia as a whole is estimated to have jumped by nearly three decades: from about forty-three years to seventy-one years. In Southeast Asia, the pattern of progress against mortality has been somewhat less uniform. Even so, estimated average life expectancy for that region has risen by over half during those same years: from just over forty years to nearly sixty-six years. In both East Asia and Southeast Asia, the tempo of mortality decline has exceeded the world average for almost half a century. In consequence, there are today only a handful of Eastern Asian locales (Burma, Cambodia, East Timor, and Laos among them) in which

TABLE 10.2

Estimated and Projected (medium variant) Total Fertility Rates for Eastern Asia

	1955-60	1975-80	1995-2000
East Asia	**5.12**	**3.13**	**1.78**
China	5.59	3.32	1.80
DPRK	5.77	2.55	2.10
Hong Kong	4.71	2.32	1.32
Japan	2.08	1.81	2.10
Macau	5.03	2.00	1.60
Mongolia	6.00	6.65	3.27
Republic of Korea	6.33	2.92	1.65
Taiwan	6.21[1]	2.73[2]	1.76[3]

	1955-60	1975-80	1995-2000
Southeast Asia	**6.07**	**4.81**	**2.86**
Brunei	6.29	4.40	2.70
Cambodia	6.29	4.10	4.50
East Timor	6.35	4.30	4.32
Indonesia	5.67	4.68	2.63
Lao	6.15	6.69	6.69
Malaysia	6.94	4.16	3.24
Burma/Myanmar	6.00	5.30	3.30
Philippines	7.09	4.96	3.62
Singapore	5.99	1.87	1.79
Thailand	6.39	4.25	1.74
Vietnam	6.05	5.54	2.97

Note: Estimates for China include Taiwan, but Taiwan is also presented separately here.   1=1952-55, 2=1975-90, and 3=1996
Sources: *World Population Prospects: The 1996 Revision* (New York: U.N. Population Division, 1998) and the *Statistical Yearbook of the Republic of China*, 1980 and 1997 eds. (Directorate General of Budget, Accounting and Statistics, ROC).

TABLE 10.3

Estimated and Reported Life Expectancy at Birth in Eastern Asia

East Asia	1950-55	1995-2000	Southeast Asia	1950-55	1995-2000
East Asia	42.9	71.0	Southeast Asia	40.5	65.7
DPRK	47.5	72.2	Brunei	604.	75.5
Hong Kong	61.0	78.8	Cambodia	39.4	54.1
Japan	63.9	80.0	East Timor	30.0	47.5
Macau	53.9	77.6	Indonesia	37.5	65.1
Mongolia	42.3	65.8	Laos	37.8	53.5
ROK	47.5	72.4	Malaysia	48.5	72.0
China	40.8	68.5	Burma/Myanmar	36.9	60.1
Taiwan	60.4[1]	74.8[2]	Philippines	47.5	68.3
			Singapore	60.4	77.3
			Thailand	47.0	69.3
			Vietnam	40.4	67.4

1=1953   2=1996

Notes: Figure for China includes Taiwan.

Sources: *World Population Prospects: The 1996 Revision, Annex II & III* (New York: U.N. Population Division, 1998).

life expectancy at birth ranks below the mean for contemporary developing regions as a whole.

Like mortality, fertility has also fallen dramatically in Eastern Asia over the past four decades (see table 10.3). In the late 1950s, only one country in that vast expanse (Japan) reported a total fertility rate (TFR)[7] that would, if maintained, possibly result in long-term population stabilization. In almost every other part of Eastern Asia, the average woman was then typically bearing five, six, or even seven children.

By the late 1990s, however, fertility levels were estimated to have dropped decisively below the replacement level for East Asia as a whole. This was a breathtaking transformation of childbearing patterns, signifying a reduction in average fertility levels by over two-thirds since the late 1950s. Apart from tiny Mongolia and possibly the still-mysterious Democratic People's Republic of Korea (DPRK), sub-replacement fertility is today apparently characteristic of each and every East Asian state—most portentously, of course, China. At this juncture, indeed, fertility levels appear to be lower in China than they are in the United States—and lower still in Taiwan, South Korea and Japan.[8]

In Southeast Asia, the decline of fertility has been somewhat more uneven, and somewhat less striking in aggregate. Total fertility rates in the late 1990s remain relatively high in some locations: Cambodia's women are thought to be bearing an average of over four children; in Laos, where sustained fertility decline evidently has yet to commence, the average is believed still to exceed six and a half. Still, fertility levels for Southeast Asia as a whole are thought to have come down by over half since the late 1950s, with most of that drop during the past twenty years. In Singapore and Thailand, fertility levels are currently believed to be well below the replacement level. In other, heavily populated, places—such as Indonesia and Vietnam—fertility levels appear to be not far above net replacement, and approaching that threshold quite rapidly.[9]

Because migration plays only a marginal role in Eastern Asia's population dynamics today, population trends between now and the year 2015 will presumably be determined basically by trajectories for mortality and fertility. Projections of Eastern Asian mortality and fertility over the coming two decades are necessarily conjectural. The United Nations' most recent update of its world population projections envisions an overall increase in life expectancy for East Asia of about four years, and for Southeastern Asia of about six years, between the late 1990s and 2015-20; improvements on this order seem entirely plausible at the moment.

Fertility trends are intrinsically more difficult to anticipate. The U.N.'s "medium variant" projections presume a gradual but slight increase in fertility for East Asia, and for Southeast Asia a continuation of fertility decline—albeit at a less rapid pace than in the recent past—until replacement levels for that area overall are reached in 2015-20. "High variant" and "low variant" projections, for their part, depict an Eastern Asia in 2015-20 in which regional fertility levels are about 10 percent above the replacement level in East Asia and about 30 percent above replacement in Southeast Asia—or, alternatively, about 30 percent below replacement and 6 percent below replacement, respectively.

There is really no way to tell which of these "variants" will prove accurate—or if any of them will. Although economic progress, mass education, and the spread of anti-natal family planning programs presumably are among the many factors that may have accounted for the tremendous change in Eastern Asian childbearing patterns over the past generation, demographers cannot confidently estimate the past impact of any specific influence on fertility trends (much less predict such impacts for the future).

Yet the contrasting fertility "variants" presently contemplated for Eastern Asia in the U.N.'s population projections do not substantially alter the region's demographic profile for the year 2015. If the "medium" variant proves accurate, Eastern Asia's population will rise from about 2 billion today to about 2.25 billion in 2015—an increase of roughly 13 percent (see figure 10.1). If the "high" variant is actualized, the region's population will grow by a bit over 18 percent; the "low variant" would make for growth of about 8 percent. In the grand scheme of things, these are not dramatic differences. Moreover, virtually everyone who will be in Eastern Asia's labor force, marriageable cohorts, or pension populations in the year 2015 is already alive today. (As has already been mentioned, demographic techniques afford some precision in projecting the survival schedules of people who already exist.) In consequence, we can paint a reasonably accurate picture for Eastern Asia's demographic situation fifteen or twenty years hence, and describe with reasonable confidence some of the demographic issues and problems that are likely to face that region in the decades just ahead.

FIGURE 10.1

Estimated & Projected Population of Eastern Asia, 1915-2015

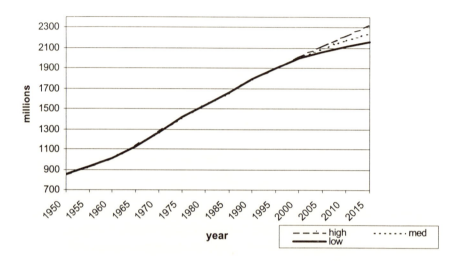

Source: *World Prospects: The 1996 Revision, Annex II, II* (New York: United Nations Population Division, 1998)

The End of "Unprecedented Growth"

In the generation just past, demographic specialists and informed non-specialists alike talked of the "unprecedented growth" in human numbers then underway in Eastern Asia. In the view of many analysts, and not a few local policymakers, rapid population growth within the region was exacerbating social and economic problems, and possibly contributing to political tensions as well. In this reading of events, Eastern Asia's "population explosion" was adversely affecting the race between food and mouths, compromising economic growth, overburdening labor markets with new job-seekers, contributing to urban volatility and reducing the ability of local governments to cope with their domestic problems.[10]

Population growth is expected to continue in East Asia and South-east Asia in the decades immediately ahead. The sorts of increases anticipated, however, can no longer be described as "unprecedented," either in relative or even in absolute terms.

For Eastern Asia as a whole, U.N. "medium variant" projections contemplate an annual pace of increase about 0.8 percent between 1995 and 2015. That would compare with Eastern Asia's estimated 1.6 percent annual rate of natural increase in 1975-95, or 2.1 percent per year in 1955-75. In absolute terms, that same "medium variant" envisions an absolute increase of 350 million persons in Eastern Asia in the 1995-2015 period. That would, of course, be a very large number—but it would be rather less than the estimated 490 million increment of 1975-95, or even the 480 million increase over 1955-75. Even the "high variant" projections for 1995-2015 point to smaller relative and absolute increases than witnessed in the recent past: about 1.0 percent a year, and a total of about 430 million additional people.

In Southeast Asia, it is true, current "high variant" projections would make for absolute population increases in the years just ahead that would be ever so slightly greater than those recorded in the 1980s and 1990s (see figure 10.2). Even those "high variant" projections, however, would imply a pace of growth slower than any recorded for the area since the end of World War II; under the "medium variant" scenario, by contrast, the net increase in Southeast Asian population would be smaller in 2010-15 than it had been between 1955 and 1960. In East Asia, for its part, "high," "medium," and "low" projections all point to smaller additions to the area's population than those experienced in the 1960s, and possibly even the 1950s (see figure 10.3).

The dramatic slowdown in anticipated demographic growth in Eastern Asia in the years immediately ahead is the direct consequence of the broad movement, already noted, toward replacement or sub-replacement fertility within the region's major population centers. Prolonged sub-replacement fertility, in fact, could bring some countries within the Eastern Asian region to the point of zero population growth, or even population decline, by the year 2015.

Under all three current U.N. projection "variants," for example, Japan's population is envisioned to shrink after the year 2010. Under the "low" set of fertility assumptions, furthermore, population growth would have virtually ceased by 2015 in both Thailand and the Republic of Korea; under that same set of hypothetical assumptions, population

FIGURE 10.2

Estimated & Projected Absolute Population Change and Rate of Increase, Southeastern Asia 1950/55-2010/15

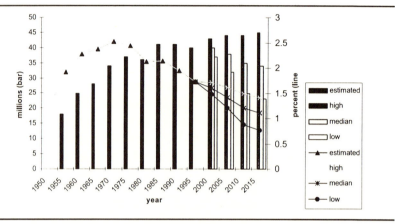

Source: *World Population Prospects: The 1996 Revision* (New York: United Nations Population Division, 1998)

FIGURE 10.3

Estimated & Projected Absolute Population Change and Rate of Increase, East Asia 1950/55-2010/15

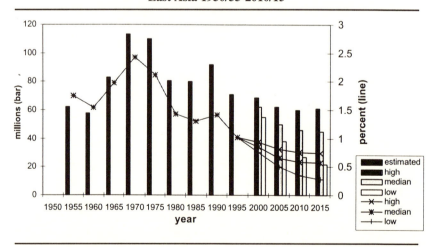

Source: *World Population Prospects: The 1996 Revision* (New York: United Nations Population Division, 1998)

decline for the East Asian area as a whole would commence around 2020.

The "population issues" of the coming decades in these parts of Asia will thus differ from those of the Cold War era in fundamental respects. Whatever the merit may have been of the widespread anxiety about rapid population increase in Eastern Asia—and one may argue that those anxieties were indeed often overblown,[11] accommodating burgeoning human numbers is likely to be ever less a pressing concern for presiding states within the region. Differential rates of national population growth may have some political and economic salience, as they did upon occasion in the past. But a host of new demographic concerns loom just on Eastern Asia's horizon. These include the ramifications of rapid population aging, declining manpower availability, and unnaturally imbalanced sex ratios.

Differential Population Growth

Though population growth will almost certainly be slowing throughout Eastern Asia in the decades immediately ahead, the pace of deceleration will not be uniform: some national populations will be growing more rapidly than others. This means that the relative demographic balance among countries within the region will be shifting over the next decade or two—in some instances, appreciably.

One should not overemphasize the intrinsic economic or strategic significance of relative demographic shifts among specific countries or regions.

In recent memory, after all, the most rapidly growing region of the world has been sub-Saharan Africa, whose share of total world population jumped by over a third between 1965 and 1995: from an estimated 7.3 percent to an estimated 9.9 percent.[12] Yet sub-Sahara's influence on the world stage hardly waxed over those same decades: instead, for much of the subcontinent, those years were marked by economic retrogression, political decay, and poignant appeals for external humanitarian, development, and security assistance.

Under certain circumstances, however, differential population growth rates can reinforce other, non-demographic pressures to alter an existing balance of international or regional power. This seemed to happen, for example, in the Franco-German rivalry during the "long peace" between the Napoleonic era and the outbreak of World War I. Whereas in

1800 there were five French citizens for every four Germans, by 1914 there were over eight Germans for those same five French.[13] Germany's ascendance in this nineteenth-century competition was arguably due to a great many factors, many of them non-demographic, but population trends nevertheless contributed to German predominance.

FIGURE 10.4

**Estimated & Projected Ratio of Chinese to Indian Populations 1950-2015
(medium variant projections)**

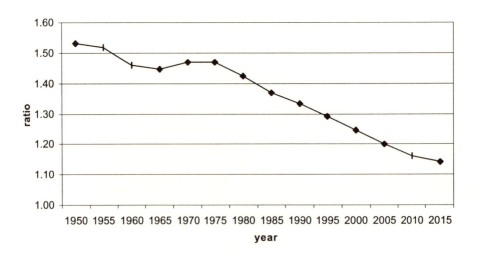

Source: *World Prospects: The 1996 Revision, Annex II, II* (New York: United Nations Population Division, 1998)

As these two contrasting examples may illustrate, there are precious few fixed rules regarding the geopolitical impact of relative population shifts between countries or regions. Clearly, for this reason, a nuanced appreciation of the *potential* role that differential population growth may play in international relations or world economic affairs is more appropriate than any more deterministic approach.

Surveying the Eastern Asian horizon, there would appear to be three settings in which differential population growth stands to change the ratio of population between neighboring, and potentially rivalrous, states. The first involves the world's two great demographic giants, China and India. Shortly after World War II, China's population is believed to have been over half again as big as India's; as late as 1970, there may still have been three Chinese for every two Indians (see figure 10.4). Since then, however, India's rate of natural increase has been decidedly higher than China's, and demographers currently expect that situation to continue in the decades immediately ahead. By 1995, the ratio of Chinese to Indians had dropped below 4:3; by 2015, if current U.N. projections prove accurate, that ratio will fall to under 6:5. And while the accuracy of long-range population projections can never be vouchsafed, the most recent projections of both the U.N. Population Division and the U.S. Census Bureau envision India's overtaking of China as the world's most populous country some time in the twenty-first century.[14]

At this juncture, though, it is not obvious that the changing Sino-Indian demographic balance will have strong bearing on the prospects for these two rising powers in the immediate future. First, the change in relative demographic weight, while appreciable, is not that radical in the period under our consideration. (There are about 30 percent more Chinese than Indians today, and there will still likely be around 16 percent more Chinese than Indians in 2015.) Second, over the foreseeable future, the might of these two states (economic, military, and otherwise) seems likely to depend far more upon their ability to mobilize and harness the potential of their given populations than in any changes in raw human numbers per se under their jurisdiction. Impending differentials in population growth seem most unlikely to alter the disposition or conduct of either Beijing or New Delhi's foreign policies between now and the year 2015. And while a demographic race might conceivably figure within the context of a great strategic struggle between these two mutually mistrustful countries, for the time being their geopolitical attentions appear to be focused principally upon developments within their own local regions of influence, rather than upon their enormous, but more distant, nuclear neighbor.

Within Southeast Asia, perhaps the most important shift in relative numbers will involve Thailand and Vietnam (see figure 10.5). Around 1950, there were three Vietnamese for every two Thais. Thereafter, for a number of reasons—not least of which was the prolonged war in Vietnam—Thailand's population grew more rapidly for three full decades. By 1980, the ratio of Vietnamese to Thais had fallen from 3:2 to under

FIGURE 10.5

**Estimated & Projected Populations of Thailand and Vietnam 1950-2015
(medium variant projections)**

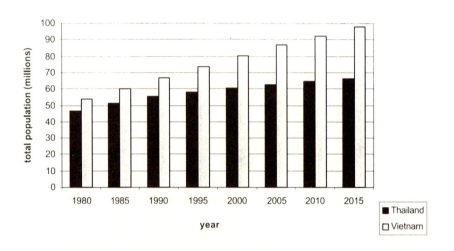

Source: *World Prospects: The 1996 Revision, Annex II, II* (New York: United Nations Population Division, 1998)

6:5. Since 1980, however, Vietnam's tempo of population growth has exceeded Thailand's, and is expected to continue to do so in the coming decades. Thus, the balance of population between Vietnam and Thailand looks likely to move back toward 3:2, and could indeed come close to that former ratio by 2015.

All other things being equal, the strategic implications of this prospective demographic differential would appear to favor Hanoi over Bangkok. Yet as we know, all other things are *not* equal today, and are not likely to be in the decades immediately ahead.[15] How these evolving population trends affect the Southeast Asian region between now and 2015 will depend in large measure upon the policies adopted by Bangkok and Hanoi, and upon the capabilities of the Thai and Vietnamese societies to cope with change—matters about which we can only speculate today.

Perhaps the most dramatic and portentous differential in rates of population growth within Eastern Asia, however, is that of Korea and Japan (see figure 10.6). In 1950, Japan's population was 2.8 times greater than that of North and South Korea combined. But fertility levels in divided Korea have been consistently higher than those in Japan; thus, despite the horrendous losses exacted by the Korean War, the demographic balance between Japan and Korea has been steadily shifting. By 1995, the ratio of Japanese to Koreans had declined from nearly 3:1 to under 2:1; by 2015, it is projected to be just over 1.5:1.

FIGURE 10.6

Estimated & Projected Populations of DPRK, ROK and Japan, 1950-2015 (medium variant projections)

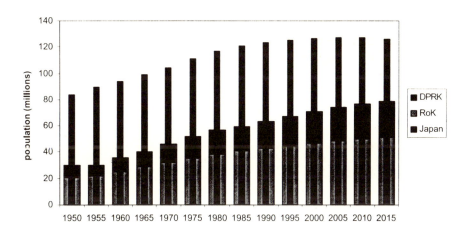

Source: *World Prospects: The 1996 Revision, Annex II, II* (New York: United Nations Population Division, 1998)

The geopolitical implications of these intraregional trends, of course, would take on an even greater significance if Korea were to reunify successfully under the government of the Republic of Korea. In 1950, the ROK's population amounted to about 24 percent of Japan's; by 1995, it was up to 36 percent. With a unification hypothetically consummated under Seoul's aegis, the ROK's population could amount to as much as 62 percent of the Japanese by 2015. A successful Korean reunification would amplify tremendously the significance of extant population trends. Positing political stability and continued rapid industrialization (quantities, as we know, that can hardly be taken for granted), such a demographic augmentation of the Republic of Korea could make the interaction of Seoul and Tokyo much more like a relationship of equals than it has ever been.

The Aging of Eastern Asia

Eastern Asia's revolution in life expectancy, in conjunction with its transition toward replacement or even sub-replacement fertility levels, has set the stage for a dramatic process of population aging within the region over the next several decades. The aging of Eastern Asia, indeed, is a future trend that looks to be all but inexorable at this point (only utter holocaust would prevent it). In many parts of Eastern Asia, the aging of national populations will proceed at an extraordinarily swift tempo. The "graying of Eastern Asia" is sure to have social and economic ramifications; it may have political repercussions as well.

As recently as the early 1980s, nearly all of Eastern Asia's populations were quite young: the median age for both East Asia and Southeast Asia stood in the low twenties or high teens. At that time, persons sixty-five years and older accounted for just over 5 percent of the total population of these regions. As recently as 1985, children under fifteen outnumbered those older people by a ratio of 5:1 in East Asia, and by over 10:1 in Southeast Asia.

The age profile of Eastern Asia will look very different by 2015. In that year, we can expect the median age of East Asia as a whole to be about thirty-seven—several years higher than the current American level and similar to levels in some of today's "gray" Northern Europe. Though overall population growth rates throughout Eastern Asia will be slowing over the coming decades, the pace of growth for every country's elderly age groups will be accelerating. Thus, the share of the older groups will be increasing, and the ratio of children to older persons will be falling. In 2015, Southeast Asia will have only four children under the age of fifteen for every person sixty-five or older—far down from the ten of 1985—and East Asia will have fewer than two.

Regional averages, however, obscure the disparate impact that aging will have on local populations within Eastern Asia (see figures 10.7 and 10.8). Some Eastern Asian countries are likely to retain quite youthful populations over the next two decades: in the year 2015, for example, the median age in the Philippines may be about twenty-six, and in Cambodia it may still be under twenty-five. By contrast, the likely median ages in Thailand (about thirty-five) and China (thirty-six) would be comparable to what can be seen in some of today's (more elderly) OECD countries. And another group of Eastern Asian locales will almost certainly contain populations "grayer" than any yet witnessed in human history. Barring radical changes in migration trends, for example, Singapore's median age in 2015 will be about forty-one; Hong Kong's will be about forty-four; and Japan's will be nearly forty-five.

At the moment, the United Nations defines an "aging society" as one in which 7 percent or more of the population is sixty-five or older. In 2015, that same age grouping is likely to account for about 8-9 percent of the total population in Thailand and China; about 10 percent in South Korea, over 11 percent in Taiwan; around 15 percent in the enclave of Hong Kong; and an amazing 24 percent in Japan.

Rapid population aging will bring profound social and economic changes to much of Eastern Asia in the coming decades. From Singapore to Northeast Asia, for example, the neo-Confucian social order will be tested by the proliferation of the elderly, as well as by the presumably concomitant vast increase in infirm and aged dependents.

For thousands of years, an East Asian tradition that venerated age and emphasized the hierarchical obligations of children to their parents and ancestors was reinforced by prevailing demographic trends: very old people were exceedingly rare while children were plentiful. By 2015, however, there will be nothing exceptional in much of Eastern Asia about achieving a ripe old age. The elderly, in fact, will be utterly commonplace. Indeed, in some of those spots (Japan, Hong Kong, possibly Singapore), grandparents will already outnumber their grandchildren. In many other places (China, Taiwan, Thailand, and the Korean peninsula), that momentous generational reversal will be quickly approaching.

In the fast-changing, skill-sensitive economic environment that we expect for the year 2015, furthermore, the age-old Confucian presumption that the elderly should be honored for the special knowledge and wisdom they possess may appear distinctly less self-evident than in earlier eras. And peoples long inculcated in the virtues of filial piety

FIGURE 10.7

Estimated & Projected Median Age in Selected Southeast Asian Countries, 1980-2015 (medium variant projections)

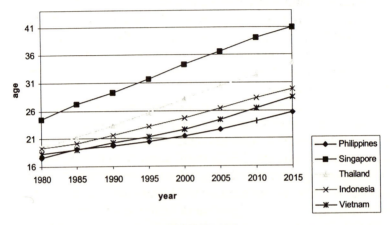

FIGURE 10.8

Estimated & Projected Median Age in Selected East Asian Countries, 1980-2015 (medium variant projections)

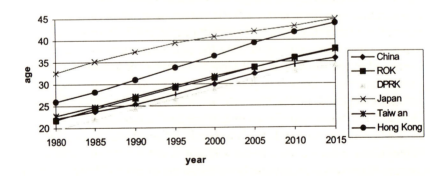

Note: Estimates for China include Taiwan, but Taiwan is also presented separately here.
Sources: *World Prospects: The 1996 Revision, Annex II & II* (New York: U.N. Population Division, 1998) and the *Statistical Yearbook of the Republic of China* 1980 and 1997 eds., (Directorate General of Budget, Accounting and Statistics, ROC)

may have an especially complex time coping with a new reality, in which inter-generational resource transfers suddenly loom large, as parents and other ancestors emerge as pervasive, and possibly major, financial burdens upon the able-bodied.

For local economies affected, rapid population aging implies an imminent advent of truly imposing pension obligations. The most extreme squeeze will be felt in Japan. By 2015, Japan is likely to be the world's most aged society. And by 2015, for every Japanese sixty-five or older, there will be barely 2.5 people "of working age" (15-64)—and not all of these will be working.

The budgetary implications of that metamorphosis are arresting. In the United States, as contemporary commentary has already noted, the unfunded liabilities of the national social security system are enormous. But according to a recent OECD study, Japan's relative liabilities are over three times greater, amounting today to an estimated 70 percent of current GDP.[16] On this budgetary path, Japan's net public debt burden would shoot up from the 11 percent of GDP recorded in 1995, one of the OECD's very lowest, to a projected 102 percent of GDP in 2015, which is envisioned to be very nearly the OECD's highest for that time.[17] (By way of comparison, America's level of net public debt, widely regarded as disturbingly high, will amount to a bit under 50 percent of GDP in the year 2000).[18] To maintain solvency under its current outlay trajectory, the Japanese national pension system would be required, according to calculations by Tokyo's Health and Welfare Ministry, to raise pension taxes on the country's basic wages from an already high 17.4 percent level to a staggering 34 percent rate by 2025.[19] Consequently, if Japan's elderly are to enjoy in 2015 the paid retirement they have been promised today, the nation will have to manage a much higher burden of debt and taxes than it copes with today.[20] (None of those pension calculations, incidentally, take into account the implications of financing health or home care for an ever more aged citizenry.)

Yet however ominous Japan's impending fiscal burdens may appear, Japan today must be seen as an affluent country with an established system of universal retirement benefits. Apart from tiny Hong Kong, no other Eastern Asian venue can be similarly described.[21] Thus, in the coming decades the conjuncture of a relatively low level of per capita income, incomplete pension coverage, and rapid population aging promises to produce a host of still unfamiliar but awkward, and possibly intense, economic problems within many parts of the region.

China's prospective pension problem deserves special mention. By 2015, upwards of 120 million Chinese will be sixty-five or older; their numbers will likely be growing by about 7 percent (about 9 million persons) each year. Despite its vaunted economic advances over the past generation, China today remains a low-income country afflicted by widespread poverty. According to some World Bank estimates, for example, China's real, purchasing-power-adjusted, level of per capita output is distinctly lower than Sri Lanka's, and its distribution of income is also rather more unequal.[22] Under any plausible pace of intervening material advance, hundreds of millions of Chinese will still live under the shadow of crushing poverty in the year 2015. As one Chinese writer has already observed, whereas the now-developed countries "first [got] rich and then [got] old," China will "first get old."[23]

At the moment, however, China lacks any official mechanism to provide for the needs of its old and most impoverished senior citizens. While China does today manage a number of separate public pension schemes (nearly all of them actuarially unsound), these programs cover only a small minority of China's populace and generally skirt the remote, rural regions that constitute the heartland of the Chinese poverty problem.[24] How China will deal with the mounting support problems that will be posed by this huge, rapidly growing, vulnerable, and currently unprotected subpopulation is a grave, and as yet unanswered, question.

Rapid aging in Eastern Asia, in sum, is almost certain to create, or exacerbate, domestic tensions. But it may also have international consequences—even far-reaching ones. For all other things being equal, rapid population aging would seem to presage a great drop in savings rates throughout much of Eastern Asia—a drop that could have spillover effects upon the global economy.

Very generally speaking, savings tend to follow the individual's "life cycle": people typically depend on their parents when they are young, accumulate resources during their working years, and then spend more than they earn during retirement. Writ on a national scale, this "cycle" would imply that a propitious "age structure" facilitates national savings, while population aging, at some point, tends to depress a country's savings level—and that rapid aging could depress that average level significantly, and swiftly.

Results from applied research on Eastern Asian economies seem to square with this theoretical schema. A number of recent studies, for example, have suggested that Eastern Asia's remarkable "savings boom" over the past generation can be understood in terms of demographic forces: that rapid fertility declines among still-youthful populations permitted massive accumulations of surplus (which, in turn, fueled local engines of growth).[25] Conversely, some OECD modeling exercises indicate that, other things being equal, "aging effects" would be expected to drive down Japan's national savings rate by 8 or 9 percentage points between the turn of the century and the year 2030.[26]

Naturally, demographic trends are by no means the only, or even the most significant, influence on a phenomenon as complex as national savings behavior. (Recall that between 1965 and 1995 "dependency ratios" in the Caribbean paralleled East Asia's, and those in Latin America tracked closely with Southeast Asia's, even though savings rates in Latin America and the Caribbean, according to the World Bank, were barely half as high as in Eastern Asia in 1995.)[27] Yet if demographic trends are indeed an important influence on national savings levels, they can be expected to exert downward pressure—potentially, even strong downward pressure—on savings levels in the decades ahead.

By definitional identity, a country's volume of savings must equal domestic investment plus its international current account balance. If savings fall significantly and investment does not, a country can easily switch from being a net exporter of capital to a net importer.

As fate would have it, Eastern Asia's two major economies (Japan and China) are both net exporters of capital today. Japan's status as a capital exporting country is by now widely known. In the period 1991-96, according to estimates by the International Monetary Fund, Japan's total exports of capital exceeded $660 billion.[28] What is less well recognized, however, is that China has also recently emerged as a net capital exporter, albeit on a more modest scale. Over the 1991-96 period, IMF estimates suggest that China exported about $17 billion more capital than she imported (this despite her continuing domestic boom in direct investment from abroad).[29]

But Japan and China will both face increasingly heavy demographic pressures on their savings rates in the years ahead. Crude calculations can show the potential magnitude of the forces at play. Against current Japanese GDP, the OECD's hypothetical eight percentage point drop in Japanese savings rate would make for about a $400 billion shift in domestic investment fund availability. But Japan's current account balance is far lower than that sum: between 1991 and 1996, as noted above, it averaged just over an estimated $110 billion a year.[30]

Do demographic trends therefore portend an inexorable reversal in Japanese and Chinese international capital positions and increasing demands upon world capital markets by other aging Eastern Asian populations? Not necessarily. It could be that slower population growth simultaneously will reduce the demand for domestic investment; some economists, in fact, believe that demographic forces will actually depress Eastern Asia's investment rates faster than its savings rates, freeing up capital funds for the rest of the world in the years ahead.[31]

This is, however, a contentious and speculative issue about which little consensus as yet exists. It may suffice to observe that rapid population aging, absent macroeconomic policy changes and other domestic adjustments, could well have an impact on Eastern Asia's provision of, and demand for, international capital—and that such changes could directly affect world capital markets, international interest rates, trade openness, and by extension, prospects for the entire global economy.

Due to the magnitude of their sudden "longevity explosions" and the precipitous nature of their fertility declines, many parts of Eastern Asia will experience a much more rapid process of population aging in the decades ahead than was recorded in developed regions in the recent past. It took forty years (1955 to 1995) for the median age of the world's "more developed regions" to rise from twenty-eight to thirty-six; East Asia as a whole will make the same transition in less than twenty years (1995 to 2015), and some East Asian countries will be growing old at an even more rapid pace. And although Southeast Asia will qualify as a relatively youthful region in 2015, given an anticipated median age of about twenty-eight, that median age will jump nearly five years between the turn of the coming century and 2015. In those fifteen years, Southeast Asia will age as much, in absolute terms, as the "more developed regions" did in thirty (1955-1985). Eastern Asian societies and governments thus have less time than their industrial European predecessors to prepare for the challenges that aging will inevitably pose.

Declining Manpower Availability

From the end of World War II through the end of the Cold War, Eastern Asian labor policies were preoccupied by the imperative of accommodating a surging growth of local manpower. Attention to, and anxiety about, this swelling wave of new job-seekers was first manifest in Occupation-era Japan[32] (the labor force of which had suddenly been enlarged by the repatriation of former soldiers and colonists), but gradually spread to nearly all other countries in the region. (These concerns were instrumental in, among other things, the establishment of Eastern Asia's many separate national—and explicitly anti-natal—family planning programs.)

By the end of the Cold War, however, Eastern Asia's great wave of entrants into the population "of working ages" had begun to crest; in some locations, its force was all but spent by the late 1990s. In the next two decades, it will begin to ebb within the region's most important economies. Overall, Eastern Asia's manpower availability will continue to expand between now and the year 2015. But thanks to the spread or continuation of sub-replacement fertility regimens and the consequent deceleration of population growth, a region that had once seemingly defined the image of "surplus labor" will be forced, increasingly, to confront the problems of "labor scarcity."

Past and prospective trends in Eastern Asian manpower availability are illustrated in figures 10.9, 10.10, and 10.11. These graphs chart changes in the "working age" population, which is defined by convention as the 15-64 year-old group. (That definition is clearly arbitrary, but not wholly unreasonable.)

In Eastern Asia as a whole, the tempo of net additions to the working-age population all but exploded between the late 1950s and the early 1980s. In the second half of the 1950s, Eastern Asia's 15-64 age group grew by an estimated 34 million people—an annual pace of about 1.1 percent. In the early 1980s, by contrast, their numbers rose over 130 million—or by almost four times as much—and were growing by about 2.8 percent per year.

By the late 1990s, that momentum had been reversed. The absolute growth of working age manpower for Eastern Asia for the second half of the 1990s is estimated at about 90 million—down about a third from the early 1980s; the pace of growth had dropped in half, to about 1.4 percent a year. In Southeast Asia, the absolute increment of new potential workers was still on the rise, although the rate of growth was falling. In East Asia, both measures of manpower change were down sharply. In those intervening fifteen years, the absolute growth of East Asia's "working age" population is estimated to have dropped by half, and the pace of growth is believed to have fallen by even more—from 2.8 percent down to 1.1 percent a year.

The cresting and subsequent attenuation of manpower growth, naturally, has followed different trajectories in Eastern Asia's diverse local settings. The absolute growth of "working age" population peaked first

FIGURE 10.9

Estimated & Projected (Median Variant) Change in Working Age Population (15-64) in Selected East Asian Countries (1955-2015)

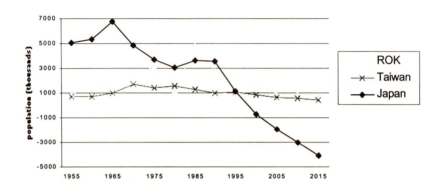

Source for Taiwan, *The Statistical Yearbook of the Republic of China* 1980 and 1997 eds., (Directorate General of Budget, Accounting and Statistics, ROC) for all others, *World Population Projects:* The 1996 Revision, Annex I, II & III (New York: UN Population Division, 1998)

FIGURE 10.10

Estimated & Projected Changes in Working Age Population Selected Southast Asian Countries (1955-2015)

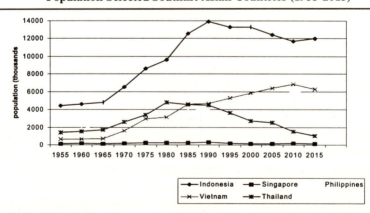

Source: *World Population Projects:* The 1996 Revision, Annex I, II & III (New York: UN Population Division, 1998)

FIGURE 10.11

**Estimated & Projected (Medium Variant) Change China's in
Working Age (15-64) Population, 1955-2015**

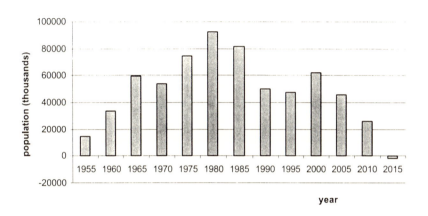

Note: figures for China do not include Taiwan
Source: *World Population Projects:* The 1996 Revision, Annex I, II & III (New York: UN
Population Division, 1998) and the *Statistical Yearbook of the Republic of China* 1980
and 1997 eds. (Directorate General of Budget, Accounting and Statistics, ROC)

in Japan, in the early 1970s; its growth dropped off sharply thereafter
(and turned negative in the late 1990s). In South Korea, it peaked in the
late 1970s; in Thailand, Taiwan, and Singapore, in the early 1980s.

Most portentously, China's net growth of "working age" manpower
reached its zenith in the early 1980s; no one alive today will ever again
see increases of that magnitude for that country.

In Indonesia, the high-water mark for the growth of "working age"
cohorts was reached in the late 1980s, although subsequent declines
have been very gradual, and will continue to be for the next several
decades.

And in a few Eastern Asian locales—Vietnam and the Philippines
most important among them—the high-watermark for incremental manpower growth is not yet in sight. At the moment, U.N. projections an-

ticipate a decline in absolute growth of both Vietnamese and Filipino "working age" populations after the year 2015. Those presumed apogees, however, necessarily depend upon projected fertility trends early in the coming century—quantities about which we can offer no precise and confident judgments today.

Between now and the year 2015, the growth of potential manpower will decelerate in Eastern Asia. Internally generated increases in "working age" population, now running at about 16 million a year, will likely fall below 5 million a year twenty years hence, implying a regional pace of growth of a mere 0.3 percent per year. In East Asia, indeed, the absolute size of the working age populace will likely begin to fall: growth (if any) in Taiwan and the Korean peninsula will be negligible; Japan's "working age" population will be shrinking; and most significantly, China's manpower growth rate will have just turned negative.

Within Southeast Asia, domestic manpower growth will have all but ceased in Singapore and Thailand by 2015. Indeed, virtually all of Eastern Asia's regional manpower growth will be accruing from just three countries: Indonesia, the Philippines, and Vietnam.

The coming slowdown, or actual decline, of available manpower resources within Eastern Asia will pose a number of new challenges to the region. Some of the most vexing challenges will be economic. Over the past generation, for example, the formula for rapid economic growth for much of Eastern Asia has relied heavily upon the mobilization of labor and capital "inputs" to speed development along.[33] In the decades immediately ahead, however, new local supplies of labor stand to be far less plentiful than in the past. As we have already seen, moreover, population aging is likely to constrain the volume of local savings available for capital accumulation. If rapid economic growth is to resume after recovery from the recent Eastern Asian downturn, a new formula will have to be devised—one far more reliant upon improvements in efficiency and productivity for sustained material advance.[34]

Declining manpower availability, unfortunately, may in itself complicate the task of productivity improvement in a number of ways. Improved labor productivity, for example, will presumably require higher levels of skill and educational attainment for labor forces within the region, but the slowdown in manpower growth stands to reduce the pace at which education-based skills percolate up into the working age population.

In almost every country within Eastern Asia, educated youth will be replacing their less well-educated elders within the manpower pool at a far less rapid pace than in the recent past. In 1975, for example, young-sters in their late teens accounted for over a fifth of South Korea's "work-ing age" population; by 2015 they will make up less than a tenth of it. Much the same will be true in Thailand, Taiwan, and, perhaps most significantly, China. Even in Indonesia, the share of 15-19-year-olds within the "working age" population is projected to drop sharply: from roughly one-fifth in 1975 to barely an eighth by 2015. Barring major changes in schooling and training processes, such trends presage mount-ing difficulties in eliciting rapid education-based improvements in la-bor productivity. East Asian governments, of course, will still have a variety of options at their disposal for augmenting manpower within their national economies, but most of these strategies offer only mar-ginal benefit and/or carry unintended costs.

Encouraging temporary or permanent immigration, for example, would be one way of coping with a shortage of labor or specific skills. Some of the smaller Eastern Asian countries have already successfully employed this device: in recent years, in fact, as much as 15 percent of the workforce in both Singapore and Malaysia was composed of non-citizens.[35] Other larger Eastern Asian countries, however, as yet appear to be markedly less capable of either incor-porating newcomers into their economy or assimilating them into their society. In particular, Japan appears to be conspicuously un-able to cope with inflows of immigrants. In 1995, resident foreign-ers accounted for a lower share of national population in Japan than in any of the European Union's seventeen member-states.[36] In 1995, furthermore, fewer foreigners were naturalized in Japan than in tiny, restrictive Switzerland.[37] Without a major influx of immigrant work-ers, however, Japan's "working-age" population stands to decline by over 10 million between 1995 and 2015.

Promoting higher rates of labor force participation would be another potential means of adding to the domestic workforce. By comparison at least with the United States, labor force participation rates for Eastern Asian women appear to be quite low in a number of locales: among them, Hong Kong, Japan, Singapore, South Korea, and Taiwan.[38] In each of these places, however, fertility levels are already noticeably lower than in America; enticing more women out of the home and into the paid workplace would likely have the effect of reducing fertility even further—and thus of relieving today's labor shortages by intensifying tomorrow's.

The Impending East Asian Bride Shortage

In ordinary human populations around the world and throughout re-corded history, the "sex ratio" for babies has exhibited a strong biologi-cal predictability: around 105-107 baby boys can be expected for every 100 baby girls.[39] Since the early 1980s, however, sex ratios at birth through most of East Asia have undergone a steady, and eerie, rise. By 1993, South Korea was registering nearly 116 baby boys for every 100 baby girls born.[40] In 1995, a Chinese national sample population cen-sus counted over 118 boys under the age of five for every 100 little girls.[41] Unnaturally high (albeit somewhat less extreme) sex ratios for infants and toddlers were also reported in the early 1990s for Hong Kong and Taiwan.[42]

In South Korea, Taiwan, and Hong Kong—places with virtually com-plete demographic registration systems—the imbalances revealed through national statistics can be taken at face value. China's birth reg-istration system, on the other hand, remains incomplete, and part of the unnatural imbalance recorded in the 1995 sample census was a statisti-cal artifact. Most of the reported imbalance, unfortunately, appears to be real. Recent U.S. Census Bureau reconstructions, for example, con-clude that the actual sex ratio for infants and toddlers in China for 1995 lay in the vicinity of 1.16 to 1.[43]

The gender imbalance that has been emerging in contemporary China can be associated easily enough with the state's grotesque and punitive "One Child Policy," which is associated with, among other things, a reported resurgence of the age-old practice of female infanticide in the Chinese countryside.[44] But in Hong Kong, Taiwan, and most dramati-cally, in South Korea—places subject neither to involuntary family plan-ning programs nor to rumors of rural female infanticide—these rising sex ratios at birth require a different sort of explanation. At the moment, it would appear that the conjuncture of sub-replacement fertility, strong son preference, and availability of sex-selective abortion are making for severely skewed sex ratios at birth throughout East Asia—irrespec-tive of income level, educational attainment, or extent of political liber-ties for the population in question.[45]

Today's striking imbalance between numbers of boys and girls in East Asia means there will be a corresponding mismatch between pro-spective husbands and brides a generation hence—or even sooner. In South Korea, for example, the ROK National Statistical Office (NSO) has calculated that the sex ratio for the country's "marriage age population" in 2010 will be over 123 men for every 100 women.[46]

For China, the dimensions of this mounting mismatch are illustrated in figure 10.12, which shows the Census Bureau's projections for the "sex ratio" for Chinese in their early twenties between now and the year 2020. Between 1995 and 2020, the number of Chinese men in their early twenties for every 100 young Chinese women from the same cohort is envisioned as increasing from 105 to 116.

In the Chinese (and the Korean) tradition, virtually all men and women who are able to get married ultimately do so. For a society with a pre-

FIGURE 10.12

**Estimated & Projected Sex Ratios, 20 to 24 age group, China 1995-2020
(men per 100 women of same age group)**

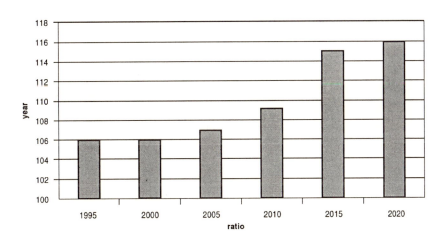

Source: U.S. Bureau of the Census, Unpublished Worksheets, March 1998.

sumption of near-universal marriage, however, the arithmetic implications of unnatural imbalances between the supply of prospective husbands and wives are straightforward, and unforgiving. If there are 116 young Chinese men for every 100 young Chinese women, and if (say) 2 percent of those young women never marry, then one out of every six of these young men must find a bride from outside of this cohort—or fail to continue his family line.

In theory, this problem could be finessed simply by marrying outside one's cohort—for example, by finding a younger bride. In the East Asian past, younger brides were often the solution to the problem of "excess" males. Given East Asia's historic (high-fertility) age structure, however, each new cohort would be larger than the one before it. In the coming decades, given today's regimen of low and sub-replacement fertility, East Asia's rising youth groups will typically be *smaller* than the cohorts born just before them.

Thus, to the degree that young men in Hong Kong, Taiwan, South Korea, and China manage to solve their mating problem by marrying younger women from within their country or place, they will concomitantly intensify the eventual "marriage crisis" facing their compatriots a few years their junior.

In many settings throughout history—including most of early modern Western Europe—bachelorhood was an acceptable social role, and the incidence of never-marrying bachelors within the total male population was high.[47] East Asia, however, was never one of those settings, and is not one of them today. Unless it is swept by a truly radical change in cultural and social attitudes toward marriage in the next two decades, both China and South Korea are poised to experience an increasingly intense, and perhaps desperate, competition among young men for the nation's limited supply of brides.

What forms will this competition take, and how will these societies be affected by it? In South Korea, a Minister of Health and Welfare has "quoted a scholar saying that if the sex imbalance ratio exceeded 120 males to 100 females, riots may take place because of the shortage of females for marriage."[48] (His pronouncement, one may note, was offered before the country's statistical authorities had estimated the imbalance would actually exceed this threshold by 2010.) As for China, a 1997 essay contemplating the country's future gender imbalance in the journal, *Renmin Luntan,* predicted direly that "such sexual crimes as forced marriages, girls stolen for wives, bigamy, visiting prostitutes, rape, adultery ... homosexuality ... and weird sexual habits appear to be unavoidable."[49]

Such assessments sound overly dramatic. Yet even if one does not take the social upheaval, or degeneration, posited above for granted, the coming bride shortages may create extraordinary social strains and tensions—especially in China.

In Hong Kong and Taiwan, the solution to the coming "bride shortage" is simple and relatively straightforward: import from abroad. To "clear the market" for marriages a decade or two hence, these entities need only secure a combined total of about twenty thousand ethnic Chinese "mail-order brides" each year—hardly an unmanageable proposition, one should think, for prospering societies so close to an enormous, and largely impoverished, Chinese hinterland.

For South Korea, the problem is more complex. Although the ROK has become a relatively affluent society and a member of the OECD, the ROK already contains over three-fifths of the world's entire stock of ethnic Koreans. Already matchmaking services in Seoul are contracting marriages with "Yanbian brides"—ethnic Koreans from communities in Northeast China. For the generation of men beginning to enter the marriage market in 2010, however, South Korea stands to face a cumulative "bride deficit" of roughly one million women—and there are fewer than two million ethnic Koreans in all of China.[50] If these prospective suitors are to find ethnic Korean mates, their only arithmetically viable solution is to look to North Korea.

For today's divided Korea, such a proposition is unthinkable. But even in the context of some future detente, or unification, on the Korean peninsula, the problems posed by the South's hunger for Northern women would be unprecedented—and at the very least, indelicate. For the DPRK—a regime that has by now all but lost its *raison d'être*—the duty of protecting the country's womanhood against outside predators might offer a new and primordial rationale for regime continuation. For a unified Korea, on the other hand, the process of healing and reconciliation might be furthered in some ways by North-South intermarriages— but the social resentment of those in the North who were left behind (or left unmarriageable) would also likely be a new force to contend with.

It is China, however, for whom the impending bride shortage looms largest, and looks most intractable. In comparison to the overseas Chinese diaspora, China itself is very poor—hardly a favorable circumstance in searching for "mail order brides." And for purely arithmetic reasons, searching abroad for Chinese wives will be a strategy of distinctly limited promise. By 2020, for example, the surplus of China's males in their twenties will likely exceed the *entire* female population of the island of Taiwan! Thus, barring a sudden and dramatic departure from existing customs, a significant fraction of China's young men will have to be "socialized" in a manner that does not include marrying and forming their own family.

Not a few of these young Chinese men might be struck by a bitter irony of their paradoxical national circumstance: at a time when (in all likelihood) their country's wealth and power would be greater than ever before, their own personal chances of possessing the wherewithal necessary to establish their own family not only look bleak, but steadily worsening.

It is easy to imagine how such a paradox could invite widespread dissatisfaction or even outright discontent. At the same time, there is very little that any future Chinese government will be able to do to address the root of the problem: the disproportion between young men and young women. As *Renmin Luntan* intoned, the involuntary bachelors from China's rising cohorts will "handle [a] punishment they have received as a result of the social and natural imbalance created by the mistakes of the previous generation."[51]

Auguste Comte's aphorism that "demography is destiny" is a dictum much overused. With intelligent policies and reasoned behavior, it is commonly possible to maximize opportunities and to minimize risks inherent in almost any given fertility regimen—that is, to make one's own "destiny" regardless of demographic trends. East Asia's mounting gender imbalances, however, are a problem that does not look amenable to any ready policy solutions today. It is a problem that has already been set in place, ready to unfold in the coming century. Until and unless sex ratios return to a more biologically natural balance, East Asia's future will be characterized by a new form of social distortion with unpredictable, but possibly far-reaching, implications.

Notes

1. By "Eastern Asia," we refer here to the continental landmass and islands demarcated by the Indian subcontinent, the ex-Soviet Central Asian Republics, and the Russian Far East.
2. "Southeast Asia" and "East Asia" are defined here in accordance with the United Nations' geographical classification of countries—with the single exception of the Republic of China, which is omitted in principle by the U.N. from such

listings, but is counted as part of "East Asia" in this essay. Estimates of the proportions of East Asian and Southeast Asian populations in the year 2015 living as of mid-year 1998 are derived from United Nations, *World Population Prospects: The 1996 Revision* (New York: U.N. Department for Economic and Social Information and Policy Analysis, Population Division, 1998). Note that these estimates are predicated on the twin assumptions that devastating mortality crises and vast upsurges in migration do not occur between now and 2015.

3. Included here is the reclusive, statistically reticent Democratic People's Republic of Korea (DPRK), which has released returns for a countrywide population count for 1993. See DPRK Central Bureau of Statistics, *Tabulation of the Population Census of the Democratic People's of Korea (31 December 1993)* (Pyongyang, 1995).

4. A new, post-Cold-War U.N. geographical designation encompassing the territories of the old British Raj (minus Burma) plus the Central Asian Republics of the old Soviet Union.

5. Numbers are projections for mid-year 1998, adjusted from estimates of mid-year 1995 populations.

6. Among them: the Korean War (1950-53); the Vietnam Wars (1954-75); China's "Three Lean Years" (1959-61); Indonesia's mayhem in 1965; and Cambodia's Khmer Rouge interlude (1975-78). Another bout of "excess mortality" may now be underway in North Korea, which has been gripped by an officially acknowledged food shortage since 1995. At this writing, however, not enough information is available about the North Korean food situation to determine its death toll.

7. The total fertility rate is a demographic measure of mean births per woman per lifetime. Note that we are referring here to period—rather than cohort—TFRs.

8. Japan's TFR, in fact, was recorded to be 1.39 in 1997. Kyodo News Service, July 10, 1998; reprinted as "Japan: Muraoka: Expert Panel Planned to Discuss Birthrate Fall," in US Foreign Broadcast Information Service (hereafter FBIS), FBIS-EAS-98-191, July 10, 1998 (electronic version).

9. So rapidly, in fact, that the U.N.'s 1996 population projections may already overstate their fertility. Whereas those U.N. projections place Vietnam's total tertility rate for 1995-2000 at about 3, slightly more recent projections by the U.S. Census Bureau give Vietnam a TFR of 2.5 for the year 1998. (Net replacement fertility for Vietnam would require a TFR of just over 2.1.)

10. Perhaps the most authoritative representation of this perspective is the U.S. National Academy of Sciences' 1971 report, *Rapid Population Growth: Consequences and Policy Implications, Volume I* (Baltimore, MD: Johns Hopkins University Press, 1971).

11. For an argument to this effect, see Nicholas Eberstadt, "Demography and International Relations," *Washington Quarterly* 21, no. 2 (1998), pp. 33-52.

12. Derived from *World Population Prospects*, Annex I.

13. Derived from Colin McEvedy and Richard Jones, *Atlas of World Population History* (London: Penguin Books, 1978), pp. 55-60, 67-72.

14. The U.S. Census Bureau's latest projections for China, India, and other countries are provided by its International Programs Center's "International Data-Base," which may be accessed online at <http://www.census.gov/ipc/idbsum>.

15. To note only the most obvious differences: Thailand is far more prosperous than Vietnam; its population is better trained and educated; and despite its recent financial travails it has already established a market-economic system and a relatively open, competitive political structure (endpoints Vietnamese leaders are still eyeing in the "transition" they are attempting to engineer).

16. OECD, *Ageing in OECD Countries: A Critical Policy Challenge* (Paris: OECD, 1996), p. 36. Calculations refer to the year 1994.

17. Ibid., pp. 83-84.

18. Ibid., p. 83.

19. Kyodo News Service, December 5, 1995 (in English); reprinted as "Japan: Government Unveils Specific Options for Pension Reform," FBIS-EAS-97-339, December 5, 1997 (electronic version).

20. For a cogent analysis of such pressures and some interesting speculations about their possible impact, see Milton Ezrati, "Japan's Aging Economics," *Foreign Affairs* 76, no. 3 (1997), pp. 96-104.

21. For information on Eastern Asian pension systems and old age programs, see U.S. Social Security Administration, Office of Research, Evaluation and Statistics, *Social Security Programs throughout the World, 1997* (Washington, DC: Government Printing Office, 1997).

22. World Bank, *World Development Report 1997* (New York: Oxford University Press, 1997), pp. 214, 222. Estimates of per capita GDP refer to "PPP" adjusted levels for 1995; estimates on income distribution refer to household income 1995 for China, and to household expenditures 1990 for Sri Lanka.

23. Lin Ying, "The Aging of the Population: A Severe Challenge," *Guangming Ribao*, April 6, 1996, p. 1; translated as "PRC: Worsening Problem of Population Aging," FBIS-CHI-96-213, April 11, 1996 (electronic version).

24. For more details, see Barry Friedman et. al., "How Can China Provide Income Security for Its Rapidly Aging Population?" *World Bank Policy Research Working Paper no. 1674* (October 1996), and Loraine A. West, "Pension Reform in China: Preparing for the Future," *Journal of Development Studies* vol. 35 no. 3 (1999), pp. 153-183.

25. See Kenneth Kang, "Why Did Koreans Save So Little, and Why Do They Now Save So Much?" *International Economic Journal* 8, no. 4 (1994), pp. 99-111; Matthew Higgins and Jeffrey G. Williamson, "Age Structure Dynamics in East Asia and Dependence on Foreign Capital," *Population and Development Review* 23, no. 2 (1997), pp. 261-93; Andrew Mason, "Will Population Change Sustain the 'Asian Economic Miracle'?" *Asia-Pacific Focus*, no. 33 (1997); David E. Bloom and Jeffrey G. Williamson, "Demographic Transitions and Economic Miracles in Emerging Asia," *NBER Working Paper*, no. 6268 (November 1997).

26. *Ageing in OECD Countries*, op. cit., p. 95.

27. Derived from *World Population Prospects*, op. cit., Table A.30; *World Development Report 1997*, op. cit., p. 239.

28. International Monetary Fund, *International Financial Statistics* 51, no. 6 (June 1998), pp. 394-95. Net capital exports are taken from "line 78 aid": "Balance on Goods, Services, and Income."

29. Ibid., p. 204.

30. Derived from *World Development Report 1997*, p. 215; International Monetary Fund, *International Financial Statistics* 51, no. 6 (June 1998), pp. 394-95.

31. Viz. "Age Structure Dynamics in East Asia and Dependence on Foreign Capital," op. cit.

32. Representative expressions of these concerns would include *Problems of Population and Economy of Japan* (Tokyo: Population Problems Research Council, Mainichi newspapers, 1951). For an early account of these SCAP-period concerns, see Irene B. Taeuber, *The Population of Japan* (Princeton, NJ: Princeton University Press, 1958), chapter 17.

33. The most extreme, and provocative, formulation of this argument is perhaps found in Paul Krugman, "The Myth of Asia's Miracle," *Foreign Affairs* 73, no. 6

(1994), pp. 62-78. A more exacting presentation of a similar perspective may be found in Alwyn Young, "The Tyranny of Numbers: Confronting the Statistical Realities of the East Asian Growth Experience," *Quarterly Journal of Economics* 110, no. 2 (1995), pp. 641-80. Other scholars, while disagreeing with this particular interpretation, have also recognized the important role "factor mobilization" has played in Eastern Asian growth. For a sampling, see Dani Rodrik, "The 'Paradoxes' of the Successful State," *European Economic Review* 41, nos. 3-5 (1997), pp. 411-42; Michael Sarel, "Growth In East Asia: What We Can and Cannot Infer from It," *International Monetary Fund Working Paper no. 95/98* (September 1995); and William Easterly, "Explaining Miracles: Growth Regressions Meet the Gang of Four," in Ito Tokatoshi and Anne O. Krueger, eds., *Growth Theories in Light of the East Asian Experience* (Chicago: University Chicago Press, 1995), pp. 267-90. For basic data on East Asian growth, labor and capital accumulation, see Angus Maddison, *Monitoring the World Economy: 1820-1992* (Paris: OECD, 1995).

34. This may even prove true for Japan, where postwar growth appears to have derived more from improvements in total factor productivity (TFP) than from mobilization of factor inputs. See Yutuka Kosai, Jun Saito, and Naohiro Yashiro, "Declining Population and Sustained Economic Growth: Can They Coexist?" *American Economic Review* 88, no. 2 (1998), pp. 412-16.

35. See *Utusan Malaysia*, January 1, 1996, pp. 1, 2; translated as "Malaysia: Government Acts to Reduce Dependency on Foreign Workers," FBIS-EAS-96-035, January 1, 1996 (electronic version); International Labor Office, *Yearbook of Labor Statistics 1996* (Geneva: ILO, 1996), p. 114; and OECD, *Migration and the Labor Market in East Asia: Prospects to the Year 2000* (Paris: OECD, 1996), p. 20.

36. OECD, *Trends in International Migration 1995* (Paris: OECD, 1996), pp. 60, 123. Roughly half of the registered "foreigners" in Japan, moreover, are ethnic Koreans who have resided in the country for up to four generations—a fact that should speak for itself.

37. Ibid., p. 60.

38. Data from Republic of Korea National Statistical Office, *International Statistics Yearbook 1997* (Seoul: NSO, 1997), p. 92.

39. Ansley J. Coale and Judith Banister, "Five Decades of Missing Females in China," *Demography* 31, no. 3 (1994), pp. 459-80; citation at 459.

40. *International Statistics Yearbook 1997*, p. 66.

41. China State Statistical Bureau, Department of Population Statistics, *Tabulation of the 1995 National One Percent Sample Survey* (Beijing: China Statistical Press, 1997).

42. *International Statistics Yearbook 1997*, op. cit., p. 66; Republic of China Directorate-General of Budget, Accounting, and Statistics, *Statistical Yearbook of the Republic Of China 1997* (Taipei: ROC Executive Yuan, 1997), pp. 16, 18. For an analysis of the Taiwanese trends, see Ming-Cheng Chang, "Sex Ratio at Birth and Son Preference in Taiwan Province of China," Korea Institute for Health and Social Affairs and United Nations Population Fund, *Sex Preference for Children and Gender Discrimination in Asia* (Seoul: KIHASA, 1996), pp. 71-89.

43. Unpublished worksheet, U.S. Bureau of the Census, International Programs Center, China Branch. I am grateful to Dr. Loraine A. West, Chief of the Census Bureau's China Branch, for generously sharing this research with me in March 1998.

44. The most comprehensive presentation of evidence on this score remains John S. Aird, *Slaughter of the Innocents: Coercive Birth Control in China* (Washington, DC: AEI Press, 1990).

45. For additional background, see *Sex Preference for Children and Gender Discrimination in Asia*, op. cit. See also Monica Das Gupta, "'Missing Girls' in China, South Korea, and India: Causes and Policy Implications," *Harvard Center for Population and Development Studies Working Paper Series*, no. 98.03 (March 1998).
46. Digital *Chosun Ilbo*, January 8, 1997; reprinted as "South Korea: Statistics Office Projects Demographic Figures for 2010," FBIS-EAS-97-006, January 9, 1997 (electronic version). Note that the NSO arrives at this estimate by comparing men aged 26-30 with women 23-27. This approach—quite reasonable, considering existing differentials in age at first marriage in South Korea today—compounds the impact of the gender imbalance within a birth cohort with the effect of sub-replacement fertility, which reduces the size of younger, rising, birth cohorts. For a more detailed analysis, see Chai Bin Park and Nam-Hoon Cho, "Consequences of Son Preference in a Low-Fertility Society: Imbalance of the Sex Ratio at Birth in Korea," *Population and Development Review* 21, no. 1 (1995), pp. 59-84. In the year 2010, Taiwan will face an even more dramatic imbalance between prospective brides and grooms than that of today's South Korea. In that year, according to recent projections by the U.S. Census Bureau, there will be almost 127 Taiwanese men in their late twenties for every 100 Taiwanese women in their early twenties. (These projections are available online, at <http://www.census.gov/ipc/idbsum/twsum.txt>.) Most of that impending marriage squeeze, however, was caused by the sharp drop in fertility in Taiwan between the early 1980s (the presumptive groom's birth cohort) and the late 1980s (the birth cohort of the presumptive brides). After 2010, Taiwan's "bride shortage" will ease considerably: by 2015, for example the country's corresponding sex ratio for marriage-age men and women will drop to about 107.
47. Cf. J. Hajnal, "European Marriage Patterns in Perspective," in D.V. Glass and D.E.C. Eversley, eds., *Population In History* (London: Edward Arnold, 1965), pp. 101-43.
48. *Korea Times*, January 29, 1995, p.1; reprinted as "Government Planning Review of Population Policy," FBIS-EAS-95-019, January 29, 1995 (electronic version).
49. *Renmin Luntan*, November 8, 1997, no. 11, pp. 50-51; translated as "China: Female-Male Population Discrepancy," FBIS-CHI-98-042, February 11, 1998 (electronic version).
50. ROK "bride deficit" calculated on the basis of U.S. Census Bureau projections of South Korean age-sex distributions for the year 2010 (available online at <http://www.census.gov/ipc/idbsum/kssum.txt>). Ethnic Korean population in China from *International Statistical Yearbook 1997*, op. cit., p. 85.
51. Cf. note 49.

References

Aird, John S., *Slaughter of the Innocents: Coercive Birth Control in China* (Washington, DC: AEI Press, 1990).
Bloom, David E. and Jeffrey G. Williamson. "Demographic Transitions and Economic Miracles in Emerging Asia." *NBER Working Paper no. 6268*, (November 1997).
Chang, Ming-Cheng. "Sex Ratio at Birth and Son Preference in Taiwan Province of China." Korea Institute for Health and Social Affairs and United Nations Population Fund. *Sex Preference for Children and Gender Discrimination in Asia* (Seoul: KIHASA, 1996), pp. 71-89.
China State Statistical Bureau, Department of Population Statistics. *Tabulation of the 1995 National One Percent Sample Survey*. Beijing: China Statistical Press, 1997.

Chosun Ilbo, January 8, 1997; reprinted as "SOUTH KOREA: Statistics Office Projects Demographic Figures for 2010." U.S. FBIS, FBIS-EAS-97-006, January 9, 1997 (electronic version).

Coale, Ansley J., and Judith Banister. "Five Decades of Missing Females in China." *Demography*, vol. 31, no. 3 (1994), pp. 459-480.

Das Gupta, Monica. "'Missing Girls in China, South Korea, and India: Causes and Policy Implications." *Harvard Center for Population and Development Studies Working Paper Series*, no. 98.03 (March 1998).

DPRK Central Bureau of Statistics. *Tabulation of the Population Census of the Democratic People's Republic of Korea (31 December 1993).* (Pyongyang: 1995).

Easterly, William. "Explaining Miracles: Growth Regressions Meet the Gang of Four," in Ito Tokatoshi and Anne O. Krueger, eds. *Growth Theories in Light of the East Asian Experience* (Chicago: University of Chicago Press, 1995), pp. 267-290.

Eberstadt, Nicholas. "Demography and International Relations." *Washington Quarterly*, vol. 21, no. 2 (1998), pp. 33-52.

Ezrati, Milton. "Japan's Aging Economics." *Foreign Affairs*, vol. 76, no. 3 (1997), pp. 96-104.

Friedman, Barry et. al. "How Can China Provide Income Security for Its Rapidly Aging Population?" *World Bank Policy Research Working Paper*, no. 1674 (October 1996).

Hajnal, J. "European Marriage Patterns in Perspective," in D.V. Glass and D.E.C. Eversley, eds. *Population in History* (London: Edward Arnold, 1965), pp. 101-143.

Higgins, Matthew and Jeffrey G. Williamson. "Age Structure Dynamics in East Asia and Dependence on Foreign Capital." *Population and Development Review*, vol. 23, no. 2 (1997), pp. 261-293.

International Labour Organization. *Yearbook of Labor Statistics 1996* (Geneva: ILO, 1996).

International Monetary Fund. *International Financial Statistics*, vol. 51, no. 6 (June 1998) and vol. 52, no. 4 (April 1999).

Kang, Kenneth. "Why Did Koreans Save So Little, and Why Do They Now Save So Much?" *International Economic Journal*, vol. 8, no. 4 (1994), pp. 99-111.

Korea Times, January 29, 1995, p.1; reprinted as "Government Planning Review of Population Policy." FBIS-EAS-95-019, January 29, 1995 (electronic version).

Kosai, Yutuka, Jun Saito, and Naohiro Yashiro. "Declining Population and Sustained Economic Growth: Can They Coexist?" *American Economic Review*, vol. 88, no. 2 (1998), pp. 412-416.

Krugman, Paul. "The Myth of Asia's Miracle." *Foreign Affairs*, vol. 73, no. 6 (1994), pp. 62-78.

Kyodo News Service. December 5, 1995 (in English); reprinted as "Japan: Government Unveils Specific Options for Pension Reform," U.S. FBIS, FBIS-EAS-97-339, December 5, 1997 (electronic version).

——. July 10, 1998; reprinted as "Japan: Muraoka: Expert Panel Planned to Discuss Birthrate Fall." U.S. FBIS, FBIS-EAS-98-191, July 10, 1998 (electronic version).

Maddison, Angus. *Monitoring the World Economy: 1820-1992* (Paris: OECD, 1995).

Mason, Andrew. "Will Population Change Sustain the 'Asian Economic Miracle'?" *Asia-Pacific Focus*, no. 33 (1997).

McEvedy, Colin and Richard Jones. *Atlas of World Population History* (London: Penguin Books, 1978).

OECD. *Ageing in OECD Countries: A Critical Policy Challenge* (Paris: OECD, 1996).

——. *Trends in International Migration 1995* (Paris: OECD, 1996).

——. *Migration and the Labor Market in East Asia: Prospects to the Year 2000* (Paris: OECD, 1996).

Ogawa, Naohiro. "The Socioeconomic Consequences of Population Aging in Japan." *NIRA Review* (Tokyo), Autumn 1998, pp. 3-7.

Park, Chai Bin and Nam-Hoon Cho. "Consequences of Son Preference in a Low-Fertility Society: Imbalance of the Sex Ratio at Birth in Korea." *Population and Development Review*, vol. 21, no. 1 (1995), pp. 59-84.

Population Problems Research Council. *Problems of Population and Economy of Japan* (Tokyo: Population Problems Research Council, Mainichi newspapers, 1951).

Renmin Luntan, November 8, 1997, no. 11, pp. 50-51; translated as "China: Female-Male Population Discrepancy." U.S. FBIS, FBIS-CHI-98-042, February 11, 1998 (electronic version).

Republic of China Directorate-General of Budget, Accounting, and Statistics. *Statistical Yearbook of the Republic of China 1997* (Taipei: ROC Executive Yuan, 1997).

Republic of Korea National Statistical Office. *International Statistics Yearbook 1997* (Seoul: NSO, 1997).

Rodrik, Dani. "The 'Paradoxes' of the Successful State." *European Economic Review*, vol. 41, nos. 3-5 (1997), pp. 411-442.

Sarel, Michael. "Growth in East Asia: What We Can and Cannot Infer from It." *International Monetary Fund Working Paper no. 95/98* (September 1995).

Taeuber, Irene B. *The Population of Japan* (Princeton, NJ: Princeton University Press, 1958).

United Nations. *World Population Prospects: The 1996 Revisions* (New York: U.N. Department for Economic and Social Information and Policy Analysis, Population Division, 1998).

U.S. Census Bureau. Latest projections for China, India, and other countries provided by the Bureau's International Programs Center's "International Data-Base" at <http://www.census.gov/ipc/idbsum>.

U.S. National Academy of Sciences. *Rapid Population Growth: Consequences and Policy Implications, Volume I* (Baltimore, MD: Johns Hopkins University Press, 1971).

U.S. Social Security Administration, Office of Research, Evaluation and Statistics. *Social Security Programs throughout the World, 1997* (Washington, DC: Government Printing Office, 1997).

Utusan Malaysia, January 1, 1996, pp. 1,2; translated as "Malaysia: Government Acts to Reduce Dependency on Foreign Workers." U.S. FBIS, FBIS-EAS-96-035, January 1, 1996 (electronic version).

West, Loraine A. "Pension Reform in China: Preparing for the Future." *Journal of Development Studies*, vol. 53 no. 3 (1999), pp. 153-183.

World Bank. *World Development Report 1997* (New York: Oxford University Press, 1997).

Ying, Lin. "The Aging of the Population: A Severe Challenge." *Guangming Ribao*, April 6, 1996, p. 1; translated as "PRC: Worsening Problem of Population Aging," U.S. FBIS, FBIS-CHI-96-213, April 11, 1996 (electronic version).

Young, Alwyn. "The Tyranny of Numbers: Confronting the Statistical Realities of the East Asian Growth Experience." *Quarterly Journal of Economics*, vol. 110, no. 2 (1995), pp. 641-680.

11

What If It's a World Population *Implosion*? Speculations about Global *De*-Population

Introduction

Over the past several years, some of the world's best demographers have begun to contemplate a global contingency that could have revolutionary consequences, but has yet to be taken seriously by statesmen, policymakers, or informed citizens. That contingency is the possibility that human numbers might finally peak, and then commence an indefinite decline, in the generations immediately ahead. This quiet reassessment of the alternative demographic future before us is implicitly reflected, among other places, in the United Nations' Population Division's biennial compendium, *World Population Prospects*—the oldest, largest, and most intensive of the various contemporary undertakings that attempt to envision and outline likely future demographic trends. The edition of that volume[1] released in 1998 includes a "low variant" projection that anticipates zero population growth for the world as a whole by the year 2040, and negative growth—that is to say, depopulation—thereafter. (See figure 11.1.)

Like the two alternative projections ("medium" and "high") also offered, this "low variant," as previous editions of the study have explained, is "thought to provide reasonable and plausible future trends."[2] And the eventual global depopulation envisioned in these projections, one should emphasize, is not calamitous—it does not result from Malthusian, environmental, or any other variety of disaster. Just the contrary: this contemplated stabilization and ultimate decline of world population is assumed to occur under what *World Population Prospects* terms, "conditions of orderly progress." The U.N. Population Division's method, in fact, specifically posits that "catastrophes such as wars, famines or new epidemics" will not take place "during the projection period."[3] This is not, to be sure, the first time that population specialists or others have raised the prospect of long-term population decline. Some sixty years ago, expectations of an imminent depopulation were widespread in the Western world. In the 1930s, in fact, "the fear of population decline," to recall a phrase,[4] was palpable in a number of European countries—or at least in their leading political and intellectual circles.[5]

FIGURE 11.1

Revised U.N. Projections for World Population, 1995–2050 (Billions)

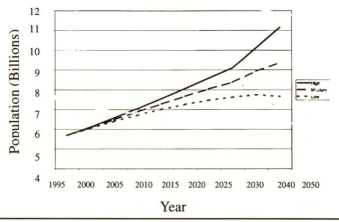

Source: *World Population Prospects: The 1996 Revision*, (United Nations Population Division, 1996), Annex II, pp. 10-11.

We now know, of course, that those predictions of depopulation were famously off the mark. Indeed, at the very time when they were supposed to be entering into permanent negative growth due to subreplacement fertility—the decades of the 1950s and 1960s—Western countries actually turned out to be in the midst of a demographic surge driven by a postwar "baby boom." There is no compelling reason to put greater faith in the predictive properties of demography in the 1990s than there was in the 1930s, as we shall see in a moment. The U.N.'s new "low variant" projections, in particular, can hardly be said to provide a sure vision of the future. But they do offer a glimpse of one *particular* and by no means fantastic version of the future: a version whose outlines as yet have scarcely been described, and whose ramifications have scarcely been pondered. At a time when all manner of potential "population problems" seem to be regularly accorded official attention by national and international authorities, the neglect that has to date greeted the possibility of a long-term reduction of human numbers is all the more striking.

In the following pages, we will survey the demographic contours of a world in which population has ceased to increase, and examine some of the political, economic, and social implications that might flow from a global "population implosion" a few decades from now, using the U.N.'s new "low variant" projections as an illustrative guide. Unaccustomed as we may be to thinking about such a world, its advent might not be that distant an eventuality. The U.N.'s projections in question imagine an indefinite demographic descent, commencing just over forty years from now—at which time most of the earth's current inhabitants will likely still be alive.

The Limits of Population Forecasting

But first, a few general words of warning about demographic projections and forecasts are in order. The uninitiated sometimes invest unwarranted confidence in the capabilities of "population sciences" to chart accurately the demographic trends of tomorrow. Those more familiar with the disciplines in question entertain more modest hopes. The paradox of long-term demographic forecasting is that its methods combine superb technique with an almost complete lack of viable predictive theory.

Mathematical demography is an elegant and sophisticated construct; it can generate detailed and internally consistent population projections once supplied with the necessary assumptions. Those assumptions, unfortunately, are precisely the sticking point. For mathematical demography will easily demonstrate that under noncatastrophic conditions, change and composition within any convened population will be dominated by fertility trends—and the "population sciences" offer no reliable framework for anticipating the fertility trends of the future.

In the modern era, the defining essence of fertility change has been the emergence and spread of sustained fertility decline. Yet the phenomenon of secular fertility decline has posed unanswerable questions to social theorists literally from the beginning. The first country in the world to embark upon long-term fertility decline did so in the late eighteenth century. That country, however, was not industrializing England, as modernization theories would lead us to expect, but rather France— then impoverished, overwhelmingly agrarian, predominantly illiterate, and by appearances devoutly Catholic. Charles Tilly has described the dilemma that European fertility decline continues to pose to historians and social scientists:

> The problem is that we have too many explanations which are individually plausible in general terms, which contradict each other to some degree, and which fail to fit some significant part of the facts.[6]

More modern fertility trends have proved no less nettlesome. Despite the almost overwhelming availability of information on conditions in contemporary industrial societies, demographers were unable to foresee either the transnational postwar "baby boom," or the subsequent OECD-wide shift to an underreplacement fertility regimen. As for developing countries, demographers have been unable to forecast either the onset of fertility decline or the trajectory that fertility change follows once it begins.

Complicating any effort at long-range population projections are two additional and highly inconvenient details: (1) population theory offers no reliable indications as to how far "normal" fertility levels may fall— or (2) whether fertility regimens will tend to converge toward net replacement after a pronounced swing away from it.

For better or worse, our only recourse in addressing these issues is to consult the empirical record. From that record, we know that the fertility level of a fairly large population under "conditions of orderly progress" can be very low indeed: Eastern Germany's post-unification level, if continued, would imply less than one birth per woman *per lifetime*.[7] By the same token, we now know that a country's fertility can drop swiftly and dramatically once the process of secular fertility decline begins: between the early 1960s and the early 1990s, for example, Thailand's estimated "total fertility rate" (TFR) plunged from over six births per woman per lifetime to less than two.[8] We know further that subreplacement fertility can characterize fairly poor contemporary societies—China, Cuba, and possibly Sri Lanka, among others.[9] Finally, we know that fertility levels can remain below replacement for prolonged periods. Japan, for example, entered into subreplacement fertility over forty years ago, and has been gradually moving further *away* from net replacement for the past quarter century.[10] All these particulars, however, furnish precious little guidance for long-range forecasts of population totals for any given country, much less the world as a whole.

Let us be clear: demographic techniques are reasonably accurate for *some* kinds of forecasts. Under ordinary conditions, for example, they are rather good at predicting how many people from a current cohort will be alive a given number of years hence. (This insight is the basis of the modern life insurance industry.) But no one has yet devised a sound technique for estimating the unborn in advance—and no one is likely to do so, so long as parental preferences determine fertility patterns.

The "Low Variant" Model

Now, back to the U.N.'s "low variant" projections. Since all population projections faithfully and mechanically reflect the assumptions embodied within them, it is worth pausing a moment to examine the particular set of assumptions that bring us to the verge of an ongoing global depopulation[11] forty-odd years from today.

The U.N.'s "low variant" model takes estimates of the world's current population composition (by country, age, and sex) and calculates hypothetical future populations based on three separate sorts of assumptions: (1) migration, (2) mortality, and (3) fertility. For 1995-2000, the model envisions a net migration of about 1.6 million people a year to the "more developed regions" (meaning the OECD countries of the early 1990s, Eastern Europe, and the predominantly European portions of the former Soviet Union) from the "less developed regions" (everyone else); this stream gradually diminishes, and ceases altogether in 2025. These assumptions are clearly arbitrary: there is no particular reason to presume they will be correct. On the other hand, given their magnitude, these assumptions exert only a slight influence on population trends for the "more developed regions"—and of course next to none on trends for the world as a whole.[12]

With respect to mortality, the U.N.'s model presumes that life expectancy at birth will rise in the "more developed regions" from roughly seventy-five today to eighty-one in the year 2050. For the "less developed regions," life expectancy is presumed to increase from the current estimated level of sixty-four to seventy-six by 2050; in the "least developed countries" (a subgrouping composed mainly of sub-Saharan countries), it is seen as rising from fifty-two to seventy-two. By the benchmarks of the immediate past, such improvements in longevity would look to be clearly feasible—and perhaps even modest. In the fifty-five years between 1995 and 2050, life expectancy at birth for the world as a whole is posited to rise by twelve years (from about sixty-five to about seventy-seven); by contrast, in the forty-five years between 1950 and 1995, global life expectancy is thought to have risen by about twenty years (from about forty-five to about sixty-five).[13]

The model's most important assumptions concern future fertility trends (see figure 11.2). By the U.N.'s estimate, total fertility rates for the "more developed regions" averaged about 1.7 in the early 1990s; the "low variant" assumes these to have fallen to about 1.5 today, and presumes they will stabilize in another decade at about 1.4 (roughly, the level currently characteristic of the nations of the European Union[14]). For the "less developed regions," TFRs averaged perhaps 3.3 in the early 1990s; these are seen as having fallen just below 3 today, declining further to about 2 in 2020, and about 1.6 in 2050. For the "least developed countries," where the average number of birth per woman per lifetime in the 1990s is estimated to have exceeded five, TFRs are posited to drop below 4 by 2010, below 3 by 2020, and below 2 by 2035.

FIGURE 11.2

**Actual and Projected Low Variant Fertility Rates by Region, 1950–2050
(Births per Woman)**

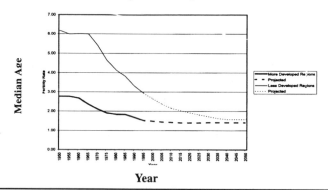

Year

Source: World Population Prospects: The 1996 Revision, (United NAtions Population Division, 1996), pp. 120-137.

Another way to look at these fertility assumptions is from the vantage point of net replacement. In the "more developed regions," the "net reproduction rate" (NRR) is already down to about 0.7—meaning that the next generation, under present patterns of childbearing and survival, would be about 30 percent smaller than the current one. The U.N.'s "low variant" assumes that the NRR will stay close to its current level for the next half-century, registering just under 0.7 in 2050. The "less developed regions," in this vision, fall below replacement around 2010; the "least developed" subgrouping, around 2030. For the world as a whole, the NRR today is placed at over 1.2; global subreplacement commences around 2010, and by 2050 it is stipulated to be 0.74—or about the same as the NRR for today's industrial democracies.

What is one to make of these postulated fertility trends? One way to assess them is in historical perspective. Over the next half century, the "low variant" model proposes a decline in TFRs of roughly 0.3 for the "more developed regions," and of about 1.5 for the "less developed regions." By contrast, as figure 11.2 indicates, over the forty years between the early 1950s and the early 1990s, actual TFRs dropped by an average of about 1.1 in the "more developed regions," and by nearly 3 in the diverse amalgam of countries within the "less developed regions."

As we have already seen, there is no possible way of telling today whether or not these hypothetical "low variant" fertility trends will eventually come to pass. Against the mirror of recent history, however, the assumptions of fertility decline built into this particular population model look neither terribly radical nor especially heroic.

The Arithmetic of Depopulation: Who, Where, When?

The arithmetic consequence of this bundle of assumptions—none of them outlandish—is a world in which population crests, and declines thereafter. By these particular computations, the human population would reach its apogee around the year 2040 at somewhat over 7.7 billion—about one-third more than the 5.8 billion thought to be alive today. Between 2040 and 2050, the world's population would fall by about 85 million. In absolute terms, such a decadal drop would hardly look immense. It would compare, for example, with the U.N. Population Division's estimates of an actual net world population increase in the early 1990s of 86 million *a year.*[15] From then on, though, world population would shrink by roughly 25 percent with each successive generation.

Negative rates of "natural increase"—death rates higher than birth rates—would characterize the "more developed regions" as early as the year 2000, although thanks to modest net immigration, absolute population totals for these groupings would not begin to fall until after 2005. For the "less developed regions," negative natural increase would begin around the year 2045. For today's "least developed countries," population growth would continue for a decade or so beyond 2050, despite subreplacement fertility, due to "demographic momentum."[16]

Given these differentials, the same trends that would result in an ultimate global population decline would also bring about a significant redistribution of world population. In 1995, the ratio of population between "less developed" and "more developed" regions stood at about 4:1; in 2050, by these projections (and today's geographical designations of those regions), it would be 7:1. The balance of population would shift dramatically not only between given countries, but even between entire continents. In 1995, for example, the estimated populations of Europe (including Russia) and Africa (including Egypt and the Maghreb states) were almost exactly equal. In 2050, by these projections, Africans would outnumber Europeans by over three to one.

In this world with negative population growth, the profile of the world's most populous countries would also look rather different from the rankings with which we have been familiar. (See table 11.1.) Only six of the dozen largest countries of 1950, by these projections, remain on the list for the year 2050. Nigeria, which did not even make the list for 1950, is postulated to be the world's fourth largest country in 2050—just edging out the United States. New additions to the "big twelve" between now and the year 2050, by these computations, would include Ethiopia, Zaire, and Iran. Whereas six of the twelve largest countries in 1950, and four in 1995, come from the "more developed regions," as currently defined, one—the U.S.—so qualifies by these projections in 2050. Just how demographically negligible the current "industrial democracies" would be in this version of the year 2050 may be illustrated with a single comparison: not a single European state—including Russia—could match the Philippines in total numbers.

The demographic forces that would propel the world to the point of depopulation would not only profoundly alter the global distribution of population: they would also utterly transform its composition. Longer lives and falling fertility would inexorably pave the way for a radical aging of the human population—a shift of a magnitude with no historical precedent.

TABLE 11.1

The World's Dozen Most Populous Countries, 1950–2050 (Millions)

	1950 (Actual)		1995 (Actual)		2050 (Projected)	
1	China	555	China	1222	India	1231
2	India	358	India	929	China	1198
3	USSR	180	U.S.A.	267	Pakistan	306
4	USA	152	Indonesia	197	Nigeria	279
5	Japan	84	Brazil	159	U.S.A.	272
6	Indonesia	80	Russian Fed.	148	Indonesia	251
7	Pakistan	72	Pakistan	136	Brazil	188
8	Brazil	53	Japan	125	Bangladesh	178
9	U.K.	51	Bangladesh	118	Ethiopia	176
10	W. Germany	50	Nigeria	112	Zaire	146
11	Italy	47	Mexico	91	Iran	143
12	France	42	Germany	82	Mexico	127

Note: 1950 reading adjusted to account for actual historical boundaries.
Source: Derived from UN *World Population Prospects 1990* (New York: UN, 1991), p. 23 and *World Population Prospects: The 1996 Revision*, (United Nations Population Division. 1996), Tables A.3, A.6.

Figure 11.3 lays out the prospective trajectories. Around 1900, the median age of the world's population may have been about twenty years—not far from what it had been in all earlier eras. Over the second half of the twentieth century, the median age for the world's population rose somewhat; it reached about twenty-five around the year 1995. By the year 2050, in this "low variant" world, the median age would be over forty-two.

FIGURE 11.3

Actual and Projected (Low Varient) Median Age of World Population by Region, 195–2050 (Median Age in Years)

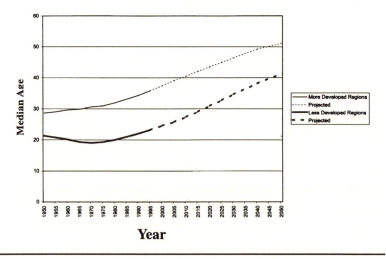

Year

Source: World Population Prospects: The 1996 Revision, (United Nations Population Division, 1996), Annex II III, pp. 12-15.

In the "less developed regions," the median age would almost double between 1995 and 2050, jumping from twenty-three years to forty-one years. To put this in perspective, it would mean that the "average" population from these regions would be more aged than the "greyest" populations in our world today. (In Germany and Japan, for example, median age is currently just under forty.) But the "more developed regions" of 2050 would be older still—almost unimaginably so, from our current vantage point. In 2050, by the "low variant" projections, the median age in this area would exceed fifty-one. In some countries, of course, the population would be even more aged: Japan's median age would be fifty-three, Germany's, fifty-five. In Italy—which is postulated in these

FIGURE 11.4

More Developed Regions: Actual and Projected (Low Varient) Populations Age 65 and Over, and 5 and Under

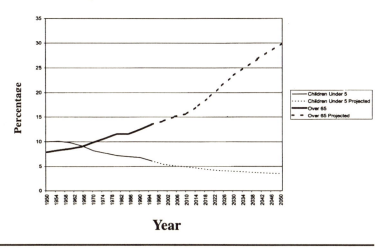

Source: *World Population Prospects: The 1996 Revision*, (United Nations Population Division, 1996), Annex II III, pp. 12-15.

FIGURE 11.5

Less Development Regions: Actual and Projected (Low Variant) Populations Age 65 and Over, and 5 and Under

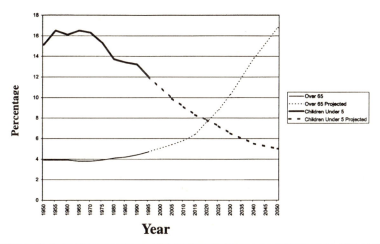

Source: World Population Prospects: The 1996 Revision, (United Nations Population Division, 1996), Annex II III, pp. 12-15.

projections to maintain the world's lowest fertility levels in the coming century—median age in the year 2050 would be fifty-eight.

This tremendous and rather sudden aging process can be considered in terms of its subsidiary implications. For the world as a whole, these trends would portend a gradual disappearance of children, and a population boom among the elderly (or let us say, groups *currently* considered elderly).

In 1950, children under the age of five composed just under a seventh of the global population. Today they make up about one-ninth of the total. In 2050, by these projections, they would account for less than one-twentieth. Conversely, persons over sixty-five made up about 5 percent of the world's population in 1950, and perhaps 6 ½ percent in 1995, but would account for over 18 percent of the total in 2050. Where there were two and a half young children for every older person in the world in 1950, there would, by 2050, be almost four persons sixty-five or over for every child. In the "less developed regions," there would be three times as many older people as young children; in the "more developed regions," the ratio would be eight to one (see figures 11.4 and 11.5). In Italy—designated here as the extreme instance of demographic aging—barely 2 percent of the population in 2050 would be under the age of five, but more than 40 percent would be sixty-five or older.

This dramatic worldwide aging would also have a particular bearing upon women. For the first time in the modern era, and possibly the first time in the human experience, "women of reproductive ages" would no longer constitute the norm for humanity.

In 1995, by the U.N. Population Division's estimates, 51 percent of all women on earth were between the ages of fifteen and forty-nine.[17] (These are designated as the childbearing years by the conventions of contemporary demography—imprecisely, but not unreasonably). Although accurate global counts are obviously not available for earlier periods (or even today), population structures generated by demographic techniques with fertility and mortality levels akin to those of earlier centuries suggest that half, or more, of the women alive at any given time may have been within those same "childbearing years."[18] Under "low variant" assumptions, however, by the year 2050 over 55 percent of the world's women will be *outside* the childbearing years. In the "more developed regions," nearly two-thirds of all women would *not* be "of reproductive age."

A final cohort worth mentioning is the fifteen-to-twenty-four-year-olds, the vigorous and exuberant adolescents and young adults who influence fashions and style, exemplify physical beauty—and happen to do most of the actual fighting in times of war. In the "low variant" version of the future, the size of this youthful group shrinks significantly in both relative and absolute terms. In the world as a whole, by these projections, there would be 100 million fewer youths in 2050 than there were in 1995; where they had comprised 18 percent of the world's population in 1995, they would account for less than 12 percent by 2050. "More developed regions," of course, would be especially youth-less: less than 9 percent of their population would be fifteen-to-twenty-four-year-olds. In this reckoning, in fact, barely half as many young people would be living in these countries as live there today.

Society, Economy, and Policy in a Depopulating World

It may not yet be possible to imagine realistically and in detail the influence that a presumption of steady and continuing—but noncatastrophic—population decline would exert on the routines of daily life, or social dynamics, or economic patterns, or the operations of government. Yet a number of issues suggest themselves immediately—along with a number of questions that are still unanswerable.

A Global Nursing Home?

If the world's population reaches the point of stagnation and incipient decline by the middle of the next century under "conditions of orderly progress," by far most of the absolute increase in human numbers in the intervening years will accrue in the ranks of the elderly. The U.N.'s "low variant projections," for example, envision a growth in human numbers between 1995 and 2050 of just under 2 billion; 1.4 billion of this presumed increase is accounted for by the group sixty years of age and older. A significant fraction of the world's population would, in this vision, be septuagenarians, octogenarians, and nonagenarians; in results calculated for some of the "more developed" countries, in fact, persons between the ages of seventy-five and eighty-five would outnumber those between the ages of zero and ten.

Such a gerontological drift would seem to raise basic and inescapable questions about the health profiles of the societies of this particular future. Would a depopulating planet be a planet of wheelchairs—of increasingly infirm and brittle senior citizens with correspondingly escalating demands for medical services and care from the rest of society? Or would the revolution in longevity envisioned in these projections be accompanied by a revolution in health that would effectively extend the boundaries of "middle age"—and thereby the scope for active, vigorous, and productive existence?

To address these questions, we might begin by examining the considerable corpus of research on health and aging that is accumulating today. That literature, as it happens, is inconclusive—or more precisely, it points in diametrically opposite and mutually exclusive directions.

One school of thought argues that the risk of illness and the direction of mortality changes are inversely related: that longer lives mean worse health for the survivors.[19] Another holds that improvements in life expectancy translate very largely into improvements in disability-free life expectancy, even for persons in their seventies and early eighties.[20]

Reviewing the points of controversy in these studies, one is inevitably struck by the mischievous ambiguity of the term "healthy life." "Mortality" is easy to define and thus (in theory) to measure: not so "health," with its infinite gradations and the intrinsically subjective nature of any self-assessment. It is possible—indeed likely—that existing data on self-perceived health status are confounded by the higher expectations of those who are better off: in the United States and elsewhere, despite physical evidence to the contrary, more affluent and better educated people often seem more inclined than their peers to rate their own health as unsatisfactory.

Reviewing the available research on old age and health, it would appear that the weight of international data today seems to support the argument that improvements in "disability-free" life expectancy rise nearly as rapidly as improvements in life expectancy for the population under eighty-five years of age—so long as "disabilities" are carefully and objectively defined. With proper health habits and appropriate medical interventions, it would appear, current know-how can already offer the great majority of persons the possibility of active and independent life well into their eighties.[21] To this extent, anxieties about the coming of an unending era of dependent invalids would appear to be misplaced.

At the same time, we should remember that the "quality of life" for older persons may at times hinge critically upon discrete but expensive medical treatments. Insofar as it is possible to imagine that those services would be more available in rich countries than in poor ones, even in the year 2050, it could be that differences in the health status of the elderly might in the future provide the same sort of summary index of "development" that the infant mortality rate is taken to offer today.

Economic Performance: Stagnation and Inadequate Demand?

In the 1930s, when the specter of "depopulation" haunted Western intellectual circles, many of the most eminent economists of the day—including Alvin Hansen, Roy Harrod, John Maynard Keynes, Gunnar Myrdal, and Joan Robinson—made the case that low fertility and stagnant or declining population could be expected to compromise economic performance. The strongest variants of this brief held that sluggish or negative population growth could exacerbate, or even precipitate, "underconsumption"—and a crisis of unemployment—by stifling demand. Less deterministic versions, however, still warned of the constraints on growth that low fertility would impose: by pressing down the investment rate, for example, or by slowing the allocation of new labor into promising and productive areas.[22]

With the benefit of hindsight, most of these arguments now look surprisingly weak. Depression-era economists were too ready to explain that great international slump—which was essentially non-demographic in nature—in terms of the fertility patterns and population trends of the day. (Ironically, barely a generation later eminent economists were attributing those same ills—inadequate investment and growth; underemployment of labor—to overly *rapid* rates of population growth.) Among the many misjudgments in these accounts that we might point to today was the tendency to underestimate the role international trade might play in linking (thus expanding) markets and in stimulating a productivity-enhancing division of labor, regardless of the population trends in a given country at a given time.

Contrary to the warnings of past and present exponents of impending "population crises," a careful review of the empirical record of our era can be interpreted as suggesting that ordinary demographic forces, whatever their character, need not be more than a secondary factor in overall economic performance.[23] That record further suggests that well-thought-out public policies, in tandem with suitable private arrangements, can capitalize upon the potential opportunities inherent in a country's population trends, and mitigate attendant risks.

In the modern era, in fact, nations have even prospered in the wake of seemingly calamitous "population problems." West Germany, Taiwan, and South Korea each flourished economically after their sudden,

forced, and tumultuous absorption of millions of refugees; Japan enjoyed rapid and sustained development after World War II even though
its life expectancy for men had been driven down to neolithic levels
during the course of its terrible defeat.

By comparison with such trials, the demographic challenges posed
by gradual population aging, and eventual population decline, look
decidedly modest. Indeed, there may even be some reasons to be
guardedly optimistic about the macroeconomic consequences of these
trends.

Surveying America's demographic prospects, for example, economist David M. Cutler and his colleagues have made the point that prolonged subreplacement fertility would actually somewhat lower the
country's investment needs and increase its living standards (consumption levels) since so much less capital would be required by new entrants into the labor force. Although expenditures on the care and support
of the elderly would naturally rise, these costs would, in their reckoning, be substantially offset by a reduced need to spend on the young. In
all, they conclude, the optimal savings rate in the middle of the next
century would probably be slightly lower than the optimal savings rate
today.[24] Other more recent work similarly casts the macroeconomic
implications of prospective population aging as a mixed array of challenges and opportunities—whose overall implications need by no means
be on the balance adverse.[25]

The demographics of depopulation, however, might well pose one
major and heretofore novel economic problem for societies of the
future: this would concern the education and training of the
workforce.

In a world where nearly half of the population was living to the age
of eighty or beyond, the ordinary person's "economically active life
expectancy" could quite conceivably be as much as fifty years—or more.
Given the arithmetic of sustained below-replacement fertility, moreover, it is not difficult to imagine circumstances half a century hence in
which the majority—even a distinct majority—of a country's workers
were over the age of fifty.

If educational systems functioned under those conditions as they do
today, most people at work would have received their final formal training over a generation previously; they would be inculcated with, and
functioning with, the knowledge and techniques of an increasingly distant past.

One should not overstate the problem: on-the-job training, "refresher courses," and the like are already familiar features of the modern workplace. The age structure changes that negative population growth would bring, however, would considerably intensify the mismatch between an educational system designed to train people when they are young and the desire of workers to enjoy a long and worthwhile career in an increasingly complex economy.

Newly embodied knowledge and techniques have been a driving force of material advance in our century. If they are to serve the same role in the coming century, and the coming century proves to be a time of pervasive population decline, the institutions and routines of higher education will probably have to be fundamentally re-examined and recast.

Pressures on the Welfare State

The possible cessation and decline of population growth in coming decades may pose no insuperable macroeconomic problems to future generations, but it stands to create enormous difficulties for the state. In a world like that imagined in the U.N.'s "low variant" projections, governments would be subject to intense—very possibly unbearable—budgetary and political pressure to overhaul the public welfare systems to which we are accustomed today. Negative population growth would place special stress on the central feature of the modern welfare state: the nationwide, tax-financed, pay-as-you-go pension program. Weighed down by unalleviable demographic burdens, it is hard to imagine how such programs could remain viable.

The government-run social security and pension schemas in virtually all of today's industrial democracies finance their operations by taxing today's workers to fund today's retirees. Since these systems were established in periods of relatively high fertility and relatively rapid population growth, pay-as-you-go pension systems had the political allure of promising generous benefits on the cheap. In an unguarded moment thirty years ago, Nobel laureate Paul Samuelson captured the reasoning undergirding this approach to public finance:

> The beauty about social insurance is that it is *actuarially* unsound. Everyone who reaches retirement age is given benefit privileges that far exceed anything he has paid in.... Social security is squarely based on what has been called the eighth wonder of the world—compound interest. A growing nation is the greatest Ponzi game ever contrived. And that is a fact, not a paradox.[26]

With below-replacement fertility and increasing longevity, however, the arithmetic of pay-as-you-go retirement programs mutates abruptly, and unforgivingly. As the ratio of employees to retirees falls, a universal pay-as-you-go retirement system has only three alternatives for preventing bankruptcy: to reduce pension benefits; to raise taxes; and/or to restrict eligibility. There are no other options.

As Carolyn Weaver persuasively demonstrated a decade ago, demographic forces had already brought social insurance programs throughout the Western world to the verge of crisis by the 1980s.[27] By that time, social security payroll taxes *alone* exceeded 20 percent in a number of Western countries, and exceeded 30 percent in at least one of them (Netherlands); unfunded liabilities were nevertheless continuing to mount.

But when Weaver was writing, there were almost six persons of "working age" (as the years fifteen to sixty-four are customarily designated) for every person of "retirement age" (sixty-five and older) in the "more developed regions." With zero, and then negative, population growth, those ratios would fall precipitously.

The dimensions of that decline are illustrated in figure 11.6, which plots changes in projected "dependency ratios" between 1995 and 2050 (see figure 11.6). (In this instance, the "dependency ratio" is defined as the number of persons sixty-five and older for every 100 persons between the ages of fifteen and sixty-four.) In 1995—under the current crisis of the Western welfare state—that dependency ratio comes out to roughly twenty—meaning that there are now about five people "of working age" for every person "of retirement age." In 2050, by these projections, the dependency ratio in today's Western democracies would be above fifty: the ratio of fifteen-to-sixty-four-year-olds to people sixty-five and over would be less than two to one. In some countries, these projected ratios for the year 2050 would be still higher: sixty for Germany; sixty-four for Japan; and an amazing eighty for Italy where there would be only 125 persons in the fifteen to sixty-four group for every 100 senior citizens.

Although populations in the "less developed regions" would not, in these projections, be so very "grey," those countries would be distinctly less capable of maintaining state-based, pay-as-you-go retirement systems in the year 2050 than OECD countries are today. For one thing, the dependency ratio of elderly to working-age population would be higher for the "less developed regions" *on average* than it is in *any* OECD country today.

FIGURE 11.6

Projected Dependency Ratio of Elderly (Age 65 and Over) to Working Age Population (Ages 15-64), Selected Countries and Regions, 1995–2050

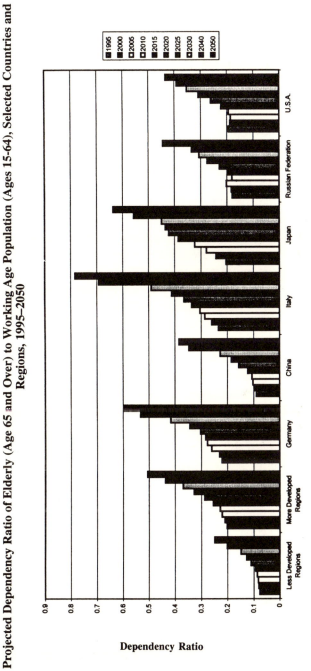

Source: World Population Prospects: The 1996 Revision, (United NAtions Population Division, 1996), Annex II III.

For another, the "less developed regions" half a century hence may not be, on average, nearly as affluent as the OECD countries are today. Angus Maddison's informative calculations suggest that even after adjusting for international differences in purchasing power of local currencies, per capita GDP of what the U.N. terms "less developed regions" was about a fifth of the "more developed countries" per capita GDP in the early 1990s—and less than a sixth of the OECD countries.[28] If these regions should enjoy long-term per capita growth rates of (let us say) 3 percent a year for the next half century, their average output level would still be nearly 40 percent lower than the OECD's today. (To get a sense of what this would mean, think of financing Western Europe's pensioner burden in the coming decade out of Western European incomes from the late 1960s.)

Already the actuarial status of state-run retirement systems in most OECD countries appears unsustainable. In the United States, according to calculations by economists at the OECD, the net present value of the unfunded deficit in our social security system amounts to only 23 percent of GDP.[29] I say "only" because the unweighted average of that deficit for the twenty OECD countries examined came to 95 percent of GDP. Even by gutting the implicit social contract underlying these systems—implementing, for example, radical limits on pension eligibility to restrict beneficiaries to less than a third to the retirement-age population—over half of them would still remain underfunded over the foreseeable future.[30]

These OECD calculations, of course, pertain to the net present value of government pension systems *today*—when people of "working ages" outnumber the "retirement" age groups by roughly five to one. In 2050—if, indeed, the ratio of "working age" to "retirement" populations were two to one, or less—the net present value of the deficit in state pension systems, as they are currently constituted, would be vastly greater.

As an abstract conjecture, it is possible that societies under such circumstances could keep their preexisting social security systems intact—if they were willing to foreswear publicly financing practically anything else, and were willing to sacrifice a good measure of future economic growth as well in the bargain.[31] But free electorates today would never opt willingly for such a choice, and it seems highly unlikely that they would do so tomorrow. Under the demographic constraints envisioned in the U.N.'s "low variant" projections, the mounting pressures would likely generate political momentum for a transition to an actuarially viable pension system.

One aspect of such a restructuring would likely be later general retirement ages, as populations made greater productive use of their extended active lifespans.[32] No less significant, such a restructuring would almost necessarily presuppose a changeover from "pay-as-you-go" financing to self-financing of retirement benefits by individuals over the course of their own lives. Though such a changeover would, of course, be consonant with a full privatization of social insurance, it is also possible to imagine the reformed pension systems operating under the aegis of government. Even under government supervision, however, it is hard to see how self-financed pensions (which explicitly acknowledge the beneficiary's creation of his or her retirement account) could lend themselves as readily to redistributive or other nonmarket objectives as pay-as-you-go arrangements have done.

Declining population growth thus might not suppress the appetites of the state, but it might well check the voting public's willingness to feed them.

From Blood Ties to Elective Affinities?

Nearly forty years ago, Jean Fourastie, the French sociologist, wrote a vivid and penetrating essay on the impact of modern mortality declines on family life and social life. The revolution in survival chances, he opined, had transformed marriage from a binding but temporary contract to a much lengthier, and possibly more tenuous, commitment; had reduced old age from an almost mystic status to a common and often pitiable physical condition; and had all but banished the procession of death and suffering that had previously conditioned all family life. Fourastie also noted that the modern revolution in mortality schedules had totally altered the ordinary person's chances of participating in "intellectual life" (which he took to begin at age twelve) and "independent life" (which commenced, in his view, around age twenty). The scope for "creative intellectual life," he observed, had been hugely expanded by improvements in survival chances: by his calculations, modern man could expect to experience between three and six times as many years of life in his forties and fifties (which Fourastie designated the peak period of creativity) as the "traditional man" of the seventeenth century.[33] (This vast extension of "creative intellectual life," one should mention, may have had a direct bearing on the process of modern economic growth, which has been so strongly driven by applied advances in knowledge.)

If a revolution in mortality has already recast social rhythms and relations within the family, a revolution in fertility may be poised to have a similar impact in the future. More specifically, the magnitudes of the fertility declines envisioned in the U.N.'s "low variant" projections would set the stage for a world never before inhabited: a world in which the only biological relatives for many people—perhaps most people will be their ancestors.

Paradoxically, the great reduction in fertility witnessed in Western societies over the past two centuries has been accompanied by a parallel reduction in childlessness. In the modern world, as the demographer Laurent Toulemon has observed, "very few couples remain voluntarily childless."[34] To date, the modern regimen of subreplacement fertility has been that only a few parents seek third children, but that almost everyone chooses to have that first baby if they can.

Under such circumstances, prolonged bouts of fertility far below the replacement level would profoundly alter the composition of the "typical family." Consider the possibilities for Italy, currently the country with the world's lowest fertility level.

At the moment, Italy's TFR is estimated to be less than 1.2; the U.N.'s "low variant projection" anticipates the continuation of this pattern to the year 2050. If Italy's current fertility regimen is extended for two generations, the modal "family" will be completely redefined. For in that future world, under reasonable assumptions about the incidence of childlessness and larger families, almost three-fifths of the nation's children will have no siblings, cousins, aunts or uncles—only parents, grandparents, and perhaps great-grandparents. Under those same assumptions, conversely, less than 5 percent of Italy's children would have both siblings *and* cousins.

Italy's position today is at an extreme within the fertility continuum among contemporary nations. But projecting the fertility rates for the entire European Union forward two generations only alters this Italian vision to a degree: about 40 percent of those European children would have no collateral blood relatives; less than a sixth would have firsthand experience of a brother or a sister and a cousin. Families in the "less developed regions" in the year 2050, in these projections, would not have evolved so fully in this direction, but this would only be a matter of time: within another generation or two, under the fertility trajectories contemplated, a family consisting of siblings, cousins, uncles and aunts would be anomalous throughout the entire world.

While it is possible to describe this new typology of the family, it is almost impossible today to imagine what it would portend. Throughout the remembered human experience, the family has been the primary and indispensable instrument for socializing a people; families presented the individual with extended bonds of obligation, and reciprocal resources—including emotional resources—upon which he or she could draw. Under the demographic projections considered here, all that would change momentously. For many people—in some places, for most people—"family" would be understood as a unit that does not include any biological contemporaries or peers.

Who will form "one's own little tribe" in such a future? Who will we play with, learn from, love unthinkingly, and fight with ferociously, knowing all the while that we can do these things because we are linked together by an indissoluble common tie? If "family are the people who must take you when no one else will," and blood relatives one's own age are simply no longer the norm, who then will take us in?

The nuclear family may have marked a radical departure from previous sorts of familial arrangements. But as we have just seen, the nuclear family does not begin to approach the limits of social atomization that may await us in a depopulating world. Difficult as the implications of these changes may be to comprehend today, we may yet manage to assess them very carefully. For it is not impossible that we will eventually experience them firsthand.

Notes

Earlier versions of this essay were presented at the New Sciences Seminar Series at the Johns Hopkins School of Advanced International Studies, and published in *The Public Interest*, no. 129 (1997). For this revised version, the author would like to thank Professor Joel E. Cohen and an anonymous reviewer for their helpful comments and constructive criticisms; the usual caveats, of course, obtain.

1. United Nations, *World Population Prospects: The 1996 Revision* (New York: U.N. Population Division, 1998). These projections, in circulation informally since November 1996, are due to be superseded by the upcoming 1998 revisions. Initial indications suggest that the 1998 revisions may accentuate the "depopulationist" tendencies embodied in the "low variant scenario" assumptions.
2. United Nations, *World Population Prospects: The 1992 Revision* (New York: U.N. Population Division, 1993), p. 84.
3. Ibid.

4. Michael S. Teitelbaum and Jay M. Winter, *The Fear of Population Decline* (New York: Academic Press, 1985).

5. For further details about these European anxieties, see D.V. Glass, *Population Policies and Movements in Europe* (London: Cass, 1967), and Joseph J. Spengler, *France Faces Depopulation: Postlude Edition, 1936-76* (Durham, NC: Duke University Press, 1979).

   European "depopulationists" in the 1930s generally did not view demographic trends in global terms, and few studies from that period considered population prospects for the world *as a whole*. Such inattention in part reflected the political realities of a day when world politics was shaped by European "Great Powers" that also ruled large overseas colonial populations.

   It may also be that population trends in the "backward areas" (as they were then called) attracted scant attention because the Great Powers did not perceive them to be a problem. From the dawn of the Industrial Age until the Great Depression, population growth rates were consistently higher in the colonizing countries than in the areas colonized. Simon Kuznets, *Modern Economic Growth: Rate, Structure and Spread* (New Haven, CT: Yale University Press, 1966), chapter 2.

6. Charles Tilly, "Introduction," in Charles Tilly, ed., *Historical Studies of Changing Fertility* (Princeton, NJ: Princeton University Press, 1978), p. 3.

7. See Nicholas Eberstadt, "Demographic Shocks After Communism: Eastern Germany, 1989-1993," *Population and Development Review*, vol. 20, no. 1 (1994), pp. 137-52.

   One may argue, of course, that circumstances in Eastern Germany today are exceptional—and, indeed, they are. Yet extraordinarily low levels of fertility today are also being registered under rather less politically extraordinary conditions. As Jean-Claude Chesnais recently noted, "In some regions of Spain (such as Catalonia and the Basque country) and of Italy (Emilia-Romagna, Liguria, Venezia-Friuli, and Tuscany), the [total] fertility rate is below 1 child per woman." Jean-Claude Chesnais, "Fertility, Family and Social Policy in Contemporary Western Europe," *Population and Development Review*, vol. 22, no. 4 (1996), pp. 729-39, citation at p. 729.

8. *World Population Prospects: The 1996 Revision*, Annex I, p. 121.

9. Ibid., pp. 121-22.

10. Government of Japan Statistics Bureau, *Japan Statistical Yearbook 1996* (Tokyo: Management and Coordination Agency, 1996), p. 62.

11. One is tempted to describe this as *permanent* depopulation—yet that would not be quite accurate.

   The projections in *The 1996 Revisions*, after all, extend only to the year 2050: its "low variant scenario" exercise, in fact, considers only a *decade* of depopulation. Even so, one may note that this fact, while technically correct, does not reflect the spirit that animates the U.N. Population Division's long-term population projections.

   That spirit is better revealed in the predecessor publication, *Long Range World Population Projections: Two Centuries of Population Growth, 1950-2150* (New York: U.N. Department of International Economic and Social Affairs, 1992), which presents a "low" variant projection in which fertility levels eventually settle at a global TFR of 1.7, and in which world population is depicted in decline for fully a century (2050-2150).

   Insofar as the U.N. Population Division's "low variant" fertility scenarios do not now assume that subreplacement fertility regimes tend to readjust up to the replacement level, we might say that those models ultimately generate depopulation "as far as the eye can see"—or more precisely, as far as the computer program is permitted to run.

12. As Joel E. Cohen pointed out to the author, there is *some* impact, insofar as the model presumes that immigrants will instantly conform to the fertility patterns of their destination country. That hypothetical impact, however, would be minuscule in comparison with hypothetical overall world population at the time of its peaking.

13. Derived from *World Population Prospects: The 1996 Revision*, Table A.27.

14. Preliminary data for 1995 put the EU's TFR at exactly 1.40. Chesnais, "Fertility, Family and Social Policy in Contemporary Western Europe," p. 730.

15. Derived from United Nations, *Demographic Yearbook 1995* (New York: U.N. Department for Economic and Social Information and Policy Analysis, 1997), p. 129.

16. For a while, in other words, the fact that rising cohorts contained absolutely larger numbers of women of childbearing age would outweigh the fact that the fertility rates for these childbearing cohorts was dropping.

17. See *World Population Prospects: The 1996 Revision*, Annex II.

18. The classic compendium for such consultations is Ansley J. Coale and Paul Demeny with Barbara Vaughan, *Regional Model Life Tables and Stable Populations*, second edition (New York: Academic Press, 1983).

19. Represented, for example, by James C. Riley, "The Risk of Being Sick: Morbidity Trends in Four Countries," *Population and Development Review*, vol. 16, no. 3 (1990), pp. 403-22.

20. For example, James F. Fries, "The Compression of Morbidity: Near or Far?" *The Milbank Quarterly*, vol. 67, no. 2 (1989), pp. 208-32.

21. See, for example, the Institute of Medicine's study on this topic: Robert L. Berg and Joseph S. Cassells, eds., *The Second Fifty Years: Promoting Health and Preventing Disability* (Washington, DC: National Academy Press, 1990).

22. For a succinct survey of these views, see United Nations, *The Determinants and Consequences of Population Trends* (New York: United Nations Population Division, 1953), pp. 241-46.

23. For two of the more authoritative recent studies elaborating on this perspective, see U.S. National Research Council, *Population Growth and Economic Development: Policy Questions* (Washington, DC: National Academy Press, 1986), and Robert Cassen, ed., *Population and Development: Old Debates, New Conclusions* (New Brunswick, NJ: Transaction Publishers, 1994).

24. David M. Cutler et al., "An Aging Society: Opportunity or Challenge?" *Brookings Papers on Economic Activity*, no. 1 (1990), pp. 1-56. Note that although Cutler and his colleagues suggest that demographic trends might lower the *optimal* savings rate in coming years, they also hold that the current savings rate in the United States is suboptimally low.

25. See, for example, David A. Wise, ed., *Studies in the Economics of Aging* (Chicago: University of Chicago Press, 1994); Richard A. Posner, *Aging and Old Age* (Chicago: University of Chicago Press, 1995); and Richard Disney, *Can We Afford to Grow Older? A Perspective on the Economics of Aging* (Cambridge, MA: MIT Press, 1996).

26. Paul A. Samuelson, "Social Security," *Newsweek*, February 13, 1967, p. 88.

27. Carolyn L. Weaver, "Social Security in Aging Societies," in Kingsley Davis, Mikhail S. Bernstam, and Rita Ricardo-Campbell, eds., *Below-Replacement Fertility in Industrial Societies: Causes, Consequences, Policies* (New York: Cambridge University Press, 1987), pp. 273-94.

28. Angus Maddison, *Monitoring the World Economy, 1820-1992* (Paris: OECD, 1995).
29. Deborah Roseveare, Willi Liebfritz, Douglas Fore, and Eckhard Wurzel, "Ageing Populations, Pension Systems and Government Budgets: Simulations for 20 OECD Countries," *OECD Economics Department Working Paper No. 168* (1996), p. 15.
30. Ibid., pp. 15-16.
31. The prospective magnitude of public pension system outlays for OECD countries in the coming decades is indicated by calculations provided in the OECD's recent study, *Ageing in OECD Countries: A Critical Policy Challenge* (Paris: OECD, 1997).

    For the twenty OECD countries considered, pension expenditures averaged about 7.4 percent of GDP in 1995. Under the assumption of future "wage indexation" (i.e., that pension benefits would grow along with wages), the average outlay for public pensions would rise to an envisioned 13.6 percent of GDP in the year 2050.

    In this exercise, the United States would be allocating 8 percent of GDP to public pension payments in 2050—roughly twice as much as today, but dramatically less than any other OECD members. In Japan, for example, the corresponding hypothetical amount would be over 16 percent of GDP; in Germany, over 17 percent; in Spain, over 20 percent; and in Italy, over 25 percent!

    And even those estimated "wage indexed" pension burdens may be arguably described as optimistically low. For as it happens, the study in question posited that fertility levels in all OECD countries would gradually and progressively rise back to the replacement level between 1995 and 2025/30. As we know, no such trends are yet in evidence.
32. Such a restructuring, we may note, would require reversal of the pervasive and long-standing international tendency toward *earlier* retirement ages for able-bodied workers during the later stages of the process of modern economic growth!
33. Jean Fourastie, "De la vie traditionelle a la vie tertiaire," *Population* (Paris), vol. 14, no. 3 (1959), pp. 417-32; selections translated as, "Jean Fourastie on the Impact of Secular Mortality Change," *Population and Development Review*, vol. 21, no. 3 (1995), pp. 653-58.
34. Laurent Toulemon, "Tres peu de couples restent volontairement sans enfant," *Population*, vol. 50, no. 4 (1995), pp. 1079-1109. Toulemon's argument concerned France specifically, but the point can be made equally about most other contemporary Western societies.

References

Berg, Robert L., and Joseph S. Cassells, eds. *The Second Fifty Years: Promoting Health and Preventing Disability.* Washington, DC: National Academy Press, 1990.

Cassen, Robert, ed. *Population and Development: Old Debates, New Conclusions.* New Brunswick, NJ: Transaction Publishers, 1994.

Chesnais, Jean-Claude. "Fertility, Family and Social Policy in Contemporary Western Europe." *Population and Development Review*, vol. 22, no. 4 (1996).

Coale, Ansley J., and Paul Demeny with Barbara Vaughan. *Regional Model Life Tables and Stable Populations*, second edition. New York: Academic Press, 1983.

Cutler, David M. et al. "An Aging Society: Opportunity or Challenge?" *Brookings Papers on Economic Activity*, no. 1 (1990).

Disney, Richard. *Can We Afford to Grow Older? A Perspective on the Economics of Aging.* Cambridge, MA: MIT Press, 1996.

Eberstadt, Nicholas. "Demographic Shocks After Communism: Eastern Germany, 1989-1993." *Population and Development Review*, vol. 20, no. 1 (1994).

Fourastie, Jean. "De la vie traditionelle a la vie tertiaire." *Population* (Paris), vol. 14, no. 3 (1959).

Fries, James F. "The Compression of Morbidity: Near or Far?" *The Milbank Quarterly*, vol. 67, no. 2 (1989).

Glass, D.V. *Population Policies and Movements in Europe.* London: Cass, 1967.

Government of Japan Statistics Bureau. *Japan Statistical Yearbook 1996.* Tokyo: Management and Coordination Agency, 1996, p. 62.

Kuznets, Simon. *Modern Economic Growth: Rate, Structure, and Spread.* New Haven, CT: Yale University Press, 1966.

Maddison, Angus. *Monitoring the World Economy, 1820-1992.* Paris: OECD, 1995.

Organization for Economic Cooperation and Development. *Ageing in OECD Countries: A Critical Policy Challenge.* Paris: OECD, 1997.

Posner, Richard A. *Aging and Old Age.* Chicago: University of Chicago Press, 1995.

Riley, James C. "The Risk of Being Sick: Morbidity Trends in Four Countries." *Population and Development Review*, vol. 16, no. 3 (1990).

Roseveare, Deborah, Willi Liebfritz, Douglas Fore, and Eckhard Wurzel. "Ageing Populations, Pension Systems and Government Budgets: Simulations for 20 OECD Countries." *OECD Economics Department Working Paper No. 168* (1996).

Samuelson, Paul A. "Social Security." *Newsweek*, February 13, 1967.

Spengler, Joseph J. *France Faces Depopulation: Postlude Edition, 1936-76.* Durham, NC: Duke University Press, 1979.

Teitelbaum, Michael S., and Jay M. Winter. *The Fear of Population Decline.* New York: Academic Press, 1985.

Tilly, Charles, ed. *Historical Studies of Changing Fertility.* Princeton, NJ: Princeton University Press, 1978, p. 3.

Toulemon, Laurent. "Tres peu de couples restent volontairement sans enfant." *Population*, vol. 50, no. 4 (1995).

United Nations. *Demographic Yearbook 1995.* New York: U.N. Department for Economic and Social Information and Policy Analysis, 1997.

United Nations. *The Determinants and Consequences of Population Trends.* New York: United Nations Population Division, 1953.

United Nations. *Long Range World Population Projections: Two Centuries of Population Growth., 1950-2150.* New York: U.N. Department of International Economic and Social Affairs, 1992.

United Nations. *World Population Prospects: The 1992 Revision.* New York: U.N. Population Division, 1993, p. 84.

United Nations. *World Population Prospects: The 1996 Revision.* New York: U.N. Population Division, 1998.

U.S. National Research Council. *Population Growth and Economic Development: Policy Questions.* Washington, DC: National Academy Press, 1986.

Weaver, Carolyn L. "Social Security in Aging Societies," in Kingsley Davis, Mikhail S. Bernstam, and Rita Ricardo-Campbell, eds., *Below-Replacement Fertility in Industrial Societies: Causes, Consequences, Policies.* New York: Cambridge University Press, 1987.

Wise, David A., ed. *Studies in the Economics of Aging.* Chicago: University of Chicago Press, 1994.

Index